AMERICAN STEPFAMILIES

AMERICAN STEPFAMILIES

William R. Beer

Transaction Publishers
New Brunswick (U.S.A.) and London (U.K.)

Copyright © 1992 by Transaction Publishers.
New Brunswick, New Jersey 08903

All rights reserved under International and Pan-American Copyright Conventions. No part of this book may be reproduced or transmitted in any form or by any means, electronic or mechanical, including photocopy, recording, or any information storage and retrieval system, without prior permission in writing from the publisher. All inquiries should be addressed to Transaction Publishers, Rutgers—The State University, New Brunswick, New Jersey 08903.

Library of Congress Catalog Number: 91-8924
ISBN: 0-88738-436-6
Printed in the United States of America

Library of Congress Cataloging-in-Publication Data

Beer, William R., 1943–
    American stepfamilies : a sociological report / William R Beer.
       p.   cm.
    Includes index.
    ISBN 0-88738-436-6
    1. Stepfamilies—United States. 2. Stepchildren—United States.
    3. Remarriage—United States. I. Title.
HQ759.92.B44 1991
306.874—dc20   91-8924
                                                                     CIP

This book is dedicated to my children,
Nicole and Joshua, who give us joy
as a family.

Contents

Preface   *ix*

Introduction   *xi*

1 An American Stepfamily   1

Part I   Inside the Stepfamily: Adults

2 Hope and Experience—Couples in Second Marriages   23

3 "Pure" Stepparents: Less Risks, Less Rewards   43

4 "Yours and Mine" Stepparents: Who's in Charge Here?   61

5 "Yours and Ours" Stepparents: Rookie and Veteran Parents   83

6 "Yours, Mine, and Ours" Stepparents: Delicate Balances   107

7	Centrifugal Children: Parent-Child Relations	125

Part II Inside the Stepfamily: Children

Introduction		141
8	Strangers in the House: Stepsibling Relations	143
9	Outsiders and Insiders: Half-Siblings	161

Part III The Stepfamily in Society

Introduction		175
10	Challenge to Society: Where do Stepfamilies Fit In?	177
11	The Bottom Line: Are Stepfamilies Successful?	197
Postface: The Way It Is/The Way It Should Be		229
Index		*239*

Preface

As I was finishing the manuscript for this book, I joined a stepfamily. My mother had died two years before, and my father remarried, to a widow whose family had lived next to mine for many years when I was a boy. In middle age I thus acquired not only a stepmother but three stepsiblings, two women and a man whom I had known and played with when we were children. During the wedding ceremony in a lovely Anglican chapel in Washington, D.C., one of the thoughts that occurred to me was that when I started doing research for this book I had had no idea that I would actually ever become a member of a stepfamily myself. As I watched the serene and love-filled faces of the newlyweds, I felt all professional distance from my subject slipping rapidly away. It was a good thing I was finishing the book now, I thought, otherwise I could never be objective about stepfamilies.

Amid the chatter under the cheerful yellow reception tent some hours later, I realized that my earlier thoughts were wrong, and that I had really been a part of several overlapping stepfamilies for a long time. One of my sisters had two children before she divorced and remarried to a man with custody of his two children from his previous marriage. Both she and her husband are, therefore, parents and stepparents at the same time, and their children one anothers' stepsiblings. That made me uncle to two children and stepuncle to two others. My other sister had a child by a first marriage and another child by a second marriage. Her children were thus half-siblings to each other, and her husband is father to one of the children and stepfather to the other; I am uncle to the children and brother-in-law to the stepfather. My wife's long-bereaved father had remarried several years before, and my son and daughter had thus acquired a stepgrandmother, while my wife gained a stepmother and a stepbrother. Her stepmother was my stepmother-in-law and her stepbrother was my stepbrother-in-law, and his wife was . . .

I am happy that my muddled speculations on kinship were interrupted by an invitation to deliver a toast, or maybe I would still be there, trying to figure out who was related to whom and how. The certainty remained that stepfamilies are so widespread that many people, like myself, are members without even being aware of it. With the realization of my personal involvement, the need to explain how stepfamilies work appeared even greater.

Among the many people who helped me in the research and writing for this book, I would particularly like to thank Ms. Terrie Rabinowitz, of the Suffolk County YM-YWHA, in Commack, Long Island. I would also like to thank Dr. Patricia Papernow of Cambridge, Massachusetts, for the help she has given on this and earlier projects. My chairman at the Department of Sociology at Brooklyn College, Dr. Laura Kitch, deserves a special word of thanks for having allowed me enough released time to work on the book's preparation and writing.

Perhaps the greatest thanks should go to those many stepfamily members, necessarily anonymous, who shared so many hours of their time telling of their joy and pain. Whether they see their words in this book or not, they should know that they not only have my thanks for the help they provided me, they also have my respect for having lived difficult lives with such grace and dignity.

Introduction

Stepfamilies are increasingly common in the United States, but they are still poorly understood, by stepfamily members and non-stepfamily members alike. Lack of public understanding leads to many misconceptions, perhaps best symbolized by the television situation comedy, "The Brady Bunch," in which a stepfamily was portrayed as being just a little bit different from a conventional family, and where when there were differences, they could be dealt with by a few jokes—in twenty-three minutes, plus commercials. At the same time, thoughtful observers wonder whether children brought up in stepfamilies are somehow maladjusted and question whether they will grow up to be happy, competent and responsible adults. The stepfamily thus presents a twofold challenge—to stepfamily members themselves, who are trying to construct family lives for themselves with little cultural guidance from the society around them, and to members of society at large, who are trying to understand if this proliferating family form is good or bad.

A stepfamily is a family in which one or both of the adults is a stepparent.[1] Stepfamilies are formed in one of three ways: divorce followed by remarriage, widowhood followed by remarriage, and marriage of a single mother to a man who is not the father of the children. They are thus evidently not new because parental death and remarriage are age-old facts of life. What is new is that single motherhood and particularly divorce have become increasingly common in the recent past, giving the stepfamily the prevalence it has today.

The rate of divorce in the United States has almost doubled since 1960, and about half of today's marriages will end in divorce.[2] Most divorces involve children, and as the divorce rate is growing, the number of children involved in divorces is growing. The result is that there is a growing likelihood that a newborn baby will experience at least the separation of his parents before he or she grows up. Four out of ten children will experience the breakup of their parents by the time they are sixteen years old.[3] The greater part of them will become stepchildren, because divorced people remarry; about three quarters of divorced women, and eight out of ten divorced men, get married again.[4] The result is that more and more marriages are remarriages; in any given year, almost half of the weddings involve at least one person who was previously married.[5]

In the past, remarriage following widowhood accounted for almost all stepfamilies. Nowadays, however, the death of a spouse generates a relatively small share of stepfamilies in which children are raised. Increased life expectancy means that women and men are much less likely to die before their children have grown to adulthood.[6]

The number of unmarried mothers has skyrocketed in the last quarter century. By 1984, more than one out of five white births were to unmarried women.[7] We do not know precisely what proportion of stepfamilies are created by the marriage of single mothers to nonbiological fathers, because in such marriages the Census Bureau does not differentiate between biological and nonbiological fathers.[8]

Considering the different ways in which stepfamilies are formed, there are many possible types of stepfamily. Remarriage alone produces eight distinct varieties: divorced man-single woman, divorced man-widowed woman, divorced man-divorced woman, single man-divorced woman, single man-widowed woman, widowed man-single woman, widowed man-widowed woman, widowed man–divorced woman. And there are three possible combinations of parents and children in a remarriage: father and children and stepmother, mother and children and stepfather, and father and children and mother and children. In theory, there are thus at least twenty-four different types of stepfamilies. If we include the possibility of multiple divorces and remarriages and the birth of "mutual" children—children born to a remarried couple—the number is even greater.[9] But while these speculations about the different possible combinations of stepfamilies may be interesting, most of them, in fact, are of one general type, the "stepfather" family.

In about 90 percent of divorces, women get custody of the children.[10] When they remarry, they bring their children with them. Therefore, most stepfamilies start with a remarrying, divorced, custodial mother. Her new husband, who may also have been married previously, may have had one or more children by this previous marriage, and since he is not likely to have custody, he will be visited by his children. The result is the common pattern of a mother, her children, and a resident stepfather, whose children regularly come to stay in the household overnight, or at most for a few weeks during vacations. A significant portion of such stepfather families will see the birth of at least one mutual child.

Because of the changes in marriage, childbearing, and divorce, we Americans have been forced to reconsider our conception of what a family is and what such broadened definitions mean for the society at large. While the typical family has long been thought of as consisting of a lifelong married couple and their dependent biological children, the numbers we have glanced at show that this type of family is being displaced by the growth of other types. This rapid change poses two potential problems. First, people who enter stepfamilies often have images of the family sharply at variance with the realities they are living. What patterns of tension consequently develop within stepfamilies and how are they different from the stresses of nuclear families? What strategies do stepfamily members devise for resolving these tensions? Second are the ramifications for society. What changes have taken place in the United States that have led to the partial eclipse of what for so long was regarded as an ideal family form? What are the consequences for society of large numbers of children being raised to adulthood in such unconventional homes?

Answering these two sets of questions is the task of this book. The argument I will make, in the first two parts, is that many of the internal processes of stepfamilies are fundamentally different from those of conventional families, but that these can be successfully negotiated, just like those in other families. The stepfamily is a type of family in its own right, with unique relationships worked out by stepfamily members with little cultural guidance. Chapter 1 sets the stage by telling the story of Randy Maxwell and using it as an illustration of how stepfamilies are unique.

Chapters 2 through 7 focus on adult relationships, beginning with the core of the stepfamily, the remarried couple. Chapter 2 describes how the nature of that relationship is different from that of first marriages. The following four chapters describe the different types of stepparent roles, building from the simplest to the most complex. Chapter 3 describes stepparents who have no children of their own and who have no children with their new spouses. Chapter 4 includes accounts of remarried people who both have children from previous unions. The addition of a "mutual" child fundamentally transforms the stepfamily in ways described in chapters 5 and 6, the former comprising cases where one of the spouses had no children before, and the latter where the parents of the mutual child were both parents already. Finishing the treatment of adult roles, chapter 7 illustrates the issues that arise in biological parent-child relations in stepfamilies.

Just as important as adult step-relationships are those between and among children, as discussed in the second part of the book. In chapter 8 we look at the nature of stepsibling relations, focusing on stepsibling rivalry and stepsibling sexuality. In chapter 9 case studies explain the dynamics of half-sibling relations.

In chapter 10 I argue that stepfamilies are proliferating as a result of social changes that have long been at work, and that they comprise a family form that matches the needs of the contemporary postindustrial United States. Stepfamilies have been around for a long time, but the contemporary stepfamily, formed from divorce and remarriage, was rare in the past. Our society today fosters values and behavior that, more than ever before, encourage divorce and remarriage. Consequently, the stepfamily, as an institution, is here to stay.

Those who greet this conclusion with trepidation need not fear. In chapter 11, I provide large-scale evidence that stepfamilies produce children who are just as well adjusted as children brought up by both biological parents, and that they will turn out to be adults who are almost as socially well adapted as those from conventional families. Stepfamilies succeed reasonably well in carrying out the child-rearing tasks we expect of all families.

To illustrate the internal workings of stepfamilies, I use case studies, based on interviews with stepfamily respondents, who explain how their families work and why they work the way they do. These accounts are by no means objective in the sense that they try to take the position of an observer outside the family and say what is "really" going on. Rather, they are deliberately subjective, revealing how the narrator makes sense of his or her family situation and lives according to this definition. This is a necessary approach to understanding stepfamily relationships because people in stepfamilies are largely on their own when it comes to constructing their lives. The accounts were provided in lengthy, recorded interviews that were subsequently transcribed and compressed into case study form. All names and places, of course, have been changed. To avoid the ambiguities that might be involved in the study of cohabiting grown-ups, the adult respondents are all legally married to their respective partners, and the children are all in legally remarried stepfamilies.

Although the last chapter makes extensive use of survey material, most of the book is based on personal narratives. The people who tell their stories therein are not "representative" in the statistical sense, nor are they meant to be. Their cases serve as illustrations of common patterns of stepfamily life that have been discerned by social scientists — sociologists, psychologists, social workers — in published studies over the last fifteen years or so. The book is aimed at the nonspecialist, and I believe that personal histories are more readable than research reports. The reader who is interested in details of these studies will find them cited in the notes. The stepfamily members themselves are given priority over the research because I believe that people themselves should be the real focus of social science.

Some of the stepfamilies described are chaotic and full of pain, and others are tranquil, loving oases. If I had used only successful families to describe the patterns of stepfamily adaptation, I would have dishonestly concealed the frequent conflicts that occur. If I had only used problematic stepfamilies, I would have neglected those that have managed to overcome the substantial obstacles in their way. Successes or failures, the stories are full of courage, dignity, humor, and the gritty determination of people trying to do their best when faced with the struggles and absurdities of life.

Notes

1. P. 199 of F. Kosinski (1983), "Improving Relationships in Stepfamilies," *Elementary School Guidance and Counseling* 7, 199–207.
2. This does not mean that all marriages are equally likely to end in divorce. Age is an important factor, with brides and grooms who marry young more at risk than those who wed when older. Marriages also collapse at different rates. The National Center for Health Statistics estimates that approximately 20 percent of all marriages will end in divorce before five years of marriage have elapsed, 33 percent within ten years, and almost 40 percent within fifteen years.
3. L. Bumpass (1984), "Children and Marital Disruption: A Replication and Update," *Demography* 21, 1, 71–82. This report anticipates that 12 out of 100 children will see their parents break up by the time they are two years old, a figure that increases to 20 by age five, to 29 by age ten, and to 38 by age 16.
4. P. Glick (1980), "Remarriage: Some Recent Changes and Variations," *Journal of Family Forces* 1, 455–478; and P. Glick (1989), "Remarried Families, Stepfamilies and Stepchildren: A Brief Demographic Profile," *Family Relations* 38, 1, 24–27.
5. National Center for Health Statistics (1986), *Monthly Vital Statistics Reports* 35, 1. In 1983, 45.6 out of 100 marriages were remarriages. Remarriage of a groom to a first-marrying bride accounted for 11.6 of 100 marriages, and remarriage of a bride to a first-marrying groom for 10.5 of 100 marriages. The remainder, almost a quarter of all marriages, held a wedding where both spouses were remarrying.
6. According to the 1980 census, only 9 out of 100 remarriages involved widows, and two thirds of them were bereaved after they were forty years old. U.S. Bureau of the Census (1985), *Statistical Abstract of the United States* (Washington, D.C.: U.S. Government Printing Office), 80.
7. U.S. Bureau of the Census (1987), *Statistical Abstract of the United States* (Washington, D.C.: U.S. Government Printing Office), 61. In 1960, barely 2

out of 100 white births were to unmarried mothers; by 1984, more than 1 out of 5 white births were to unmarried women.
8. One estimate is that about 12 percent of all children are in this type of stepfamily, but it is likely that most of these stepfamilies are black. D. Mills (1988), "Stepfamilies in Context," in W. Beer (ed.), *Relative Strangers: Studies of Stepfamily Processes* (Totowa, NJ: Rowman & Littlefield). There are thus important racial differences between stepfamilies. While blacks tend to divorce more than whites, they remarry much less. On the other hand, far more black births than white births are to single mothers. The result is that black stepfamilies tend much more to be composed of single mothers who then marry men who are not the fathers of the children, while white stepfamilies tend to comprise remarried divorced mothers. Because of the distinctive nature of black stepfamily structure, this book focuses only on white stepfamilies. A parallel, in-depth study of black stepfamilies needs to be written also.
9. Different writers have developed many different ways of classifying stepfamilies. For one, see M. Ihinger-Tallman and K. Pasley (1986), "Remarriage and Integration within the Community," *Journal of Marriage and the Family* 48, 395–405. For a typology that takes children's perceptions as the organizing principle, see P. Gross (. . . . .), "Defining Post-Divorce Remarried Families: A Typology Based on the Subjective Perceptions of Children," *Journal of Divorce* 10, 1/2, 205–207.
10. L. Weitzman (1985), *The Divorce Revolution* (New York: Free Press), 257.

1

An American Stepfamily

Randy Maxwell

Randy Maxwell left his wife, Doris, in the spring of 1985. He left behind three children—Samuel, Vera, and Alex. By June he was dating Linda Parnell, who was in the process of divorcing her husband, Michael, and had custody of their two children, Susan and David. By August, Doris and Randy's relationship was serious enough for him to move in with her and the two children. Both wanted a fresh start, so they moved from the town where they had both previously lived to one farther from New York City.

Linda's situation was complicated by the fact that Michael was seeing the children very infrequently, and when Susan and David did see him, they would return very upset. He was also several thousand dollars in arrears on child support. Because Linda initiated an action for nonpayment against him, he has not seen his children for several years. But her divorce-related problems were simple compared to Randy's.

Early in 1986, Randy's daughter Vera, who was fifteen at the time, declared that she wanted to live with her father. Samuel had already left to go to college, so Vera was living with her mother and her brother Alex. Alex is emotionally disturbed, which made life in the household hard for the girl, and by Randy's account,

> The relationship between Vera and her mother was never very good. For some reason her mother always favored the boys and always put her down. Quite a lot of times she compared them unfavorably.

Vera aggravated things by standing up to her mother, both because of her stubborn character and because of her growing adolescent independence.

Randy's reaction to the request, at first, was hesitant. He had grown comfortable with his new stepfamily and was not sure if he or they would welcome the new addition. Even more important, the four were living in a small apartment, and Susan had just gotten her own room, for which she had longed for years. He was not sure if Susan would welcome an older teenage girl with whom she would have to share it. And yet more important than the physical space of the room, Randy points out,

> Susan had been the boss of the house, and along comes an older child. Who's going to boss her, or who is going to be the boss? Does Susan boss her brother as she had done in the past or does Vera because she is older?

But the Parnells spoke as one when Randy revealed Vera's desire, saying "Take her."

From then on, Vera's mother seldom saw her, just as Michael was cut off from his children. Randy believes that this made things simpler and helped the family to consolidate: "Both girls had something in common, in that they both had a parent whom they saw quite negatively." There were initial settling-in problems because the girls came from households with different rules. Linda's household was strict, and Vera's was very laissez-faire. Susan was neat and Vera was sloppy. So Linda and Randy jointly decided that the girls should both be responsible for the neatness of their room. They typed up a new set of rules, made the girls sign it, and posted it on the refrigerator. There was even a need to settle apparently minor issues with some original arrangements:

> We had to make rules for Cat Night, meaning who got to sleep with the cat. Cat Night was based on cable TV. Two girls were sharing one room in an apartment where there was one cable TV. Now, Vera likes to go to bed around nine, but Susan likes to go to bed around eleven. Susan likes the shows on

cable TV, and Vera likes different ones. So we had to set up a rule that on Monday, lights go off at nine o'clock, on Tuesday they go off at eleven o'clock. Vera gets control of the TV one night and Susan the other. But whoever gets to control of the TV, the other gets to cuddle with the cat for that night! It was the only way to handle this.

By such diplomatic and ingenious parenting, Randy and Linda were able to lead the girls to a reasonably harmonious stepsiblinghood.

What also helped was that in spite of much legal wrangling, Randy's divorce from Doris was imminent, and Randy and Linda could think of getting married themselves. At this point, after returning from a vacation trip, Linda discovered that she was pregnant. She and Randy did a lot of soul-searching about whether they wanted to keep the baby. Her divorce was not yet settled, and her parents strongly suggested she get an abortion. They decided to go ahead and have their mutual child. This helped speed Linda's divorce:

Linda appeared in court with her case against her now-ex-husband, five months pregnant. We think that Linda's belly made an impression on the judge, and he granted a divorce. It's very unusual to get this kind of divorce on the first try. So lo and behold, all of a sudden, Linda's divorced. We got married eight days later. We were saying, come on, hurry up, let's get married before he appeals. We learned that Michael did file an appeal, and we had a running joke about how long we we were going to be married, because if he won the appeal it would make the kid illegitimate!

At that point, in the fall of 1987, the stepfamily consisted of Linda and Randy, and Vera Maxwell, Susan and David Parnell and the new baby, Adam Maxwell. But the family did not have long before another shock struck, from one of Randy's other children.

Unlike their sister, neither Alex nor Samuel Maxwell had sided with their father in the divorce. Samuel was most hostile and bitter, and is at present entirely estranged from his father. He shared much of his animosity with his brother Alex, who is eight years younger than he, but who has psychological difficulties in addition. Though Alex expressed the same emotions, Randy still managed to see him, though often at the appointed visitation time Doris simply informed him that his son was not available.

Then a strange thing happened. Alex was being neglected. There was solid evidence of that. His hair was very long, he came in clothes that didn't fit, they were dirty. He was unbathed for a month, according to him.

Randy initiated a neglect action against his ex-wife, which initially she fought.

Suddenly, after three months, she capitulated and declared in court that she could not handle Alex, and that she was requesting that custody be transferred to Randy. Randy, however, was living in extraordinarily cramped quarters with his stepfamily and did not have room. What is more, since Randy was busy working several jobs, Alex's emotional disturbance meant that it would fall to Linda to be constantly called to school to deal with the boy's frequent crises, not to mention the impact Alex would have on the day-to-day operation of the stepfamily.

Well, this was one of the toughest decisions of my life. I still have a lot of guilt. I thought that whatever the good it might do for Alex, it would ruin a lot of other lives. So we went back to court. His mother said, "I don't want him," and I said, as nicely as I could, "I don't want him." So Alex was put into a foster home.

Two weeks later, Doris remarried, to a man named Peter Jenkins. Randy suspects that his ex-wife ejected Alex because she feared that her prospective husband would not be willing to marry her if the difficult boy were part of the package.

In any case, three months later, Alex was taken out of foster care by his now-remarried mother, but he blames Randy for the entire episode. He now lives with his mother, his stepfather, Peter, and Frances, one of Peter's two children. His other stepbrother, Charles Jenkins, is away at college. But after even more maneuvers in family court, psychiatric consultations and forensic examinations, Alex now regularly visits Randy's household, too.

In the midst of all these events, a dear aunt of Randy's died and left him with a sizable inheritance. With the proceeds, the Maxwells subsequently bought a new house. In the new home, not only do Vera and Susan each have their own rooms, but so do David and Adam. And there is even a room of his own for Alex when he comes to visit. Thus, after its lengthy saga, the stepfamily is stabilized today.

Of course, there are some continuing problems and tensions that Randy must try to cope with as best he can. Fortunately, the bedrock of the stepfamily, his marriage to Linda, is secure.

> I think it's a cornerstone of my relationship with Linda that we've gone through all of this together. I think the decision to have Adam was quite important. It was a joint decision. We've made lots of heavy decisions on major issues and we made them all together.

Their union is further strengthened by the fact that Linda has succeeded in forming a good stepmother-stepdaughter relationship with Vera. Randy says,

> Linda has such a good relationship with Vera that Vera once said—and she was only half-joking—that if Linda and I ever split up, Vera wants to go with Linda. Linda is a far better mother to her than her own mother.

Unfortunately, Randy thinks that Linda has been much more successful as a stepmother than he has been as a stepfather to David. Randy is puzzled by David, because he is an unusually compliant person, "the most plastic individual I've ever met." He is always agreeable, always cheerful, always helpful. He is "everybody's friend." Randy says he worries a bit about that, because often it is the child who does not make a fuss who is in the most pain. Randy says,

> He had an eye problem. He was getting blurry vision, something that glasses wouldn't correct. The diagnosis is that it must be something psychological. So he must be harboring an awful lot inside of him that doesn't come out.

Perhaps more disturbing to Randy is the fact that instead of being kindly and fatherly with David, he finds himself often getting angry with him—"I yell at him an awful lot." He is mystified at his own behavior. As he puts it, "He's always helpful, the exact antithesis of Alex." Randy feels his resentment comes in part from David's succeeding in every way that his own son fails. And one throwaway comment is even more revealing: "As a matter of fact, David looks exactly like his father." One can understand, if not endorse, a stepfather's irritation at a "perfect" boy whose physical presence is a constant reminder of the man who once shared his wife's bed.

It is fortunate that, for her part, Linda has managed to succeed as a stepmother, because one of the tensions in the family is between two teenage girls who are jealous of each other. Stepsibling rivalry is a major issue. Linda has to be careful to buy something for one if she buys something for the other. But besides physical shows of attention, each girl needs special time with both Linda and Randy, because each has her own needs.

> Susan has school crises. She's very much worried about her performance in school. She works like a beaver and sometimes with the pressure, she cracks. She'll come home screaming and crying and then Linda will go shopping with her. But Linda will always have in the back of her mind, "How will Vera feel? Here I am spending time alone with Susan, now what am I going to do with Vera?"

Vera has her own special needs, too.

> Vera has a weight problem. She needs to lose about thirty pounds. But she's quite pretty. Susan doesn't have a weight problem, she's quite thin. And Vera is jealous of that. Susan's very thin and she's doing better in school than Vera. Vera says, "You must love Susan better because she does well in school."

Another issue of stepsibling rivalry is the problem of age order and who is the top dog among the youngsters. Susan used to be the oldest, and got to boss around David. But Vera has become a kind of mother-caretaker for her stepbrother David, which is similar to the semicustodial role she played with Alex in the old household, although David is much better adjusted. Now, not only is Susan no longer the oldest child, but she resents how close Vera has gotten to her brother. As Randy puts it, "They still haven't got the roles worked out."

The latest addition to the family, Adam Maxwell, helped to cement Randy and Linda's relationship, but had different effects on different children.

> David was thrilled when Adam was born. He thinks it's wonderful. He's taken quite a mothering role with the baby. Susan thought it was a good idea, but worried about the infringement on her time. So with her there's a lot of sisterly feelings involved, but I think she has somewhat of a resentment.

It was Vera who had the greatest fears about Adam's birth, because for her what makes her special is being Randy's only biological daughter:

> Vera didn't want the child born at all. She said if it was a girl, she'd leave home. So thank God it was a boy. She still probably would rather us not have a baby at all.

With the exception of Vera, the birth of the new member of the family was generally a welcome development.

One other quasi-member of the household is Alex, the periodic visitor:

> David is the only one of us who can control Alex. He will say, "Alex, you have to pick up your toys now, you can't leave them in your room."

Everyone else in the household is relieved when Alex leaves because of the noise he causes, but compliant David usually says, "Oh, things went well. Alex had a good time."

And finally, of course, there is Samuel, whose estrangement causes his father great pain.

> I think he blames me for wrecking his life, that he had a nice life all set together and here I am going in and breaking it all up. He's just wrong. But he's still my son and it hurts.

Nonetheless, Randy is fairly satisfied with his stepfamily, and is optimistic that, considering all that has gone on before, things will turn out well for all. Yet he is aware that much is beyond his control:

> I'm very frustrated that I can't make everybody happy, I can't make Vera lose weight, I can't make her feel good about herself. I can't solve Susan's problems when she worries too much about school. I can't solve Alex's problems. I'm just worried about, how do I solve all of these things, and a lot of them I can't.

Even in a successful stepfamily, one with loving and dedicated and creative parents, there are persistent problems, some stemming from ordinary aspects of family life and some peculiar to stepfamily existence, that cannot be solved.

Randy's story demonstrates that stepfamilies are, in their genesis and dynamics, utterly different in many ways from conventional families. Let us enumerate and explain these ways.

How Stepfamilies Are Different from Other Families[1]

Randy Maxwell's stepfamily is more complex than many, but is by no means exceptional. It raises, in capsule form, most of the special issues of stepfamilies that will be discussed in this book.

A Streetcar Named Our Family

A stepfamily is like a streetcar, with people getting on and getting off as time goes by. Conventional families have a relatively fixed cast of characters. With a married couple at the core, members are only added and subtracted by birth, death, and the marriage of an adult child. Randy's family, by contrast, saw people joining and leaving as a result of such life events, but also as a result of the mechanisms of the legal system, and of children's decisions about whether to join the family or cut themselves off from it.

Consider that this stepfamily went through four distinct phases, depending on who was a member of the household. Phase 1 was when Randy went to live with Linda and Susan and David. Phase 2 ensued when Vera decided she wanted to join them in their apartment. Phase 3 was ushered in by the birth of Adam. Phase 4 is the present one, when Alex, after the agonizing experience with foster care and rejection by both his parents, now joins the stepfamily periodically as an outcome of bitter legal arguments. Samuel, for reasons of his own, has so far not even consented to get on the trolley, even temporarily.[2]

The Family Maze

Stepfamilies are complex in comparison to conventional families. Their complexity is due to the fact that most persons, in addition to having the standard roles appropriate to conventional families—father, husband, son, brother, etc.—have additional roles, whose multiple demands pull people in different directions, added on.

Take, as an example, Vera Maxwell. She is Randy's custodial daughter. She is also Doris Jenkins' noncustodial daughter. She is Linda Maxwell's stepdaughter, and is also in a kind of stepdaughter relationship to Peter Jenkins, the new husband of her mother, even though she rarely sees him. She is sister to Samuel Maxwell and Alex Maxwell. She is stepsister to Susan Parnell and David Parnell, but is also in a different kind of stepsister relationship with Frances Jenkins and Charles Jenkins, the children of her mother's new husband. Finally, she is half-sister to Adam Maxwell. Not all these roles are of equal importance—certainly her stepdaughter relationship with Linda is more important than the one she has with Peter Jenkins, for instance—but after a certain point, the fact that there are so many more of them makes her life far more complicated than it would be in a nuclear family. Examination of the position of any other person in the family would reveal the same kind of multiple, overlapping roles.

Who's In and Who's Out?

Stepfamilies have unclear boundaries. They are extended families in the literal sense of the term; relatedness radiates out from the conjugal couple to increasingly remote relations, so that it is hard to say where the family begins and ends. Susan and David Parnell are part of Randy and Linda Maxwell's family because Linda has legal custody and the children's father avoids any contact with them. Yet Michael is biologically part of those youngsters' family, even though he is not part of Randy and Linda's household. Strangely, then, he is "family" to two of the people in the Maxwell household but not to the others. Vera is part of Randy and Linda's family, by dint of her preference, her mother's indifference, and the decisions of family court. Yet her brother, Samuel, is deliberately estranged from his father, and only tenuously a member of her family; he has practically never seen her half-brother, and he detests her stepmother. Doris Jenkins is emphatically not part of the Maxwell family, even though she is the mother of Vera, who is a member of that family. Alex is a puzzle, because nobody seems to be quite able to figure out just which family he belongs to. Only Adam Maxwell is unequivocally part of Linda and Randy's family because he is their biological child.[3]

Who's Who?

The English language provides fairly clear terms for defining relationships in conventional families. The words, *father, mother, sister, brother, son, daughter*, and so on have clearly defined meanings. Most people would have trouble differentiating between a "second cousin twice removed" and a "first cousin once removed," but since extended kinship relations like these are rarely important to Americans, the lack of clarity of such terms is not a problem. But in stepfamilies, our language has very few terms, and this terminological gap can be a serious obstacle to defining who family members are in relation to each other.

Some terms must do double duty, describing relations that are very different from each other. Randy Maxwell is Susan Parnell's stepfather, and Peter Jenkins is also Vera Maxwell's stepfather. Yet the actual content of these relationships is very different. Susan lives with Randy and her mother, and she apparently has come to accept Randy as a fatherlike figure in her life, to the extent that she ardently competes with her stepsister for his affection. Peter Jenkins, on the other hand, although he is Vera Maxwell's mother's new husband, does not live with Vera at all; he rarely sees her, and has no fatherlike relation with her whatsoever. The same ambiguity is true of the term *stepsister*. Vera Maxwell and Susan Parnell are stepsisters, and are deeply interdependent emotionally. Frances Jenkins is also Vera Maxwell's stepsister, yet they rarely see each other.

For certain stepfamily relationships, there are no words at all. Linda Maxwell is Randy's new wife, and Peter Jenkins is Doris's new husband. Linda and Peter therefore have a definite kinship link between them for which there is no descriptive term beyond "my spouse's ex-spouse's new spouse"—words that are not apt to spring to everyone's lips when describing family relations. True, in this particular extended stepfamily there is little contact between Linda and Peter. Yet in many stepfamilies, there is a great deal of interaction between such people, mainly organized around visitation of children from one household to the other.

Another example is provided by the relation of David and Susan Parnell to Charles and Frances Jenkins. Equipped with our limited vocabulary, David could only describe his relation to Charles by calling him "my stepsister's stepbrother," an accurate enough term, but one that would require most people to stop and think for several minutes before understanding what it meant. In the Maxwell-Jenkins stepfamily there is not much chance they will get together, given the bitterness of the divorce and postdivorce relations, but in many other stepfamilies, such children have long and close contact with each other.

Why is the lack of family terminology a potential problem? It may be difficult to think clearly about a relationship when the words to describe it are inaccurate or when there is no word at all. Being unable to think clearly may make it more difficult to decide how to behave.

Needed—A New Rule Book

Most everyday behavior is governed by rules we obey so implicitly that we only become aware of them when they are violated. This is true for nuclear families, but not for stepfamilies. For example, the husband is expected to be the primary breadwinner in conventional families. Notwithstanding the increasing number of married women who work outside the home, it is almost unheard of for a married man to stay home and require his wife to support him. Our expectations that married men must be the main support of their families—and their expectations of themselves match this— are so implicit that the rule only becomes obvious in the rare cases where it is violated.

For Randy Maxwell, the rules are confusing and contradictory, however. As a married male, he is under the commonsense requirement to be his family's primary breadwinner; as it happens, Linda does not work outside the home, so in fact Randy is the family's sole support. Yet the law has an entirely different set of prescriptions. Michael Parnell is legally the support for David and Susan; in theory, Randy is under no obligation to provide them with any support whatsoever. The fact that Michael is in such arrears in child support that he would be subject to arrest is of little practical help to the Maxwell family. Nobody would accept it if Randy refused to clothe or feed his stepchildren under these circumstances. He is therefore pulled in two different directions by two different types of rules—commonsense family rules and the clumsy rules of the law. What Randy has to do is to make his own rules through a judicious reworking of everyday rules and those of the legal system.

Alex Maxwell is also in an anomalous position. In nuclear families, there are commonsense expectations about discipline. Children are ordinarily required to submit to parental discipline with, of course, a normal degree of rebelliousness, evasiveness, and manipulation. Yet Alex is faced with a dilemma. The child rearing imposed by his mother is quite different from that of his stepmother. Doris's rules are, by Randy's account, much more relaxed than Linda's. When Alex is living at home, he must abide by one set of rules, but when he is visiting his father, he must obey a distinctly different one. Of course, children can be taught that they must obey different adults in different houses, depending on where they happen to be staying. But this variable obedience is not part of commonsense knowledge about parental discipline of the sort fostered in conventional families. And it puts all obedience to adults in a kind of conditional state: Alex obviously does not have to obey Doris when he is with Linda, and vice versa.

Finally, for one pair of people, there are no clear rules at all. Linda Maxwell and Doris Jenkins will have a definite relationship with each other as long as Linda and Randy are married. But there is no commonsense knowledge about how they are supposed to behave. How is a woman supposed to behave towards her husband's first wife? How is an ex-wife supposed to behave towards her ex-husband's bride? In the case of Doris Jenkins and Linda Maxwell, the relations are quite distant; one could not even call them hostile, since there is little interaction. Yet in some of the stepfamilies discussed in this book, first and second wives have cordial, if not warm relations, and in others the relations are little short of murderous.

The rules are complex, contradictory, unclear and in some cases nonexistent. What all this means is that stepfamilies mostly start out on their own when it comes to deciding how to run their lives. They are like engineers in a locomotive who not only have to drive the train but must survey the land and lay the track too, all at the same time. This may sound like an appealing kind of freedom, but having constantly to renegotiate rules can be wearing.

Hello! We're Your New Family!

Ordinarily, a couple gets married and has a certain period of time to get used to one another before a third little person joins the family. Courtship and life as a couple are supposed to prepare a couple for the arrival of their first child, although the latter is often a shock anyway. Husbands often feel excluded and jealous of their wives' relationship with the newborn; mothers are frequently astonished at the sheer amount of time and energy required to take care of such a tiny thing. Unless they have a multiple birth, the trio will have at least a year or so to get used to one another before new family members come along. In short, in conventional families, people adjust to the family in stages, as it is formed.

In a stepfamily, though, the adjustment comes *after* the family is formed. People need to get used to living with each other immediately after the adults have married or started cohabiting. The whole process of adjustment is telescoped into a short span of time. No sooner had Randy moved in with Linda and David and Susan when, out of the blue, Vera declared her wish to live with them and her mother made it clear that she did not want to live with her daughter. A family conference ensued and, in spite of the inconvenience, Susan consented to share her room with the relative stranger. Since then, their relations have combined features normal to adolescent siblings with some related specifically to stepsibling life. But when, shortly thereafter, Doris attempted to transfer Alex from her household to the Maxwells', the line was drawn. Even though Linda and Randy had decided to add another person to the household through having a child of their own, all of the family members (with the possible exception of David, who always got along well with Alex) foresaw that an additional arrival from outside would jeopardize the existing stepfamily. The painful result was that the boy was rejected by both households for a while.

Intimate Invaders

Rivalry between children is normal. Brothers and sisters compete among each other for parental affection, for one anothers' approval, and for the approval of peers and teachers.

Stepsibling rivalry is also to be expected, though it has a different texture from sibling rivalry. While the latter has its origins in early childhood competition over parental love—usually stemming from the jealousy of an older child toward a younger who seems to be favored—stepsibling rivalry usually erupts over simpler issues, such as sharing space, clothing, and household items.

Vera and Susan are competitive in ways normal to all teenage girls, and like many teenage girls, are easily upset about real or imagined shortcomings. With Susan, it is her schoolwork and with Vera her weight problem. Like siblings, they compete over Linda's affection. Yet Susan complains that Vera is closer to Linda than she is and Vera claims that Randy loves his stepdaughter better because she does better in school. More than most adolescents, they are obsessed by the parity of what they receive from adults. Their rivalry over purchases, time, and affection reminds one of the behavior of five and six year olds; in the case of Vera and Susan, they are working out these rivalries ten years behind schedule, at the same time as they are going through adolescence.

Power Shift

Children in all families have a kind of pecking order based largely on age. The eldest usually gets to boss around the younger ones, although he or she ordinarily has more responsibilities. The youngest usually gets all the attention, yet as the baby of the family is least powerful of the siblings. There is much speculation but little certainty among psychologists about the long-term consequences of birth order and age order when the children grow up. Whatever the ultimate effects may be, the everyday relations of children are strongly influenced by these factors.

When sets of stepsiblings are combined in a single household, children's hierarchies are often changed. This is actually a special case of stepsibling rivalry, where competition revolves around treasured positions in age order. An oldest child becomes a middle child, a youngest becomes a middle child, an only child can become oldest, youngest, or middle. Such changes are often a shock, and the Maxwell household was no exception. Susan Parnell "went from being the oldest kid in the house and bossing around her brother to not being the oldest kid in the house." Vera Maxwell "had an older brother and now she doesn't have an older brother." As Randy says, "they still haven't gotten the rules worked out. . . . They're still not clear on that."

Sex and the Stepfamily

Sexual relations within conventional families are controlled by strict rules and are restricted to the adult couple. Sexual relations between generations and between the children are strictly forbidden by a set of negative rules ordinarily known as "incest taboos."

In a stepfamily, though, these rules are not clear. It would be considered unacceptable for Randy Maxwell to have sexual relations with Susan Parnell. Yet this prohibition only exists as long as he is married to the young woman's mother. If the two should divorce, assuming he has not legally adopted her and she is not a minor, there is no legal or other obstacle to his marrying his former stepdaughter. So, too, with stepsiblings. Although few adults would find it acceptable when they are living together, sexual relations between Vera Maxwell and David Parnell (assuming no age differences implying statutory rape) would not be legally incestuous, and there is no law against their marrying when they become adults.

So the sexual rules in stepfamilies are ambiguous. This is more important than first meets the eye, because in many ways stepfamilies are highly sexualized. A couple goes through their honeymoon phase almost literally in the presence of their children. Watchful little eyes miss nothing in the intimate conditions of a household, and no matter how discreet they may be, the adults' physical infatuation with each other is obvious to all. Sexuality, therefore, is more salient than in conventional families, but it is also governed by less clear-cut rules.[4]

I'm Not Finished Crying Yet

The death of a loved one is followed by predictable stages through which survivors must pass in order to resolve the loss. The stages of "grieving" are denial and isolation, anger, bargaining, depression, and acceptance.[5] Children and adults go through analoguous stages of grief following a divorce. What they are mourning is not the death of a person but the death of the family as they knew it.

Children and adults have individually different "grieving schedules," whose duration depends on age, personality, sex, and myriad other factors. Optimally, by the time a parent remarries he, his ex-spouse, and all the children involved will have successfully worked through all these stages. But the likelihood of everything happening so neatly is extremely remote, and the chances are that at least one of the children, and perhaps one of the adults, too, will still be "stuck" at an early stage of grieving by the time the stepfamily is formed.

Probably the person most clearly "stuck" in grieving in the Maxwell-Jenkins-Parnell extended family is Samuel Maxwell. His rage at his father, his blaming Randy for the divorce, his refusal to have any contact with his sister Vera or half-brother Adam, all indicate that he is still at a stage somewhere between "denial and isolation," and "anger." Why Samuel seems to have resolved the loss of the old family less successfully than Vera and even than Alex is not explained in Randy's story. It probably has much to do with his being the oldest, having had the most time and emotional investment in the old family, and the fact that Linda and Randy got married and started their new stepfamily just as Samuel was in late adolescence and was taking wing as an adult on his own. Only time will tell if he will ever work through to accepting Randy and Linda's marriage and their family.[6]

One consequence of children's not coming to terms with the end of their parents' marriage is the dream that someday they will get together again. This means that the self-perceived interests of children in stepfamilies may be quite different from those of children in conventional families. In the latter, the children want their parents to stay together, and the possibility of divorce, if raised, is frightening. For stepchildren, at least at first, they will wish for, if not actively abet, the breakup of parent and stepparents. Remarried couples, therefore, often have to struggle to stay together in spite of the efforts of the children in the house.[7] David Parnell, however, has not exerted any centrifugal force on the marriage, because his father neglected to see him for so long that he has evidently given up the fantasy of getting the parents together again.

It's All My Fault

While most people start life in a nuclear family with feelings of hope for the future, guilt tends to pervade stepfamilies at the beginning. Adults feel guilt because of feelings of failure and disappointment over the divorce; no matter how necessary the divorce may have been, few ex-spouses can look back without any feelings of self-reproach. As parents, the adults may feel particularly guilty because of the pain that the divorce caused to children. Even a never-married person who marries a divorced spouse may be accused of having broken up the other marriage, of being the "other woman," even when the sequence of events contradicts this. Children feel guilty after divorce, too. Small children tend to think that the divorce was their fault, however irrational this may be. Older children may feel guilt because of the power they have to undermine the new marriage. Even in cases of bereavement, guilt can enter in, where a remarrying spouse feels he or she is betraying the memory of the loved one, or when children feel guilty because they begin to love a stepparent and thereby are disloyal to their dead parent.

This typical feature of stepfamilies was least clearly revealed in Randy Maxwell's story, perhaps because Randy's account was the only one sought. In his case, though, he is admittedly tortured by guilt over the pain suffered by his son, Alex. Intellectually, he knows that the survival of the new marriage and the new family required their rejection of the boy. But such a course of action ran directly counter to his instincts as a father.

There are traces of guilt in the behavior of other family members as well. David Parnell, for instance, almost certainly feels responsible for the divorce of Linda and Michael in some way. His overconformity and quick compliance to any adult probably stems from the notion that if he is perfect, everything will be all right, since the disruption of his parents' marriage was, he thinks, due to some imperfection in him.

The Mutual Child

In a conventional family, a couple's decision to have another child is a function of age, money, space, and family relationships. As we saw from Randy's account, the decision of a remarried couple to add another child to the family is based on all these, plus more. The birth of "our child," in addition to "his" and "hers" children fundamentally transforms the family. It ceases to be an arrangement based on law and affection, and becomes a system where everyone is related by blood through the mutual child.

The decision to have Adam was obviously very serious for Randy and Linda. Not only did it mean trying again, after failed marriages and bitter divorces. That Randy and Linda had serious problems to confront when deciding whether or not to have Adam, and that they successfully dealt with them as an adult team, is evidence for him of the closeness of their marriage.

The range of reactions displayed by the children is typical of stepfamilies. David was overjoyed by the birth of his half-brother, and Susan was somewhat less sanguine. The half-sibling most disturbed by Adam's birth was Vera. If the baby had been a girl, Randy fears, she would not have been able to stand it. That Adam is a boy makes him just barely acceptable. From Vera's point of view, this is understandable. She is a late arrival in the family; first there was Linda and Susan and David, then there was Randy and Linda and Susan and David. Vera was like a guest arriving at a party where everyone else had had a long time to get to know one another. Her position was the most marginal (which also helps to explain the acerbity of her competition with Susan). The birth of another child meant the arrival of another potential competitor for family acceptance, one who had the added legitimacy of being Randy and Linda's mutual child. If that child had been of the same sex, the competition for affection would have been unwinnable, in Vera's eyes. No wonder her acceptance of the baby is so grudging.

A Family Not Like Any Other

A stepfamily "looks" like a nuclear family. Outsiders see a household composed of a married adult couple and their dependent children and have certain expectations about how the relationships work. From the foregoing, we can see that this is not so, but stepfamily members themselves can remain trapped by these illusions, particularly what has been called "the myth of the recreated nuclear family." Bothered by guilt over previous real or imagined failures, and inspired by their newfound love, stepparents may imagine that this time, they'll do it right, this time they'll make the family work, and it will be a happy home, the way the first one should have been. The irony is that because the workings of a stepfamily are unique, the harder a married person tries to make his or her family into a family like any other, the more he or she will fail. The first step on the road to success as a stepparent is taken by giving up the desire to shape the family into a nuclear family ideal.[8]

Randy has not taken this step yet. He has not sorted out the extent to which his family is unlike any other. He is bothered by his own aggressive behavior toward his stepson, David Parnell. It is as if he sees himself doing it without wishing to; acknowledging that the boy is flexible and adaptive, he dislikes his own attitude toward him. At the same time, he sees that his son is the opposite of his stepson, and is puzzled that David is so capable of coping with Alex's behavior when no one else can. He is angry that his other son Samuel has alienated himself so. But above all, he is stymied by the fact that he is in a family but has little power to control how things go for the other family members. Remember his words, "I'm very frustrated that I can't make everybody happy. . . . I'm just worried about how do I solve all of these things and a lot of them I can't." Part of Randy's frustration comes from the necessarily limited role of the stepfather, and part comes from the dawning realization that his family is different from others. While parents in nuclear families can never shape the family entirely to their desires, the roles of adults in stepfamilies are much more limited, and Randy is still trying to come to grips with that fact.

Something unusual is going on in stepfamilies. Their members, young and old, are often unprepared for the unique patterns of life in their new families. Because the stepfamily's uniqueness is seldom understood, people who have difficulty in making such families work often feel they or their partners or children are somehow remiss, whereas the fault simply lies in being unaware of the terrain of the new family territory they are traversing.

Notes

1. The framework for this subsection was based on R. Beer and W. Beer (1989), "Step by Step: Stepfamily Issues for Educators," *Family Life Educator* 7, 3, 4–8; see also Clifford Sager et al. (1983), *Treating the Remarried Family* (New York: Brunner & Mazel), 23–37, and Lucile Duberman (1975), *The Reconsti-*

tuted Family: A Study of Remarried Couples (Chicago: University of Chicago Press), 125–130.
2. For an argument that the stepfamily should be seen as a process, rather than a fixed structure, see R. Marotz-Baden et al. (1979), "Family Form or Family Process? Reconsidering the Deficit Family Model Approach," *Family Coordinator* 28, 1, 5–14.
3. K. Walker and L. Messinger (1979), "Remarriage after Divorce: Dissolution and Reconstitution of Family Boundaries," *Family Process* 18, 185–92.
4. E. Visher and J. Visher (1982), "Children in Stepfamilies," *Psychiatric Annals* 12, 9, 832–41, esp. 833.
5. E. Kuebler-Ross (1973), *On Death and Dying* (New York: Macmillan).
6. On mourning divorce, see J. Rosenbaum and V. Rosenbaum (1977), *Stepparenting* (Corte Madera, Calif.: Chandler & Sharp), 8, 9–14.
7. J. Visher and E. Visher (1978), "Common Problems of Stepparents and Their Spouses, "*American Journal of Orthopsychiatry* 48, 2, 252–61.
8. For discussion of stepfamily myths, see G. Schulman (1972), "Myths that Intrude on the Adaptation of the Stepfamily," *Social Casework* 53, 3, 131–39; and D. Jacobson (1979), "Stepfamilies: Myths and Realities," *Social Work* 24, 202–7.

Part I

Inside the Stepfamily: Adults

2

Hope and Experience – Couples in Second Marriages

Samuel Johnson, in a well-known aphorism, said that remarriage demonstrated the triumph of hope over experience.[1] Let us begin at the core of the stepfamily, looking at a sketch of one remarried couple, and at how they managed to combine hope and experience.

"I came home from work one day and my apartment had been broken into, down on Thirtieth Street, and I got very uptight. Right after that, one of the nurses in the central Harlem office was raped, and one of the nurses in our office was found dead in her apartment. I decided I'd had enough of Manhattan. So I got an apartment in the suburbs. My girlfriend introduced me to my husband. By the time I had gotten the apartment, my husband and his ex-wife had basically split in that period of about a year. From there we went to our little honeymoon phase where his boys would come visit. And they were basically good times. He didn't want to get married. I wanted to get married. Before that, I had never wanted to get married, I never wanted children, that was what had attracted him to me!

"So then we got married, and we got custody. And that changed our relationship markedly. We couldn't spend all weekend in bed;

you had to get up, you had to do the laundry, go shopping for groceries. You had to go through, 'Mommy's in the kitchen cooking dinner.' 'Who's done their homework and who hasn't done their homework?' And 'Why is there a note saying that so and so hasn't been to geometry in six weeks?' It killed the honeymoon. It definitely changed it. The basic strength of it always was there but day-to-day activities, the physical things, like whether you stayed in bed all day or went out or took a walk, what you talked about. It went through a lot of changes because all of a sudden you were talking about how you were going to shoot three children and have them tarred and feathered for dinner tomorrow night, because it was the only possible solution. 'Who's going to fix that broken window?' You didn't call the super any more because you were the super. So the issues that you had to deal with in the honeymoon phase were just what was the relationship between two people, and then all of a sudden that really changes. We had a hard time focusing on five people. Before it was just two people, but once we had custody, the major issues were five.

"I've never really felt they were driving us apart. I think they would have liked that. I remember them talking about it, and I remember my husband and me saying to them, 'As hard as you try, you're not going to do it.' It was definitely right out there on the table. The boys on some level felt that they had caused the divorce between their parents. And when their father and I were together they felt that if they did that to their mother and father they were going to do that with us also. They needed to be reassured that they couldn't, though I think at some level they wanted us to split, because in their fantasies their mother and their father would get back together. I remember at one point my husband saying, 'Even if your stepmother and I split, you have to understand that your mother and I are incompatible. You should be able to see that by now. We can barely stand to be in the same room.'

"The attic turned out to be the saving grace. We spent a lot of time up in our little room for that purpose. We had a TV, we had a stereo, we had a nice comfortable chair, it was like a little apartment. I think that anybody who gets into a stepfamily situation should have a little apartment someplace. Because it was away from everything; nobody could just open the door and be there, there was something very special about that.

"His ex-wife would call me up, and want to know how come I had kept her husband from coming back home. And I'd say 'Well, I don't have him tied to a chair here. If he wants to . . . ' She took us to court every six months. Like clockwork. She wanted more. She was getting the mortgage of the house, child support and alimony, and medical expenses paid, and he was left with fifty bucks a week — and she wanted more. And the judge would look at that and laugh and say, 'Case dismissed.' But every six months she took us anyway. Until recently we were still paying alimony. I was basically supporting him. I was paying the rent. I was paying everything."

The relationship of the remarried couple is fundamental to the success or failure of the family, as with conventional families, but remarried spouses must face forces that are absent for first-married families:[1] To begin with, divorced spouses must come to terms with effects of the previous marriage. Remarriage takes place after the legal constraints of divorce — child support, allocation of marital resources, custody, visitation, limits on travel — have been set down, so that remarrying spouses have limitations imposed on them with which they must come to terms. Their economic remarriage is complicated because even though finances are generally better as a result of remarrying, the family accounts are often in a state of disequilibrium because of incoming and outgoing support payments. Parental remarriage requires husband and wife to adopt a role as a stepparent at the same time as becoming a spouse again. And a person must join a world of friends, neighbors, and acquaintances as a part of a couple; this usually means relinquishing a circle of single friends, since circles of married couples tend to exclude unattached individuals. Remarriage also has a psychological dimension, because it demands that a person change his or her self-definition from that of an individual to half of a couple; a divorced person must re-form a committed and loving relationship with a new person.[2]

Remarriage thus begins on different terms from conventional marriage. It has definite advantages, as well as special stresses, which make it a unique type of relationship.

The Quality and Nature of Remarried Couple Relations

In general, how do remarriages compare with first marriages? Remarriage may well signal the triumph of hope over experience, but it might equally well indicate that the person who remarries has learned from his or her mistakes.

To start with the basics, sex is probably better in remarriage, if frequency of coitus is any measure. Citing a national fertility study, Leslie Westoff points out that coital frequency is, on average, ten times per month for women under twenty-five who have been married once, while for women remarried less than five years, it is eleven times per month.[3]

One study of happily and recently remarried couples reported three major differences between first and second marriages. Communication was better, because the couple found more compatible spouses as a result of the learning experience provided by the first marriage and because of the self-understanding resulting from the divorce. Conflict was reduced, and couples were more able to perceive such conflict as there was as an inevitable and nonthreatening part of family life. Power was more equally shared between the spouses; women felt on a more equal basis with their husbands, and housework was more equally shared. Maturity was one of the central themes, together with the realization that a married couple consisted of two distinct people, rather than two merged into one.[4]

Overall, sociological reports show slight differences in happiness between first and second marriages. According to one study, remarried people report high levels of marital satisfaction, though not significantly higher than people in first marriages. The exception to this is when both spouses have divorced and remarried; in such cases there is less marital satisfaction.[5] Happiness in remarriages also depends on other factors, such as gender, education, prior cohabitation, and presence or absence of children.

With regard to gender, one survey shows that 71 percent of men in first marriages say they are "very happy," compared to 68 percent in second marriages. For women in first and second marriages, the figures are 70 percent and 61 percent, respectively.[6] Remarried men are happier than men in first marriages, according to yet another researcher. But the same study found that remarried women are less happy than men in first marriages, because men are more likely to be better off financially and occupationally. In addition, because of older men's greater range of choices in the marriage market, they have a greater likelihood than women of finding a second mate who suits their taste. Also, ties with friends and kin are disrupted by divorce, but these same ties are not restored by remarriages. Since these relationships are ordinarily more important for women, the lack of their reestablishment affects women more.[7]

The role of economics thus has considerable influence over whether women remarry and whether they are happy in their remarriages. There is no difference between well-off and poorer women in their desire to remarry, but the wealthier ones remarry less. They have more dates, meet more men, and have more steady relationships. But their behavior is not conducive to remarriage, since they do not flatter men as much, do not tolerate abusive relations, and break up with men more.[8] In a word, wealthier women can be choosier about the men they remarry. For those who are less financially independent, remarriage does alleviate the considerable hardships associated with divorce.[9] Women who remarry, therefore, are somewhat more likely to have done so for financial reasons in addition to emotional ones. They may have settled for a certain spouse, and be relatively less satisfied than men tend to be in remarriage.

Education is also important. Lucile Duberman's study confirms that the quality of the relations between husband and wife is strongly correlated with the "solidarity" of the stepfamily. She found that about 25 percent of the degree of integration of the stepfamily was explained by the quality of the relation between husband and wife. Certain other factors, in turn, were found to influence whether or not these relations were good. One of the factors was the husband's education. When husbands were more educated, relations were more likely to be said to be "excellent." So, too, with a family's social class.[10]

The effect of children on remarriage can be dramatic. One study compared the quality of family life in those remarriages where there were and those where there were no children from previous marriages. The results showed clearly that the presence of stepchildren detracted from the quality of life in remarriage.[11] The story recounted at the beginning of the chapter suggests some reasons why this may be so.

Couples who lived together before remarrying, according to a 1981 report, showed greater "family strength" than those who had not. These couples, who tended to be younger than a control group who had not lived together before remarrying, also were more likely to rate their remarriage as successful, and to perceive that support from children, relatives, and friends was greater.[12]

Finally, there are the prospects for divorce. Remarriages are not notably more stable than first marriages, since the redivorce rate is somewhat higher than the divorce rate. But if one compares the rate of divorce among people in first marriages after excluding couples who are unlikely to divorce under any circumstances because of religion (i.e., Catholics, fundamentalist Christians, and some others) with the rate of divorce among remarried people, the former is about 45 percent and the latter about 40 percent. All things being equal, then, remarried people are slightly less likely to divorce than first-married people.[13]

This is partly because people entering remarriage do so with a sense of maturity and choice. Men in particular, because of their previous experience, will be more flexible and willing to share family tasks.[14] Remarrying spouses may be more capable of intimacy because of the greater personal insight resulting from the self-analysis that accompanies divorce. Spouses are more likely to be realistic in their expectations of one another because of the disillusionments of their previous marriage. They are also simply older and thus presumably more mature.[15]

In one study, remarried couples explained how they went about re-forging a marital bond. Looking back, they considered that it was necessary to make a definitive break not only with their former spouses but with their families of origin, upon whom they had relied in the divorced phase. In "recoupling," the couples said they had had to re-establish trust and become "best friends" with their spouse. They had come to perceive differences between them as beneficial rather than threatening, had seen the changes in their lives as leading to greater maturity and contentment, and had reevaluated priorities and developed greater flexibility in relationships. They said each individual also had certain tasks. This required giving up one's image of oneself as single, and often involved wives giving up careers to cede top priority to their families. The individual also had to understand why the first marriage did not succeed and to see the divorce as a learning experience. Couples had to learn to manage conflict between them, particularly that stemming from interaction with the children and former spouses. They thought that the strength of the remarriage was based on a commitment to remarriage; the remarriages seemed to work because they "worked" at it.[16]

Certain predictable pitfalls need to be successfully negotiated for a remarriage to succeed. A couple needs to come to an agreement about a definition of a family; the stepparent may see the couple as central, while the biological parent may see the children as central. The spouses also need to agree on approaches to parenting; a likely pattern will be one in which a stepfather will see himself as the central authority, laying down the law, while the biological parent will be more tolerant and easily manipulated. Finally, disagreements about the former spouse must be resolved; a first-marrying spouse may see her husband's "ex" as an inconvenience to be tolerated at best, while the second-marrying spouse may see her own ex-spouse as an object of intense hatred or responsibility.[17]

In sum, happiness, sex, and the quality of the relationship is somewhat better in remarriages than in first marriages, although these satisfactions are affected by gender, education, social class, children, and premarital cohabitation. It is probably just as well that remarriages tend to be more satisfying, because the stresses on a remarried couple are considerably greater than those on first-married couples. Pressures come mainly from leftover effects of past relationships. The remarried couple is not as autonomous as first-married couples, because it is embedded within a wider and more complex system of stepfamily relationships. Finances and decisions about what to do with children from previous marriages must be negotiated with an ex-spouse, and perhaps with ex-in-laws. While a first-married couple has a difficult enough time learning to negotiate problems between two people, a remarried couple must coordinate decisions and relations with numerous others, principally ex-spouses, children from previous marriages, and in-laws. The role played by ex-spouses is the concern of the rest of this chapter, since their influence stands like a stage backdrop behind all the stepfamily scenarios that follow.

Second Wife, Second Husband

Mary Peters is a second wife, a previously divorced mother to one child and visited stepmother to two. Here is her description of her relationship with her husband's ex-wife.

"We were living together for two years when she had a bad back one summer. We offered to take the kids for a week or two. We had been involved for two years, and my husband had been out of the house, but she said, 'Why don't you just come home? What's the difference who you sleep with anyway?' Like, what's the difference where you put it?' That was basically what she said. A very warm, loving person.

"I think she is the most difficult thing in the whole situation. She hasn't remarried. Out of spite, out of spite. I'm sure it's out of spite. If she remarried, she would lose the house. She would have to sell, even though I'm not sure she even considers that as a possibility, because she is just so totally in her own world . . .

"I have a lot of anger about this. I could get really crazy about this. She plans a lot of our time with the children. For instance, now the children have birthday parties this weekend, and in her head she thinks there's nothing wrong with my husband driving back out to her house on Saturday, spending four hours, and driving the children back here. She doesn't view our weekends with them as visiting, she views them as baby-sitting. It pisses me off, because I'm not a baby-sitter. She thinks nothing of asking for extra time. Our weekends without the children are important for me, and I'm not willing to give up a Saturday night so I can baby-sit for her. I also really find myself frustrated and angry when I know my husband is driving back out there three days in a row because the kids may have a birthday party.

"I feel that she doesn't see him as a person. But then again, it's his place to exert his personhood on her. I'm not sure that he does. There's another person in our relationship.

"I'm in both situations—I have a daughter who goes and visits her father on Sunday afternoons, and I don't feel myself getting crazy with him the same way she gets crazy with my husband. My ex-husband has been living with somebody for three years. She supposedly is 24 or 25. She really doesn't look it, she looks around 38 or 39. She has graying hair and an old face. I feel sorry for her. And yet I know I didn't want to live with him, and I was the one that wanted out of that relationship and I came out of it without a pot to piss in. It was important for my survival to get out of that relationship. I was dying. I can't fathom why she would be in that relationship with him.

"I'm sure my husband's ex-wife could probably say the same with me except that he was the one that finally walked out of that relationship. So I think that there's a difference. I think she feels a great deal of competitiveness with me, and her power is the children."[18]

Stuart Solomon is a second husband, a divorced father, and stepfather to one child, Lara, whose mother is named Marianne. His comments about Lara's father, Jack, complement and contrast with Mary Peters's.

"In the last year or so he started to pay child support for the first time. Though we know for a fact that he lies about how much he makes, and child support is based on that, we know a lot of things we don't even bring up to him because it's pointless. He pays very minimal support. I make a very comfortable income, and we don't need his money, but just on principle I want him to pay. I support this little girl. I always did, from the time we met. I pay for every little thing. He does absolutely nothing for her. He doesn't even pay what he's required to pay. And he does, but it's always late, a couple of months late, or the check bounces.

"He knows I won't allow it. When my wife wouldn't allow it, it didn't matter. He wouldn't listen to her. When I don't allow it, he realizes something has changed. He comes around, and he does eventually catch up now, to some extent.

"My wife still says everything he does has a motive, an ulterior motive. She can't deal with that. I feel one thing is important—if we can get anything out of Jack, that makes Lara feel good—whatever his motives are don't count.

"Right now, for instance, we're talking about Lara's Bat Mitzvah next year. All of a sudden, when we started talking about the Bat Mitzvah, this summer he's taking her to Manhattan to go to camp there. He's paying for it. He's taking her a couple of weekends here and there, and he wants to pay—he claims he will pay, but we've only talked about this on the phone—for half the Bat Mitzvah and to have his family there.

"I'm willing to talk about it with him. Marianne and he don't get along well enough to talk. It always ends up in a verbal battle. I volunteered to talk to him. But I'm still waiting to sit down and make an appointment with him. He called me again yesterday, and he told me, 'You know, I'm not trying to stall this.' (Which he is.) He's going to claim he'll cooperate, he's going to tie everything up, make a mess of it, and then he's going to back out and not pay me. I know that. Which I won't allow, so I'm just going to take a very strong stand. This time I'm going to tell him I need to be paid up front before we do anything. That's it, or you're not involved, and we have a Bat Mitzvah without you. I don't want Lara to have a Bat Mitzvah without her father, though. Marianne doesn't care. She'd rather he not be there. I don't think that's fair.

"He's married to a woman who has no interest in the Jewish religion—she's not Jewish, obviously—but she has no interest in the Jewish religion. She has knocked it on many occasions, and she wants to take part in the Bat Mitzvah also. So Marianne, being a more faithful Jew than I am, doesn't want a mockery made of this either, which I understand.

"But since this all came up, he's been cooperating with everything. Marianne claims his ulterior motive is to look good for his family. He's lied to everyone for so many years that he supports his kid, he sees her, he makes her whole life pleasant, and now all of a sudden he's excluded from a Bat Mitzvah that I'm making, his family is going to see right through him and they'll know, like we do, that he's an out and out filthy liar. I know that she's right. That is his ulterior motive. But I have an ulterior motive, too, and that is that Lara wants her father there. Simple as that.

"She's no longer hurt. She knows her father's a liar. She knows that when he says he's going to give her an allowance not to expect it. She'll never see it. She knows, from Marianne not getting support checks, that she's not going to get any money he promises either. He just talks and talks and doesn't do anything. She's pretty hardened to it, I guess you could say. She doesn't expect much.

"He now knows that he can call up and talk to me because he doesn't have to fight with Marianne. Having me as a buffer, he knows he can talk to me and not have a battle. He knows he won't have to call and talk to Lara and say 'We're doing this and that,' and have Marianne get in the middle and say, 'You dirty, filthy liar! You're not going to do that. Why do you lie to your child?' Because I wouldn't let her do that. I would say, 'Let the child see he's lying, let him make his false promises, let him break them, and let her see it.' And that's pretty much what it comes down to now. He makes all his false claims and Lara listens and doesn't expect much and she knows what kind of a person he is, and she doesn't hate him for it.

"He considers me her father. He knows he does shit. He knows he does absolutely nothing for her. He knows that if she wants a father image, or money, whatever it may be that you look for in a father, he knows that she gets it from me, not from him."

The War of the Exes

It is a truism that divorce is based on negative emotions. Even many years after their legal rupture is complete, former spouses will often feel some animosity. The probability that one or more ex-spouses will be exerting some sort of disruptive influence is thus almost assured for most remarried relationships. Even if there were no hard feelings between the ex-spouses, the relationship is a delicate one because there is no clear, accepted role for divorced spouses. Because our society does not like to admit the fact of divorce, no etiquette for the ex-spouses' relationship is universally accepted.[19] The result is that there are no guidelines for resolving issues between ex-spouses except for those provided in the law, and the law is a clumsy, unpredictable instrument. Some ex-spouses, such as Randy Maxwell and his ex-wife, do regularly resort to family court because of the lack of accepted norms, but the adversarial nature of court proceedings almost guarantees that in such cases relations will be further strained.

One study discerns five distinct styles adopted by ex-spouses toward each other. "Perfect pals" were friends before the divorce and remain so afterward. "Cooperative colleagues" cooperate in their role of parents. Less harmonious types include "angry associates," for whom anger is still the basic element in their relationship, and "fiery foes," for whom rage is such a dominant residue of their love that they cannot cooperate on anything. Finally, there are "dissolved duos," who have no contact at all with one another. In the stories related below, all of these types turn up.[20]

The ex-spouse generates two separate types of jealousy. One is competition between first and second spouse over a common spouse; these are issues of sex and loyalty. The second wife knows that her husband was once a sexual partner and helpmate of the first wife, and the same is true for second and first husbands. The second type of competition arises between first and second spouses over children. These are issues of parental competence and influence. Since ex-spouses usually both still love their children, their subsequent disenchantment and animosity lead both to call into question the other's qualifications for parenthood.

When the second spouse is also a stepparent, the potential for hostility is increased. The ex-spouse of one's present spouse has two roles: (1) divorced spouse of present spouse, (2) parent of your stepchildren. These are always potentially conflicting roles, because the former implies competition and the latter requires cooperation.[21] Even when a stepparent is doing the right thing—maintaining a common front with one's spouse against the ex, or encouraging children's communication with their noncustodial parent by refraining from saying bad things about him or her—he or she is thus bound to be acting in implicitly contradictory ways.

It is estimated that about half of remarried spouses have "strained, openly hostile, or nearly impossible" relations with former spouses. One study differentiates between four types of difficult ex-spouses. The *intruder* strives constantly, by fair means or foul, to exert control over the new family by pointing out life-style differences to children, favoring one child over another, manipulating money, making appeals to loyalty, and refusing to communicate directly. The *chaos-creator* carries out constant threats, personal attacks, and lawsuits against the remarried spouse. The *absentee parent* is financially reliable and nondisruptive to the couple, but affects them by being emotionally unavailable to his (or, rarely, her) children and, in effect, telling them that they are unloved by him and unlovable. The *abuser* is an alcoholic or drug addict, or subject to other compulsive disorders, and may be physically, sexually, or emotionally abusive to the children when they are in his or her care. The stress on the remarried couple from this kind of ex-spouse comes from the constant anxiety about the children's welfare.[22]

The characters in Randy Maxwell's story illustrate all of these. Linda Maxwell's ex-husband Michael is an extreme example of the absentee parent, since he is neither financially reliable nor emotionally available to his children. Randy portrays his ex-wife as a chaos creator, in that she not only insisted that Vera come to live with the Maxwells immediately, but also that the emotionally disturbed Alex live with them. All of Doris's attempts to create chaos use family court as a crude but effective tool. Randy Maxwell himself probably plays the role of the intruder as far as Doris is concerned, since he sees it as his job to make everybody happy, rather than leave them alone. His presentation of his life-style as superior to his ex-wife's is his way of undermining the children's relationship with their mother. It has worked with Vera, been only half-successful with Alex, and has failed entirely with Samuel. Doris, at least for a while, was abusive to Alex through her neglect of his hygiene and dress. The other accounts we have looked at also yield illustrations. Marianne Solomon's ex-husband is an absentee parent; Mary Peters's husband's ex-wife is an intruder, controlling the couple through manipulation of access to the children.

Ex-spouses intrude upon a remarriage because in a sizable number, anger and resentment are still present in spite of the divorce having become official. One out of every four couples who are divorced include one member who did not want it.[23] An unwilling divorced person is almost guaranteed to try to maintain control over, or at least contact with, the ex-spouse.

Gender influences feelings toward ex-spouses. About three-quarters of divorces are initiated by women. A former spouse is more likely to adjust to divorce if he or she was the initiator, because initiators tend to see the consequences of the separation as good. Since most initiators are female, women adjust more easily to divorce than men.[24] In one study, 41 percent of a sample of remarried men expressed negative feelings about their ex-mates, compared to 29 percent of remarried wives. Ex-wives were less hostile than husbands because ex-husbands were under a continuing financial burden, which may be exacerbated by the resentments of their new wives against the ex-wives as recipients of financial assistance. Ex-wives also have custody and thus control over access to children via visitation and bad-mouthing.[25]

Because women are more likely than men to initiate divorces, a woman's first husband is likely to harbor unresolved anger from the start. He will resent both his ex-wife and her new husband, with whom his rivalry is potentially acute. His ex-wife is likely to have custody of his children, and they will be living with the second husband. The second husband is, in all likelihood, supporting the ex-wife—and she may be working as well. The first husband thus fears that the second husband is "taking his place" with his children—although this is usually not what really happens. Though the second husband is under no legal obligation to pay for his stepchildren, his support for his wife and the household may be seen that way. Therefore, the first husband can come to see his payments to the household as superfluous, since another man is in charge. These resentments are particularly likely to arise in less-prosperous income groups, where incoming and outgoing child support payments are of crucial importance.

Children will be less of an issue between first and second husbands because the male role with children is typically less influential, though rivalry over the children can persist. The first husband feels that he should have a voice in how the children are raised because he is their father. The second feels that he should have the predominant voice since the children spend most of their time with him. His relationship with his wife is intimately tied up in this competition.[26]

Children are the major issue between wives and their first husbands. Commonly, children are both weapons and pawns in warfare between ex-spouses who have not completed their emotional divorces even though the legal divorce has been accomplished and one or both have remarried. As conduits for messages, as receivers of disparaging information about the other parent or his or her new spouse, children can be used for attacks on former spouses.[27]

The principal weapons at the first husband's disposal are unreliability regarding visitation and irregularity of child support payments. He knows that he can throw the household of his ex-wife into chaos by not honoring visitation commitments — by showing up late, returning the children late, and requesting different time slots. But most powerful is paying or withholding child support, a weapon often used.

The second husband is vulnerable to the first husband, because the ex-husband is a source of power outside the household that threatens his role as a male. Because second husbands are ordinarily married to wives who have custody of children from the first marriage, an obvious fact is that the first husband was married to his wife previously, and their past sexual intimacy is evident in the everyday presence of their children. The children themselves thus may threaten his primacy because of their emotional and biological solidarity with the first husband, as we will see in the chapters on stepparent-stepchild relations.

The economic power of the first husband means that the second husband is not the primary male breadwinner in the family. Being a breadwinner is one of the most important qualities a male is supposed to have in American society. In one report, 82 percent of Americans stated that "being a good provider" was an important quality for a man to have, compared to only 42 percent who thought this was an important quality for a woman.[28] Being a second husband to a custodial wife is thus a role that deviates significantly from cultural norms about masculinity; men in this role are consequently vulnerable.

There is a difference between the hostility felt by first wives toward second wives and that of second wives toward first wives. The first wife feels jealous of the second wife because of worries about her influence on the children.[29] This jealousy will obviously be less intense if the children are merely visiting the second wife, than if the ex-husband has custody and the second wife is living with the children. Money is a principal reason for the first wife to resent the second wife. Rightly or wrongly, the second wife is perceived as a factor contributing to child support delinquency.

The hostility of second wives toward first wives is extraordinarily intense. Two quotes will illustrate:

"I want her out of our lives. There's nothing positive about her. I've never felt enmity toward anyone the way I do toward her. I don't think I've ever hated anyone till now. I can really understand how people kill other people. I hate what she does to our lives. She's constantly involving herself."

"When I see his former wife, I feel like I'd like to kill her. I feel there is a knife inside me whittling away. I wish she'd just leave us alone. Stop calling. Drop off the edge of the world. Let her go away and do her thing and leave us alone. That's the thing I want more than anything. It spoils our day when she calls. I can see my husband's stomach churning over. Since she didn't want him you'd think she'd have as little to do with him as possible."[30]

Money, in the form of alimony and child support, is also the principal basis for resentment felt by second wives against first wives. If the second wife has been married before and has custody of children from that marriage, she may be receiving child support payments from her ex-husband at the same time as her husband is sending money to his ex-wife. In this situation, her resentment of the first wife is probably tempered by her being a recipient of payments herself, although she will probably not be receiving these payments regularly. But if the second wife has never been married, she is particularly likely to see the first wife as a drain on her household's economy, someone taking money for herself and her husband's children and depriving the second wife of luxuries and necessities. In either case, the financial pressure on a remarried man without custody is considerable. If his wife wishes to stay home, to be a full-time housewife and mother, this may only be possible if he becomes delinquent on his support payments to his first wife.

Remarriage of both ex-spouses is likely to reduce hostility all around. The anger of ex-spouses depends to a great extent on whether they have found a satisfactory new relationship. The resentment of a still-single ex-spouse is based on jealousy of his ex-wife's or her ex-husband's happiness, the fact that the remarriage represents the finality of the divorce, and that the new household symbolizes something he or she cannot control but which drastically affects his or her everyday life.[31]

Remarriage of the ex does not solve everything, though. It may reduce competition between first and second wives, since the first wife is more likely to feel secure if she has remarried. But if the remarried couple is noncustodial, the complicating factors of visitation increase. The ex-spouse will become a member of a family with whom visitation needs to be arranged; visits to the dentist, vacations, illnesses, and myriad other factors particular to the remarried first spouse's household will affect a remarried couple's relationship. And if the remarried first spouse is a noncustodial male, the financial pressures on him will probably increase, further undermining the financial autonomy of the remarried couple's household.

Remarriages thus have strengths that first marriages do not have, yet are subject to stresses that are absent for other couples. Stepfamilies are built on such shifting sands. The relations between adults and children are even more potentially problematic. A childless remarried couple, after all, may do the best they can to make their marriage work, but if it does not, they can call it quits with little harm to anyone. When children are thrown into the equation, though, the marital calculus becomes much more complicated. Ex-spouses may be kept at a distance, but children from a previous marriage cannot. They must somehow be integrated into the remarriage for a stepfamily to work. The dynamics of remarriage alone are thus much less complicated than those of stepfamilies. In the following chapters, therefore, we look at the varieties of stepparenting.

Varieties of Stepparenting

Stepfamilies are defined by the presence of a stepparent, but stepparents have different roles in different types of stepfamilies. Some have children of their own, while others do not; some have "mutual" children with their new spouses and others do not.[32] We start with the simplest type of stepparent relation first, to look at its barest essentials. Then we will look at increasingly complex types of stepparenting.

Maynard Howard became the husband of Francine, who had five children by her former husband. Bonnie Roberts provides the story of a visited stepmother; she married Ethan, who had three sons from a former marriage. Neither Maynard Howard nor Bonnie Roberts have children of their own, from a previous or their current marriages. They are *"pure stepparents."*

Eugene Brown, who married a woman with three sons from two previous marriages, has two daughters from a previous marriage. One of his daughters lives with him and his new wife, and the other has remained with his ex-wife. Eugene is therefore a resident stepfather to two sons (one other is grown up and lives in another state), as well as resident dad to one daughter and visited noncustodial dad to the other. Heather Norris is the obverse of Eugene; she has custody of two daughters from a previous marriage, and has been visited regularly for many years by her husband's daughter by a previous marriage. She is thus resident mom to two daughters and visited stepmother to one. Eugene Brown and Heather Norris are both simultaneously stepparents and biological parents. Their spouses are, too. Because both spouses have children from previous marriages but no children from the current one, this kind of stepparent is called the *"yours and mine"* stepparent.

Brenda Campbell's husband, Albert, did not get custody of his daughter and son by a previous marriage, but the teenagers were so unhappy when their mother moved out of state that they insisted on moving back with their father. Brenda has subsequently had two children with Albert, so that she was in the situation of being a resident stepmother of two with two mutual children. Less longstanding was the case of Monica Morrison, whose husband Daniel did not obtain custody of his son and daughter. Two months after Monica and Daniel had the first of their two children together, Daniel's son came to live with them, and stayed for three years; Daniel's sister remained with their mother. During the boy's turbulent teens, then, Monica was resident stepmother to the boy, visited stepmother to Daniel's daughter, and resident mother to two daughters by Daniel. Brenda Campbell and Monica Morrison represent variations on the previous theme; because they are both stepparents and parents of mutual children, they can be called *"yours and ours"* stepparents.

The most complicated type of stepfamily is one in which both spouses have children from a previous marriage and a child or children from the current marriage. Brad Henderson has two daughters from a previous marriage. His present wife has a daughter from a previous marriage. Two years ago, they had a baby boy together. Brad's daughters live with his ex-wife and her new husband in another state but visit frequently. Brad's wife's daughter lives with them, but visits her father and his new wife and their two children regularly. Andrew Stewart has a son by a previous marriage, who lives with his mother in another state. Andrew's wife has a daughter by a previous marriage, who lives with them, but often visits her father, his new wife, and their son. Andrew and his wife also have a three-year-old son. The reader will also recognize that Randy Maxwell's story, presented at the beginning of the book, also exemplified this type of family. Randy's Brad Henderson, and Andrew Stewart are *"yours, mine, and ours"* stepparents.

While each of these types of stepfamilies have much in common, the addition of roles, by increments, makes them qualitatively different. After we have looked at *pure stepparents, yours and mine stepparents, yours and ours stepparents* and *yours, mine and ours stepparents*, we can go on to look at the other sets of stepfamily relations.

Notes

1. Crosbie-Burnett says that remarried couples account for 10 percent of overall stepfamily happiness, while stepparent-stepchild relations account for 59 percent. Yet remarried couple relationships are deeply affected by whether one's spouse gets along with one's children. Remarried couple relations, therefore, are probably considerably more important than she argues. See M. Crosbie-Burnett (1984), "The Centrality of the Step Relationship: A challenge to Family Theory and Practice," *Family Relations* 33, 459–63.
2. A. Goettig (1982), "The Six Stages of Remarriage: Developmental Tasks of Remarriage After Divorce," *Family Relations* 31, 213–22.
3. L. Westoff (1977), *The Second Time Around: Remarriage in America* (New York: Viking), 126.
4. J. Keshet (1987), *Love and Power in the Stepfamily: A Practical Guide* (New York; McGraw Hill), 31.
5. L. White and A. Booth (1985), "The Quality and Stability of Remarriages: The Role of Stepchildren," *American Sociological Review* 50, 689–98.
6. N. Glenn and C. Weaver (1977), "The Marital Happiness of Remarried Divorced Persons," *Journal of Marriage and the Family* 39, 331–38.
7. L. White (1979), "Sex Differentials in the Effect of Remarriage on Global Happiness," *Journal of Marriage and the Family* 41, 869–73.
8. A. Ambert (1984), "Separated Women and Remarried Behavior: A Compari-

son of Financially Secure and Financially Insecure Women," *Journal of Divorce* 6, 3, 43–54; see also A. Ambert (1986), "Remarried Men and Remarried Women: How Are they Different?" *Journal of Divorce* 9, 4, 107, 113.
9. J. Jacobs and F. Furstenberg (1986), "Changing Places: Conjugal Careers and Women's Marital Mobility," *Social Forces* 64, 714–32.
10. Duberman, *The Reconstituted Family*, 47.
11. P. 696 of L. White and A. Booth (1985), "The Quality and Stability of Remarriages: The Role of Stepchildren," *American Sociological Review* 50, 689–98.
12. S. Hanna and P. Knaub (1981), "Cohabitation Before Remarriage: Its Relationship to Family Strengths," *Alternative Lifestyles* 4, 507–22.
13. T. Halliday (1980), "Remarriage: The More Compleat Institution?" *American Journal of Sociology* 86, 3 (November), 630–35.
14. Rosenbaum and Rosenbaum (1977), *Stepparenting*, 17.
15. Keshet, *Love and Power*, 154ff.
16. J. Kvanli and G. Jennings (1986), "Recoupling: Development and Establishment of the Spousal Subsystem in Remarriage," *Journal of Divorce* 10, 1/2, 189–203.
17. Keshet, *Love and Power*, 38–45.
18. For a book-length description of the role of the second wife, see Jean Baer (1972), *The Second Wife: How to Live Happily with a Man who Has Been Married Before* (Garden City, N.Y.: Doubleday).
19. J. Keshet, *Love and Power*, 167ff.
20. C. Ahrons and R. Rodgers (1987), *Divorced Families: A Multidisciplinary, Developmental View* (New York: Norton), 114–21.
21. Keshet, *Love and Power*, 150–51.
22. N. Hafkin (1987), "The Difficult Former Spouse: Establishing Strategies, Extinguishing the Problem," *Stepfamily Bulletin* (Spring), 2, 4, 6, 8.
23. L. Westoff (1977), *The Second Time Around: Remarriage in America* (New York: Viking), 21.
24. E. Petit and B. Bloom (1984), "Whose Decision Was It? The Effects of Initiator Status on Adjustment to Marital Disruption," *Journal of Marriage and the Family* 46, 3, 587–95.
25. Duberman, *The Reconstituted Family*, 77–83.
26. Keshet, *Love and Power*, 168.
27. Westoff, *The Second Time Around*, 49–50.
28. *Public Opinion*, December/January 1979–80, 143–44.
29. Westoff, *The Second Time Around*, 52.
30. Ibid., 47.
31. Keshet, *Love and Power*, 163.
32. Different writers have developed many different typologies of stepfamilies. For one, see M. Ihinger-Tallmann and K. Pasley (1986), "Remarriage and Integration within the Community," *Journal of Marriage and the Family* 48, 395–405. For a typology that takes children's perceptions as the organizing principle, see P. Gross (1986), "Defining Post-Divorce Remarried Families: A Typology Based on the Subjective Perceptions of Children," *Journal of Divorce* 10, 1/2, 205–17.

3

"Pure" Stepparents: Less Risks, Less Rewards

Maynard Howard

In 1969 Maynard Howard was discharged from the navy after more than a decade on active duty. Although he had been married briefly years before, he was single then and had no children. He went to stay with his married sister and found a job as a custodian in a nearby school. One of the physical education teachers in the school was a woman named Francine, who caught Maynard's eye. Francine was a mother of five children who had been divorced for eight years. When she and her husband had broken up, to make ends meet she had taken her teaching job and remortgaged the house that she had obtained in the divorce settlement.

Maynard's decision to take up with Francine and eventually marry her seems to have been based as much on practical considerations as on romantic ones.

> I got friendly with her and she seemed like a nice person and I asked her if she was available to go out. We started to date. She got a little serious and I knew I had to get out of my sister's house and this house was here. I said I'd help her out and help her with the house and be a good father to the children. So we decided we'd get married, so we did, in May of 1970.

Francine's oldest daughter, May, was living away from home at college. Still at home were sixteen-year-old Vincent, fourteen-year-old Wallace, eleven-year-old Maxine, and Vivian, age eight. The children seemed uncertain about the new arrangement.

> I sat them down and I said, "I'm going to be your father. You don't have to call me father, just call me Maynard." The kids just sat there and looked at me like, "What the hell are we getting into here?"

From the beginning, Maynard conceded the job of disciplining the children to his wife. "Francine would tell them what to do, and they went along with that." Significantly, the youngest child was the only one who accepted Maynard as a source of discipline in his own right. "Vivian was the only one who really came to me and asked me if it was all right to do this, if it was all right to do that."

As time went by, Maynard developed a close relationship with the teenage boys, with whom he worked on many projects around the house. One incident stands out in Maynard's memory.

> We had to dig a hole for the cesspool, because we needed a new one. I got hold of Wallace and Vincent and I said we'll save a couple of hundred dollars if we dig our own hole. Money was a little tight. So they said, "You get a couple of cases of beer, and we'll get our gang and we'll dig you a hole." So I said okay. Vincent was seventeen Wallace was fifteen. They got a bunch of guys over here with shovels. And I told them the size of the hole and I marked it out. They started digging. It cost me four cases of beer. Towards the end of the day, they had gone way down. The well was ten feet deep, four feet in diameter. All you could see was the dirt coming up out of the ground. None of them were really drunk but they were all having a good time. That's the kind of relationship I had with them.

Maynard got along well with Vivian, the youngest girl, from the very start. "Vivian was the apple of my eye. I doted on her." She was a third-grade student at the school where Maynard was working as a custodian. It made her feel special to be able to say hello to her stepfather during the day in the halls. Vivian's own adjustment, however, was tempered by her feeling of guilt about having somehow caused the breakup of her parents.

> It was right after Vivian was born that Marcus left this house. Vivian always had the feeling that it was her fault. She got a complex about that, that it was her fault that this marriage broke up. She lived with that for a long time.

Things were less harmonious with Maxine, who was rebelling against all authority at the time. The teenager began associating with delinquent high school students and became a regular abuser of marijuana. She also became a compulsive overeater. She hid food in caches throughout the house and became obese. Her stepfather's efforts to get her to change her habits were markedly unsuccessful.

> I went up to her room once and she'd say, "Get the hell out of my room! You're not my father! I don't ever want to catch you in my room again!" She said to me, "You know the best thing that could happen to this house is for you to get the fuck out!" Those were her words. I'd been in the house about two and a half years. I couldn't reach this girl.

Maxine new very well how to provoke her stepfather, which aggravated the tension. On one occasion, Maynard had permitted her to have a party with her friends from school, but the next day, "I found out about some things that had happened at the party and got very upset about it. I blew my cork and had a cerebral hemorrhage from losing my temper. I ended up in the hospital."

At age sixteen, Maxine moved out of the house. Francine could not dissuade her and Marcus did not try.

> We couldn't do anything. As a matter of fact, when she moved out, I helped her move. I had a van. I helped her move the furniture. I was happy she'd moved. I swear to God I was happy this kid moved out of the house. She was a real thorn in my side.

Two years later Maxine moved back. Whether because she was older and had had her rebellion, or because Maynard had given up any attempt to control her, their relations improved. She presently lives in Florida, and the two are on reasonably good terms.

Even before Maynard and Francine married, the children had regularly visited with their father, Marcus, a successful real estate investor. Maynard and Marcus developed a cordial relationship and saw much of each other when the children were living for or returning from visiting. The basis for the mutual acceptance was that each fulfilled the other's expectations. "I guess Marcus was more interested in how I was going to be for his kids," and he was apparently satisfied that Maynard was neither trying to replace him nor neglecting them. As for Maynard's perception of Marcus, he said with approval, "He was a regular visiting father during those eight years.

At Christmas time, there were always presents from him. And Francine got her support money from him all the time."

When May got married, she was given away by both Marcus and Maynard; Marcus was a welcome participant in all the subsequent weddings of the children as well.

Thus, with the exception of the rocky relations between stepfather and teenage stepdaughter, the stepfamily was stable and harmonious from the start. Eventually, three of the children married and were successful in their careers. May became a schoolteacher and married a high school principal in the Midwest, and Maynard is stepgrandfather to their son Emory, a two-year-old boy. Both Wallace and Vincent became land surveyors, and they, too, wed. Wallace and his wife, Sybil, live about twenty miles away, and from them Maynard has three more stepgrandchildren, Cody, Helga, and Adrienne, age ten, five, and three respectively.

Vincent's tale is less happy. He married a girl named Alma. While Alma was pregnant, Vincent discovered that he had a rash, which was diagnosed as leukemia. Throughout most of Alma's pregnancy, Vincent was in the hospital. Just before the birth of the baby, Desmond, he went into remission.

> We became very close, Vincent and I, at that particular time, closer than normal. I spent a lot of time with him. I'd go out there and pick him up, and drive him to the hospital, whatever, for therapy.

But the remission ended, and in spite of a bone marrow transplant, Vincent died when he was thirty-two.

Maynard thinks of the stepfamily as successful. Its success, for him, is demonstrated by the fact that the children all come back to him and Francine during the holidays, in addition to visiting their father. For the stepchildren, his house is as much a home to them as their father's, even though Marcus can offer them more in the way of material comfort.

> Marcus has been a very successful man; financially he's done very well. The kids go out there and visit with him, and he treats them royally. But come the holidays, they'll all be here. They'll be here this summer. And Christmas. It's a regular thing. They choose to come here.

The Sideline Player

Maynard Howard represents the "pure" stepfather not only because his role was not complicated by biological parenthood but also because he lived with a divorced woman who had custody of children from a previous marriage and received child support from her ex-husband. His resident stepfatherhood reflects the prevailing pattern of child custody arrangements preceding remarriage. His story illustrates several other common patterns of stepfatherhood as well.

Although at first sight it is dauntingly complex, the factors that affect the stepfather's role can be grouped into five broad categories. First, there are the stepchildren themselves—their age, number, gender, and attitudes. Second are the relations between the stepchildren and their natural father, and the amount of time he spends with them. The third factor is the attitude of the stepfather himself, his ability to adapt to and communicate with the other family members. Deeply affecting his success in this area is the attitude of the children's biological mother, how she conceives of and communicates her husband's role and how flexible she is willing to be. The final factor is the presence or absence of biological children, the custody arrangements the stepfather has with them, and their feelings about joining the stepfamily.[1]

Maynard Howard tells a tale of a largely successful stepfamily, as far as can be assessed from one person's point of view. The children who grew up in the family seem to have settled into reasonably stable adult lives. Maynard and Francine have successfully weathered great pain and conflict, and continue to rise above present-day family frictions. Which factors have helped or hindered this success?

Starting with the last point first, Maynard's childlessness greatly simplified his job. He was able to be as flexible and adaptable as he was to his new family's needs because he was unencumbered by previous relationships. His long bachelorhood in the navy made it possible for him to start fresh with Francine. As for Francine's ability to communicate with Maynard about her perceptions of what he should do as a stepfather, there is only negative information. In the course of the interview, Maynard said nothing about any criticism of his stepfathering on Francine's part.

Maynard was eager to be a stepfather. At loose ends after his separation from the service, he was ready to fit into the lives of Francine and her children. The strongest evidence for this is his friendly attitude toward Francine's ex-husband, Marcus. The children had and continue to have a warm relationship with their father, whom they visit frequently, who provides financial support and when necessary employment. Maynard's friendly attitude toward a father whom his stepchildren love is not only an illustration of his adaptability but an explanation for why he has been successful as a stepfather. His acceptance of Marcus was greatly aided by Marcus's success and wealth, which Maynard respects and admires. This may have helped to prevent any attempt on his part to take the place of the children's father. Stepfathers tend to be more self-conscious and self-critical than natural fathers anyway.[2] Maynard's parental deference to Marcus comes through clearly in the narrative.

Of course, his success was not unqualified. It depended on the age, gender, and attitude of each of the children. The relationship with the boys worked well because they were at a point in adolescence when peers were important and when the normal search for identity made it likely that they would accept another male role model. Other research has demonstrated that the presence of a stepfather can have a highly beneficial effect on boys whose father is absent as a result of divorce.[3] Their acceptance was increased by the fact that Maynard did not try in any way to compete with their father for their affections. He therefore did not present them with any of the loyalty conflicts that not infrequently afflict children in stepfamilies.[4] Loyalty problems are particular pitfalls with adolescents.[5] Maynard approached being a stepfather to them as a quasi-peer, doing yard work with them, drinking beer with them, and acting out a sort of all-purpose masculine part. The boys obviously appreciated it. But it was not all sweat and camaraderie. Maynard talks of how when Vincent was dying of leukemia how close he became with his stepson, and how happy he is that he could help to ease the young man's suffering.

"Pure" Stepparents: Less Risks, Less Rewards 49

As for the girls, Maynard's success was more mixed. The oldest stepdaughter, May, had already left home for college, moved far away, and was peripheral to the household after he arrived. Vivian, by contrast, was quite young when he arrived, and his description is that of a girl who was at an age when she needed a daddy. She had not yet entered the storms of adolescence, but had grown beyond the early years of Oedipal confusion and had partially recovered from her fantasy of having caused her parents' divorce. Maynard came along when Vivian needed him.

The greatest conflict was with Maxine; Maynard seems to have arrived at just the wrong time for her, although certainly not all of her problems can be explained as a result of stepfather-stepdaughter conflicts. She was just entering puberty, and much of the ordinary rebelliousness of a girl that age was directed against her stepfather. She evidently knew what kind of behavior enraged Maynard and deliberately engaged in it. That her stepfather suffered a cerebral hemorrhage attests to her success in provoking him.

Maxine's conflicts with Maynard illustrate a pattern that has long been recognized in stepfamilies. Numerous studies have shown that girls have more difficult relationships with stepfathers than boys.[6] This is partly due to the potential for sexual attraction between stepfathers and their adolescent stepdaughters. The result is that both stepfathers and stepdaughters are likely to feel uncomfortable; he will react with unusual strictness and she with unusual rebelliousness. Other research has shown that stepparents of either sex tend to have more trouble with stepdaughters, though the reasons for this are not clear.[7]

Part of the reason for the difficulty was the stage in Maxine's development at which Maynard became her stepfather. Children who are adolescents at the time of remarriage take longer to feel part of the family, because at that time they are also learning to separate themselves from their families.[8] This seems to have been more of a problem for Maxine than for Wallace or Vincent, probably because of their sex and because they were older, with a more secure sense of independence. Maxine also had individual psychological problems reflected in her becoming overweight, and abusing food and drugs. One study showed that a stepchild's satisfaction with a stepfather is directly related to the child's self-esteem.[9] Maynard was least successful with the child who evidently had the lowest self-esteem.

Another factor that explains those areas in which Maynard was successful and those in which he was not is that of the age of the stepchild when the remarriage took place. If a stepparent joins a family when a child is very young, his relationship to the child is likely to be much like that of a biological parent. Conversely, if the child is grown up, he or she will probably have cordial but distant relations with a stepparent. Vivian and May partly illustrate these two extremes. It is in between, particularly in early adolescence, that the difficulties are most likely to arise, as illustrated by Maxine.[10] The difficulties are mitigated by the sex of the stepparent and the stepchild, being lower for stepsons than for stepdaughters, particularly when the stepparent is a stepfather.

Some research has indicated that stepfamily success is more likely in higher socioeconomic brackets.[11] Ostensibly, people who are more well-off have more freedom of choice than those who remarry out of financial necessity and may be more likely to select a compatible partner. Maynard Howard, a school custodian with a modest income, does not confirm this. There is some indication that part of his decision to marry Francine was motivated by the need to move out of his sister's house, and that Francine's financial situation in part impelled her to marry Maynard. Yet by all appearances Maynard and Francine are compatible, regardless of the financial exigencies.

Maynard Howard succeeded as a stepfather because he did not try too hard. He stepped into a ready-made family structure, where routines were already set. He accommodated to the needs of these stepchildren who seemed to need him, though in different ways. He accepted Francine's former husband, and is pleased by the success of the one stepdaughter who never lived in the household. The only stepchild with whom he did not succeed in establishing a warm relationship, at least at first, was the one with whom he tried too hard. There does not seem to have been much interest on the part of other family members, aside from Francine, to accommodate to him. Research has shown that stepchildren tend not to understand their stepparents well, and to relegate them to a secondary status in comparison to their biological parents.[12]

Childless in his previous and current marriage, Maynard Howard has been content to remain on the sidelines, and this undoubtedly accounts for much of his success, as does the fact that his stepfamily has a relatively simple structure. Other sorts of stepfathers will appear in later chapters—Eugene Brown, who has children by a previous marriage as well as stepchildren; and both Brad Henderson and Andrew Stewart, who have children from previous marriages, stepchildren, and children from current marriages. Like Randy Maxwell, their successes have been much more ambiguous, because for them stepfatherhood was so much more complicated.

Bonnie Roberts

For twelve years Bonnie Roberts's husband, Ethan, was married to Rosemary, by whom he had three boys. At present, Nick is twenty-one, Carl is eighteen, and Mark is sixteen. Ethan and Rosemary were divorced eleven years ago, and Ethan and Bonnie married soon afterward. Rosemary has not remarried. She lives with the boys in the house where she and Ethan had lived. Ever since the remarriage, the boys have visited Bonnie and Ethan every other weekend, alternate Mondays and on every Thursday. For most of the time, Bonnie and Ethan's home has been within easy walking distance of Rosemary's, and particularly since they had a swimming pool, the boys also often dropped in unexpectedly for a brief visit.

Since the boys were eleven, six, and five when Bonnie married Ethan, Bonnie suddenly assumed stepmothering duties without any previous child-rearing experience. Since the boys were present only intermittently, though, Bonnie was an "instant visited stepmother." In her recollection, it was only difficult at first.

> Ethan had to go to work on that first Saturday morning. This was the first time that the children were going to be staying over. He brought them out on Friday night and Saturday morning here I am with three kids. I'm a teacher and I do deal with children, but suddenly chaos was reigning supreme. I was

overwhelmed—it was three little kids and me. They were running around and I was having a lot of difficulty at that point.

I remember calling Ethan at the office, and I remember he said, "Do whatever you have to do. If you have to end up spanking the kids, if they're not behaving, I'm giving you permission to do it."

So he really gave me license to make me feel comfortable. And I think once he just said that, it freed me up and I was able to deal with the kids. I never really had a problem after that.

Immediately afterward, Ethan and Bonnie sat down with the boys, and Ethan explained that since Bonnie was their stepmother she had as much right to discipline them as he did when they were staying in that household. The youngsters accepted the ruling, and from then on, Bonnie felt secure and was met with little resistance.

As time went by, Bonnie developed more particular relationships with each of her stepsons individually. Nick, she feels, was most damaged by his parents' divorce, and remains a highly sensitive young man. "He's very aware of special occasions and birthdays, very tuned in. . . . Very well disciplined, quiet, and obedient."

Nick was also a very poor student in high school, and at one point his grades were so bad that Ethan proposed that the boy come to stay with him and Bonnie for a while. He was receiving little adult supervision, since his mother was spending a great deal of time away from home, on her job.

> The boys would come home from school and there was nobody in the house. They could do anything they want, like blast the stereo.

Rosemary could not argue with Nick's poor grades, and was frustrated at the failure of her efforts. So it was agreed that Nick would live with his father and stepmother on a temporary basis, going home to his mother on weekends.

For Bonnie, this meant switching from visited stepmotherhood to resident stepmotherhood. Consequently, her ordinary activities were affected, as was her degree of involvement with Nick, since a lot of the everyday child care fell to her.

> Nick needed more of the structure and regimentation we could offer—when Ethan said something, it was the word, there was no room for interpretation. But after Nick came to live with us, I was the one who really spent time with him.

But more importantly, her privacy was affected, as was her feeling of freedom with her husband:

> It was an adjustment. We were used to our time alone. I felt invaded, less spontaneous. We couldn't run around naked if we wanted. Whatever you want to do on a mere whim, you can't do that when you have a child there on a full-time basis.

But as Nick's attitude changed and the quality of his schoolwork improved, Bonnie came to see it as a worthwhile sacrifice, particularly since her role as a stepmother was producing such evident and gratifying results:

> As I saw him blossom, to do much better, I felt it was worth it. I used to sit with him, and ask him questions, and I showed him how to do certain papers. I gave him interaction that he might not have been getting at all.

After six months, Nick moved back with his mother. Rosemary had always expected him back eventually, and Bonnie suspects that Nick still wanted the relatively unstructured atmosphere at his mother's house.

Mark was the most difficult of the three children, but, being the youngest, has had the most intense relations with Bonnie.

> I remember times when I would have to give him a spanking because he was just so difficult. Once he was visiting on a Saturday morning when Ethan and I were sleeping, and Mark got up very early. I had told him the night before if he got up early to be very quiet and just turn on the television. Well, at seven o'clock in the morning we hear the TV on and Mark is making a lot of noise. And I come tearing out of the room upstairs saying, "Mark! Be quiet!" Then the same thing happens a little later. At this point, Mark is flying down the stairs with me holding onto his arm, and he's flying through the air. He and I will never forget that!

When Mark entered high school, he ran into the same problems his eldest brother had. With his mother absent in the afternoon, Nick at college, and Carl a senior, there was no control, and he seldom did his homework, preferring to watch television for hours on end. When he also began acting up in class and receiving negative reports from his teachers, Ethan and Bonnie suggested the same solution that had worked with Nick. After more hesitation, Rosemary agreed.

> I really worked with him, studying, doing term papers, checking on him. He wasn't allowed to watch television except when he got home from school for

one hour. He worked hard, got his grades up, and ended up passing everything.

Eventually, after five months, Mark went back to live with Rosemary, too. But Bonnie says that she would be happy if Mark continued to live with her and Ethan. Not only is he the child she has nurtured the most, she feels she is closer to him than his mother is:

> He and I can talk about anything. He's said he feels closest to me because I don't judge him. Mark and Rosemary tolerate each other, but they don't have the kind of relationship he and I do.

In contrast to her supportive role with Nick and her close involvement with Mark, Bonnie's relations with Carl, the middle boy, have always been distant. Carl is independent, aloof, and, because he was always an excellent student, never needed the kind of intervention from his stepmother that his brothers did. On the other hand, Bonnie does not feel that this is because he preferred Rosemary, since he avoids his mother, too.

> We once said, "Carl, you were the only one who never spent time living with us." He basically said, "Well, that's okay, because there's no freedom." And Carl likes his total freedom. He would crack if he had to live with us.

There has always been a tacit undercurrent of competition between Rosemary and Bonnie, as first and second wives. But only at the beginning, "when we were all feeling one another out," was this more than a subtle tone to their relations.

> Say we were going away on a given weekend, and it happened to be a given weekend that we were supposed to have the children. Depending on Rosemary's mood, she might play games as to whether or not we would be able to have the kids the following weekend. She might say, "No, I'm sorry, it's my weekend and you forfeited because you were going away." She would just as soon have them, because there wasn't much going on in her life, and it took away some of the loneliness.

But this was only at the beginning. After everyone got used to the new arrangements, there was little friction: "She allowed the children and myself to have a great relationship, never interfering or putting a damper on it." Thus in one potential area of competition, Bonnie feels that Rosemary has not interfered with her exercise of stepmotherly functions, particularly in her closeness with Mark.

As we saw in the chapter on remarried couple relations, money issues are another potential problem, and this case is no exception. Bonnie resents the fact that Rosemary is still, after all these years, and after much financial success of her own, collecting money from Ethan:

> She still gets alimony; she collects a nice check. We're sick of spending money. At this point it's been a lot of years. I wish some other arrangement could be worked out. It just seems that this is going to go on forever. This legal arrangement was done twelve years ago, and at that point she wasn't working. That was in the agreement that she would collect alimony until she remarried. Or death. It's a constant albatross.

Ethan originally agreed to such a settlement, because he did not want Rosemary to have to remarry for financial reasons. He feared that if she did remarry, the stepfather would jeopardize his relations with his sons. Now that the boys are grown or older, both Ethan and Bonnie ardently wish Rosemary would wed.

Like Maynard Howard, Bonnie thinks of her stepfamily as a successful one. Being a stepmother has had its drawbacks:

> I think the greatest drawback would be regimentation. Not having flexibility. It's every other weekend, every other Thursday. Like clockwork. We did that for eleven years, where you knew that that time was set and sometimes you just had to deviate a little from it because you could just go crazy from it.

But the rewards more than outweigh the drawbacks. Bonnie feels that she has had an important role in the upbringing of her three stepsons. Not only did she have the rescuing role of providing vital discipline and remedial instruction for two of the boys; she thinks of herself as a confidante, someone who is an adult, but more morally neutral than a mother would be:

> In a sense they look at me more as a friend that they feel comfortable with — yet I get great Mother's Day cards! Mark thought I was objective and I am not in the role of parent. Nick and Mark may tell me something, and I have to make a decision, depending on the severity of what they tell me, whether it has to be kept between us or I have to go and discuss it with Ethan. Sometimes if they wanted it to get to Ethan, they knew I'm kind of like a clearinghouse.

The Rescuer

In some ways, Bonnie Roberts is typical, but in other ways unusual. She is typical in that most stepmothers like her are married to noncustodial divorced fathers. Since their husbands usually do not have custody of their children, they are visited by their stepchildren, rather than living with them. Thus stepmothers, in general, are much more likely to be "visited" as opposed to "resident" stepmothers. What is uncommon about Bonnie is that she has no children, from her previous marriage or from her marriage to Ethan. Although most stepmothers do not live with their stepchildren full time, they do eventually have their own children. In this sense, Bonnie is a "pure" type stepmother, but in a far from common situation.

There are indications that being a stepmother is more difficult than being a stepfather.[13] One survey of college undergraduates showed that stepmothers were ranked lowest in an ideal parental rating scale, while stepfathers were well received. Much of the explanation for the latter is that for children of divorced parents with a stepfather, the chances are great that they will have lost or greatly diminished contact with their biological fathers. Stepfathers appear "better" than biological fathers by contrast, while this does not happen with stepmothers.[14]

Part of the explanation also is that in most families, fathers tend not to be as emotionally involved with their children as mothers, since their primary responsibility is making a living and supporting dependents. Indeed, this is the basis on which mothers tend to be awarded custody of their children, since it is believed that for children to be taken from their mother's care and put in their father's would be more emotionally damaging than vice versa. Thus, a stepfather, it is believed, has a relatively simple job, in the sense that fathers are more emotionally distant from children anyway, and putting a stepfather in place of a father is not as wrenching a change as putting a stepmother in place of a mother. If a stepfather pays the bills, plays with the children sometimes, and helps out around the house, he can feel that he has done his job adequately.[15] In a word, fathers are more replaceable than mothers, and this is what makes the stepmother's job more difficult. Yet the difficulty would seem to be of a different nature, depending on whether the children are visiting or resident.

Nick, Carl, and Mark are, according to one terminology, "weekend children," and Bonnie a "weekend stepparent." One writer claims that this is the most difficult stepfamily relationship, since the weekend stepparent is the most marginal relationship to the children. The youngsters are there for the purpose of seeing their parent, and the stepparent therefore lacks authority and importance. Switching back and forth from being a regular spouse in a regular couple to being a hostess to young people who come and go as they please in her home is extremely difficult.[16]

Another study confirmed that being a live-in stepparent was a more positive experience than a visited one. Both resident stepmothers and stepfathers were found to be closer to stepchildren than those who where only visited; the stepmother role was more difficult than the stepfather role, and this was partly because stepmothers were visited by their stepchildren while stepfathers were more likely to live with them.[17]

A visited stepmother role is much more likely to be artificial and marginal. She is marginal, because on the visits the children, at least at first, are interested only in seeing their father. From the couple's point of view, the stepmother is obviously indispensable, but from the children's point of view she is very dispensable. Her husband, too, may resent her attempts to get involved in the visits. This is "his time" with the children, and if she pushes her way in, it may diminish the intensity of the visit for father and children. Ethan Roberts, to his great credit, overcame any temptations of this sort that he may have had. From the beginning, when he had to be in his office that Saturday morning and Bonnie was in charge of the boys, he let her and them know that she was in charge.

The visited stepmother's role tends to be artificial in the beginning of the remarriage, because the children and her husband want the visits to be a "good time." Her husband is so happy to have the children and eager for them to enjoy their time with him that the pressure is on her to play the hostess. If she insists on normal family routines and chores, she may be perceived as a wicked stepmother trying to spoil people's fun. Yet children in this type of situation may be in particularly acute need of rules.

When the boys live at Rosemary's, they have little discipline. The greater likelihood of undisciplined behavior of children, particularly boys, in single-mother homes, is well-known. Indeed, things were so lax that two of the three boys were in serious academic difficulties because their absent working mother could not impose order on their lives. To rescue them, Bonnie and Ethan took them in and provided the kind of structure they needed. Rosemary, like most single mothers, must work to support herself, in spite of her alimony check from Ethan. Because she is away most of the time, the boys have no authority figure in the home.

This theme is echoed throughout the following stories. An ex-wife has custody of children, and her household is in a state of relative disarray because she is overwhelmed by the dual responsibilities of work and child rearing. The visited stepmother sees herself as a kind of a rescuer, providing discipline and manners and order to children whose home lives are chaotic. She sees herself as relatively superior to the biological mother, not only more responsible but more attractive because the biological mother was rejected by her husband, and because very frequently she is younger. Compounding this is resentment about the financial drain caused by the biological mother. Thus Bonnie, and other visited stepmothers, does run the risk of being seen as an ogre because she imposes rules upon children bent on having a fun visit. Yet at the same time, the visited stepmother almost always comes off better, as a woman and an adult, in comparison to the custodial mother; the role is thus the source of much satisfaction.

Bonnie is articulate about the disadvantages and advantages of her role. The visits of children imposed limits on what she and her husband could do. Their presence was inexorable and confining, "like clockwork." On the separate occasions when Mark and Nick came to live with them temporarily, she felt a real disruption in her private life with her husband, even though the inconvenience was compensated for by the success she had in getting the boys back on track in school—another way in which she could prove her superiority to Rosemary. Yet at the same time, she can take pride in the achievements of her stepsons and be touched by their expressions of affection. She is important enough to them that they will occasionally bring a problem to her that they would not bring to their father. She can act as a buffer between them, since she is more neutral, a "clearinghouse" in her word. And there is no doubt that her affection for them, as expressed at the end of the interview, is genuine. As a pure-type stepmother, in spite of the inherent pitfalls of the role, Bonnie has managed to glean many of the advantages of motherhood without all of its burdens.

Both Maynard Howard and Bonnie Roberts are successful stepparents, not only in that they see themselves as such, but in that their marriages are of long duration and their stepchildren appear to be doing as well at life's tasks as most other children. A successful stepfamily has been defined as one that has lasted more than four years, since by this time 40 percent of remarried couples are redivorced.[18] Both stepfamilies easily satisfy this criterion.

Although the fact does not detract from their accomplishments, much of the success of both of these families is due to the relative simplicity of their stepfamily structures. For all of the complications and ambiguities of Maynard's role as a sideline player and Bonnie's role as a rescuer of another woman's children, their tasks are made easier because they have no children from previous or current marriages.

In the next chapter, the stories of Eugene Brown and Heather Norris show how adding children from two previous marriages provides a further dimension to the basic portrait of stepparenthood that we have painted above.

Notes

1. M. Rosin (1987), *Stepfathering: Stepfathers' Advice on Creating a New Family* (New York: Simon & Schuster), 71.
2. B. Robinson (1984), "The Contemporary American Stepfather," *Family Relations* 33, 381–88, esp. 384; P. Bohannon and R. Erickson (1978), "Stepping In," *Psychology Today*, January, 53–59.
3. H. Oshman and M. Manosevitz (1976), "Father Absence: Effects of Stepfathers on Psychosocial Development in Males," *Developmental Psychology* 12, 5, 479–80.
4. With regard to loyalty problems, see I. Fast and A. Cain, (1966), "The Stepparent Role: Potential for Disturbances in Family Functioning," *American Journal of Orthopsychiatry* 36, 485–91.

5. P. Lutz (1983), "The Stepfamily: An Adolescent Perspective," *Family Relations* 32, 3, 367-75.
6. See, for instance, J. Santrock, R. Warshak, C. Lindbergh, L. Meadows (1982), "Children's and Parents' Observed Social Behavior in Stepfather Families," *Child Development* 53, 472-80; J. Fischman (1988), "Stepdaughter Wars," *Psychology Today*, November, 38-42.
7. W. Clingempeel, E. Brand, and R. Ievoli (1984), "Stepparent-Stepchild Relationships in Stepmother and Stepfather Families: A Multimethod Study," *Family Relations* 33, 465-73; D. Camfield, "Cross-Sex Parent-Child Relationships in Stepparent Families," *DAI* 43, 3125.
8. A. Dahl, K. Cowgill, R. Asmundsson, and R. (1987), "Life in Remarriage Families," *Social Work* 32, 40-44.
9. J. Anderson (1982), "The Effects of Stepfather/Stepchild Interaction on Stepfamily Adjustment," *DAI* 43, 1306.
10. C. Bowerman and D. Irish (1969), "Some Relationships of Stepchildren to Their Parents," *Marriage and Family Living* 24, 2,113-28. This is what I have elsewhere called a "parabolic" relation between a child's age and the ease or difficulty of stepparent-stepchild relations; difficulties are lowest at the two age extremes, but rise in the middle stages of a child's development. (W. Beer, *Strangers in the House: The World of Stepsiblings and Half-Siblings* [New Brunswick, N.J.: Rutgers: Transaction, 1989].) For a quantitative study confirming the importance of a stepchild's age when the stepfamily was formed, see L. White, D. Brinkerhoff, and A. Booth (1985), "The Effect of Marital Disruption on Child's Attitude to Parents," *Journal of Family Issues* 6, 5-22. One other study questions the importance of child's age at parent's remarriage, but this study is based on *parents*' perceptions and may thus be biased. (E. Palermo (1980), "Remarriage: Parental Perceptions of Steprelations with Children and Adolescents," *Journal of Practical Nursing and Mental Health Sciences* 18, 4, 9-13.)
11. E. Visher and J. Visher (1979), *Stepfamilies: A Guide to Working with Stepparents and Stepchildren* (New York: Brunner & Mazel), 47-48.
12. T. Perkins and J. Kahan (1979), "An Empirical Comparison of Natural-Father and Stepfather Family Systems," *Family Process* 18, 2, 175-83.
13. Visher and Visher *Stepfamilies*, 48.
14. L. White, D. Brinkerhoff, and A. Booth (1985), The Effect of Marital Disruption on a Child's Attachment to Parents, *Journal of Family Issues* 6, 1, 5-22.
15. Pp. 49-50 in Keshet (1988), "The Remarried Couple: Stresses and Successes," in W. Beer (ed.), *Relative Strangers: Studies of Stepfamily Processes* (Totowa, N.J.: Littlefield Adams), 29-53.
16. Kalter, S. (1979), *Instant Parent: A Guide for Stepparents, Part-time Parents, and Grandparents* (New York: A&W Publications).
17. A. Ambert (1986), "Being a Stepparent: Live-in and Visiting Stepchildren," *Journal of Marriage and the Family* 48, 795-804.
18. A. Bernstein (1980), *Yours, Mine and Ours: How Families Change When Remarried Parents Have a Child Together* (New York: Scribners).

4

"Yours and Mine" Stepparents: Who's in Charge Here?

Eugene Brown

Eugene and Vanessa Brown were married for about twelve years. In 1985 they separated, when their two daughters, Ingrid and Kay, were eleven and ten respectively. Vanessa obtained custody of the girls and was given the house where Eugene had lived until then. Soon after the breakup, he met a woman from the West Coast who was in the same business as he. Patricia had herself been divorced for about ten years and had been raising three sons—Ernie, Colin, and Alan—from two previous marriages. The two of them got along so well that a year later, Patricia moved East with Colin and Alan and they married. At that point, Ernie, the oldest, was on his own and did not join them; he seldom communicates with them now. A year or so after the wedding, Ingrid came to live with Eugene and Patricia; Kay stayed with her mother, although she still visits regularly. For the past four years, then, the household has been headed by adults who are both resident stepparents, who both also have one or two biological children present, as well as a biological child living elsewhere.

From the beginning, Eugene's relations with his resident stepsons were impaired by the fact that neither one of them had wanted to come to the East Coast. Much of their reluctance stemmed from the fact that with Patricia as the sole disciplinarian, they had lived in an atmosphere essentially free of limits. In Eugene's words,

> Ernie, Colin, and Alan walked all over Patricia for years. They got away with murder, figuratively. They got away with a lot of things that they shouldn't have been allowed to do, but triple-teaming went on and Patricia got worn down to the point where it was easier to let them do whatever they wanted to. So that they were not used to being responsible for doing anything, including simple things like cleaning their rooms or taking care of themselves or anything.

Things changed when Patricia remarried, obviously, because Eugene was willing to back her up. This was difficult for Colin and Alan to accept.

The new regime was difficult for Patricia as well, because the boys continued to attempt to manipulate her and she felt torn between solidarity with her new husband and loyalty with her sons.

> We established standards of behavior and responsibility, and made sure they were enforced. It was hard for her to start doing it. They would play all their little mind games on her and try to wear her down even though I was here saying that they weren't going to. So that caused a certain amount of tension for our relationship, because she was torn.

Colin was obliged to come with his mother because under Oregon law he was a minor until he was eighteen years old. He had finished high school, but did not have a job and had not gone on to college. This inertia continued after he moved in with his stepfather.

> When he got here he would do absolutely nothing. He would lounge around and occasionally get up and make himself something to eat. He would hang out with his buddies and play football on Saturdays. He enrolled in a course at a community college, but he ended up not going.

At length, Eugene gave him a job at one of the companies he owns. The experiment was not a success.

Colin's job was to pass printed circuits through a machine that printed more information on them. It was not difficult, but it had to be done carefully. As Eugene says, "The hardest thing about the job is to keep from falling asleep." But his mistake was to guarantee Colin a certain weekly income. Colin's reaction was to infer that it did not make any difference whether he marked ten thousand or two thousand circuits, so he did as little as possible, coming in later and later and doing less and less. Eugene then offered to pay him on a piece work basis; this was not successful, either, since he produced huge numbers of circuits but often they were flawed.

> I had to fire him. He created serious survival risks for the business. I sat down with him three or four times and tried to work on checks and double checks, but he was still basically careless and dishonest about his carelessness. Within a day or so of my firing him he had gone out and found himself a job driving a cab from 6:00 P.M. to 6:00 A.M.

In addition to the employee-employer relations Eugene and Colin had, the boy was showing signs of even more serious distress. A year before the interview, Colin had attempted suicide by slitting his wrists. He has been in psychological counseling ever since. Eugene feels that part of the progress Colin has made since then is indicated by his ability to get a job for himself and stick to it. He also feels that he might have tried to do too much, to be too involved in Colin's life. He does feel that they have come to have a mutual respect for each other, in spite of the trying times.

Alan's reaction to coming East was, if anything, more negative than Colin's. He had watched his older brother and half-brother growing through their teens without any restraints and had imagined he would have a similar hell-raising adolescence. But his mother's remarriage put an end to all that. He feels "gypped," in Eugene's words. From the very beginning, he was truant, went from A's to F's, and was a serious behavior problem when he was in school. He has been so uncontrollable that the school and Eugene and Patricia have initiated a "PINS" (Persons in Need of Supervision) procedure against him — a quasi-legal measure that indicates that he is out of control.

> Alan has said practically right from the start he didn't like me and the reason was that it was cramping his style.

The boy continued to attempt to manipulate his mother, but Eugene would not permit it. As the stepfather persisted in backing up the mother, the boy's frustration grew and grew.

Eugene thinks that, in addition to losing his freedom, Alan's acting out is related to his own role as a stepfather.

> He has some problems in reconciling his feelings of his image of his father with me. I would try to do things for him and provide him with opportunities and was met with rejection. I think it's because here's this stranger from New York who walks into his life and is trying to do good things for him, when his father, who lived five miles away from him, on the West Coast, did very little for him. He saw him when it was convenient for him but never went out of his way to do anything for him.

Alan saw very quickly that rebellion and outrageous behavior were a way of keeping the focus on him. Being the family and class cutup made him feel special. Unfortunately for him, it has backfired. Eugene and Patricia came to believe that he was jeopardizing the whole household.

> You start to shift away from saying, "Boy, he's got a lot of problems, and he's had a lot of upset in his life," to the point where you start to do triage. You say, "Okay, you've had your turn, now it's time for ours. You're dragging us down. If you're not going to change, obviously you're not part of this family. For the protection of the rest of the family, you've got to go."

So the decision has been made to send the boy back West, to a father he does not know well. As Eugene explains it, the alternative was a state school or a foster family, which could well have made things worse for the boy. And perhaps the discipline that he will receive from his father will make him realize that most male authority figures require standards of decency and obedience, not just some "jerk of a stepfather."

Eugene also thinks that Alan's rebelliousness may have had other motivation as well:

> His father was married briefly, and Hannah, who was his wife, is a really sweet person, and Alan lived with them for about a year when he was seven or eight. It's one of the glowing moments in his life, because he was the center of Hannah's attention, she doted on him. I often wonder if he doesn't figure once he gets to Oregon he can get his father so pissed off that he'll go live with Hannah.

If this is indeed Alan's secret agenda, he is bound to be disappointed. Hannah has remarried and has discreetly informed Eugene and Patricia that she has no desire to have Alan live with her. Moreover, with his father, who is a career military man intolerant of dissent,

Alan will face discipline much stricter than he has faced in the family that expelled him.

The stepfamily has worked out more happily for Eugene's daughters, but not without a few bumps on the way. Ingrid, by his account, wanted to live with him from the beginning, but her mother would not permit it. However, things deteriorated between mother and daughter.

> Her relationship with her mother had reached the point where they were battling all the time and bordered on getting physical. And she just finally decided she had to get out and she called me up one day and I went and got her and brought her over here.

In her new home, in contrast to the change encountered by her stepbrothers, Ingrid faces a much less restrictive atmosphere. Vanessa's values are very different from Eugene's, and by his account more superficial and materialistic—looking just right and dressing just right are important to her. With Eugene and Patricia, there are standards, but they are pared down to essentials such as school work, chores, and manners. Technically, Vanessa still has custody, since Ingrid is sixteen but has chosen not to fight the move.

> The first few weeks she had some problems at school. When she moved here she started cutting classes. And with the discussions we had with counselors and all that, it seemed that the previous year she had attempted suicide three times. When she was living with her mother. I wasn't aware of that. Her mother didn't know. What she did was take a bottle of aspirin and got sick to her stomach. Although it wasn't life threatening, it was extremely serious, if nothing else because she was crying out for help.

Moving to the new home seems to be what Ingrid needed, because in the ensuing years she has blossomed.

> She's done very well. She's back to being the self-assured person she was. She knows where she is at. She may not know exactly what career she's going into, but she has turned from a kid who was totally depressed, who was going to quit school as soon as she was sixteen, to somebody who's talking about going to college and deciding where she wants to go. And she's got her act together with her social life; she's really come around.

The only significant adjustment problem faced by Ingrid has been created by her stepbrother, Alan, who seems to have grated on everyone's nerves. But "she's established her own turf, and

Alan's turf," in Eugene's words. In any case, Alan will soon be leaving.

Kay visits but does not live in the stepfamily household. Eugene has no explanation for why she consents to stay with her mother and her sister did not, beyond describing her as living independently of her mother, too:

> Kay structures her life so that she's very busy. She doesn't come home a lot; she very often spends the weekend with friends. She has created other environments to live in that minimize the contact with her mother. She's very involved with dancing, with lessons up the kazoo, she's involved with band, orchestra, chorus at school, and she's very involved with life. It requires a minimal amount of time with her mother.

Eugene does not express regret that she does not live with him, as he evidently sees her as living almost as independently as Ernie.

He is realistic about the strengths and weaknesses of the stepfamily he and Patricia have tried to forge. He acknowledges that he did not succeed, insofar as he had any control over what happened, in integrating Alan into the home. he also sees the accommodation with Colin as partial, at best. Of the boys, he says, "I love both Alan and Colin like they were my own kids, and I want to help them as much as I can." After his failed attempts to help both boys, though, he is now obliged to see that his power to help them is severely limited. He sees that both his daughters have adapted well, and attributes this in large part to the success of his marriage to Patricia—which certainly passed a test of fire at the hands of Colin and Alan—and to his daughters' affection for their stepmother:

> They love Patricia very much, both of them do. They call her "Mom" and really mean it. It's a very good feeling that they have. Ingrid and Kay, really, almost from the word go, felt very strongly about Patricia. It's very clear they love her and Patricia feels the same way. They say to me, "Well, it's nice you made the right choice the second time around, Dad."

Triage

When medical personnel are presented with the wounded from an accident or a battle, they carry out an agonizing procedure known as *triage*. The injured are separated into three groups—those whose wounds are sufficiently superficial that care for them can be deferred, those whose wounds are serious enough to require immediate attention, and those whose wounds are so serious that there is no reasonable expectation that they will survive.

In Eugene Brown's family, the stepparents have practiced a form of triage. Patricia's son Ernie and Eugene's daughter Kay are walking wounded; neither lives in the stepfamily household, and insofar as they have suffered from the warfare of divorce and its aftereffects, they can manage on their own. Eugene's stepson Colin, and Patricia's stepdaughter Ingrid were more seriously wounded; both attempted suicide, both showed signs of serious depression. Both live in the stepfamily household, and while this was a trial for Colin and a balm for Ingrid, both seem to have benefitted in their separate ways from living with the family. But for Alan, things are different. The twists and turns of his family history were so sharp, occurring at decisive stages in his growing up, that the adults cannot allow him to stay, in spite of their best efforts. By Eugene's account, Alan's very presence threatens the stepfamily's survival. What kinds of stepfamily dynamics can produce this result?

Parental authority is almost automatically more legitimate than stepparental authority.[1] The specific nature of the parent's authority is likely to have been consolidated over a period of time when the children were in a single-parent situation with the custodial parent. Relationships established during this prestepfamily era are likely to involve intensely proprietary feelings between parent and child, which are strongly resistant to change when the parent remarries.

During the single-parent phase, which usually takes place in a single-mother family, the parent comes to rely on her children in the absence of her spouse, for emotional fulfillment and for practical tasks. Because she is probably overwhelmed by the triple tasks of being sole resident parent, homemaker, and supplementary or primary breadwinner, she is likely to consult with the eldest about decisions, share experiences, and communicate emotional ups and downs. Children, especially the eldest, are thus elevated to quasi-adult status. And when the eldest is a male, his position is particularly privileged. He has inordinate power as well as responsibility, in comparison to his peers in nuclear families, and he has become "the man of the house" in emotionally very satisfying ways, particularly in that he has taken his father's place. When an adult male arrives in the household to break up this comfortable interdependence, rage and frustration are likely among the children, especially the eldest, particularly if they are boys.

In the case of Patricia's children, this process was particularly intense, because she had been their single parent for a comparatively long time, and all three of them were boys. They became masters at manipulation on the occasions when their mother did try to assert her authority, and Eugene's allusions suggest that these were fairly rare. Eugene's marriage to Patricia drastically changed the power relationships between Colin and Alan and their mother. To make the change even more painful, the boys were forced to move from Oregon to Long Island. Although their home is in an attractive suburb, they saw the move as a grievous loss, not only of freedom but of friends and a more casual style of life.[2]

What is more, Patricia was successful in transferring her priority from her biological relations with her sons to her marital relation to Eugene. Although Eugene's account is indirect, it is apparent that Patricia had considerable difficulty in putting her marriage bond to Eugene above her maternal relationships. For a stepfamily to succeed in the long run, a division of authority between generations that runs directly counter to the parent-child team that flourishes during the single-parent phase must be reestablished. Difficult as this is for a remarrying parent, it may be even more so for a child, to whom it appears as a betrayal.

Along with anger at loss of power, remarriage marks other kinds of loss. Not only do stepfamilies stem from a previous loss, either divorce or death; remarriage itself is a loss from the children's point of view. It is an event that confirms the earlier loss, and in the case of divorce spells an end to the dream children often have of reuniting the biological parents. That this dream contradicts the power the children have over their custodial parent does not diminish its appeal. Remarriage also confirms the divorce because the children are now living with a stepparent rather than the biological parent.[3] These losses make for much acknowledged or unspoken sorrow.

When anger and sorrow are coupled with powerlessness, as is usually the case with children, it takes other forms. One of the youngsters, Colin, simply withdrew for a while; his extreme passivity and inertia are certainly signs of depression. The only arena where he could take revenge on what he saw as the agent of his misery was in a kind of pointless and petty guerrilla warfare against his stepfather's company while he was employed there. It was petty because it only confirmed his stepfather's power and pointless because he was bound to be caught. He seems to have felt so defeated by everything—the loss of his friends, of his old neighborhood, of his freedom, by his feeling of intellectual inadequacy in junior college, by the prospect of employment, and by life in his new neighborhood—that he simply gave up and eventually attempted suicide.

Alan's reaction was more extreme in a way, because of the stage of life he was in when the remarriage took place. In addition to all the frustrations that confronted Colin, Alan's were compounded by their taking place in his early adolescence, when he was beginning the process of separation from his family and establishment of himself as an individual. For his brothers, this stage had been unconfined—as male adolescents with an overburdened single mother, they must have had a lot of fun with few responsibilities. But just when he was about to enjoy being a teenager as his older brothers had, Alan's life was turned upside down by his mother's remarriage. His rage and frustration at the situation, rather than being turned inward, as they had with Colin, were directed outward, against everyone and everything.

This does not mean that Alan's ejection from the stepfamily was inevitable. It is probable that Alan became the focus of other conflicts in the family through a process called *scapegoating*.[4] Parents who unconsciously wish to conceal discord between each other or other family members identify one child as the source of all disorder, the scapegoat. The child cooperates by acting disruptively, if only because it draws attention to him. Besides, scapegoating confirms his self-centered belief that he is the cause of everything; children, especially younger children, tend to believe that they are to blame for parental divorce, and their feeling of narcissistic omnipotence continues into the remarriage.

Finally, children actually do have greater power in stepfamilies than in conventional families, at least to the extent that the biological tie between them and their parent gives them an edge. If a stepparent should be so foolish as to say, "It's him or me!" a child knows—consciously or unconsciously—that the stepparent might be the one to be rejected. A scapegoated child acts out in part because of the relatively greater power to disintegrate marriages that children really do possess in stepfamilies.

The background to scapegoating in this context is called *pseudomutuality*, a desire on the part of parents to maintain the pretense that the family would otherwise be healthy if it were not for the symptomatic child. Such false closeness is effectively reinforced to the extent that other family members unite against the disrupter. Family solidarity really can thereby be maintained—at least for a while—by the common front in the face of the alleged source of all the problems.

The importance of maintaining pseudomutuality is much greater in the stepfamily than in conventional families because of the threatening nature of intrafamily conflict. People in stepfamilies formed by divorce and remarriage tend to perceive interpersonal conflict as a possible sign that the family will fall apart again. Such hostility did, in fact, lead to a family's dissolution before, so that this fear is not entirely unfounded. From the children's point of view, this may be something to encourage or discourage, depending on whether the child wishes to exert a centrifugal or centripetal force on the remarried couple. If the child wants to disrupt the remarriage, there are plenty of opportunities to do so, and he or she has a much better chance of success than in a nuclear family. If the child wants the marriage to continue, he may tend toward overconformity, attempting to be perfect in every way, refusing to rebel or disagree, and seeing himself as responsible for the success or failure of the marriage. The parents, wishing to make this marriage work, this time, may tend toward pseudomutuality because of the memory of the dire consequences of interspousal hostility in their previous families.

To what extent does Eugene Brown's stepfamily illustrate scapegoating? Ingrid is unhappy with Alan's presence, enjoys her closeness with her stepmother, and would just as soon see her stepbrother leave. Patricia seems to have reluctantly reached an agreement with Eugene that Alan has to go for the sake of the family. Colin, by Eugene's account, does not seem to feel particularly strongly one way or the other. The person who sees Alan as the source of much family disruption is Eugene himself, who really believes that the family's survival is at stake. Where this stepfamily does not conform to the general model of pseudomutuality and scapegoating is in Eugene's recognition that Colin's and Ingrid's problems stem from sources other than Alan's rambunctiousness. Moreover, in the typical scapegoating situation, the symptomatic child is kept in the family, because his disruptiveness is so important to family solidarity. In the case of Eugene Brown's stepfamily, the boy is actually being expelled. One wonders whether the family will function better or worse in the future, without Alan to serve as the alleged source of misery.

Eugene Brown presents an interesting contrast to Maynard Howard, revealing the essential differences between the two types of stepfather. Maynard is clearly a more marginal player than the more authoritative Eugene. Although Eugene was entering a long-standing single-mother family, the boys and their mother moved to Eugene's part of the country, and moved to the neutral ground of a new house that none of them had lived in before. Ernie, Colin, and Alan had not had a close relationship with their father to counterbalance Eugene's assertions of authority. It appears also that Eugene is a more active father and stepfather, while Patricia's ex-husband seems not to have been active in the life of the boys. In this sense, Eugene is stepping into a vacuum that was not there in the Howard family, because Marcus, Maynard's stepchildren's father, was always involved. Eugene's greatest asset is the fact that he has daughters from a previous marriage, one of whom deliberately chose to come to live in the new stepfamily. He thus has a biological ally to counterbalance the possible biological solidarity that might persist between Patricia and her sons. In sum, a resident "yours and mine" stepparental family is much more balanced and symmetrical than a pure stepparental one.[5]

As a "yours and mine" example of a stepfamily, Eugene's family contains a resident stepmother, Patricia, but her relations with her stepdaughters, one resident and the other visiting, are apparently harmonious. For Kay, who only visits, Patricia provides a noncompetitive contrast with Vanessa. For Ingrid, the important fact is that she voluntarily came to live with her father and stepmother.

Legally, Vanessa had and still has custody of her. Eugene's account of the divorce does not depict it as having been bitter, and his reproaches against his ex-wife consist of disagreements about values rather than accusations of delinquent motherhood. We are not privy to the details of what went on between Ingrid and her mother, but Ingrid's nonthreatening suicide attempts probably attest to her desire to escape her mother's household. Patricia's success as a stepmother is also partly due, as was pointed out above, to her ability to weaken her biological tie to her sons in favor of her marital tie to the girls' father.

Eugene and Patricia are both biological parents and stepparents of children in the same household. They are less typical, in the statistical sense, than a household in which both adults have children by a previous marriage but only one set of children lives there full time, while the others visit. The next "yours and mine" stepfamily is described by a remarried mother whose biological children live with her and whose stepdaughter visits them and her father.

Heather Norris

When Heather and Lloyd Norris met five years ago, both were divorced. Heather had two daughters, Audrey and Doreen, who were twelve and nine respectively. Lloyd had a daughter, Laura, who was then seven years old. Heather's ex-husband Jacob had remarried, to a woman named Matilda. At the time they met, Lloyd's ex-wife Rhoda had not yet remarried. When they started dating, Heather was living in Poquott, a town on Long Island fairly far from New York City, and Lloyd was living in Queens. Lloyd's breakup with Rhoda had been fairly amicable, and she had voluntarily allowed him to live for six months with Laura, which was the temporary arrangement at that time. The children were part of the dating from the very beginning.

> We are both very involved with our children, and that was a very important part of who we were, and when we came together dating it was natural that they come together as well. Lloyd and Laura might come out to Poquott early in the morning, we might go biking, go out to dinner, go out to a movie.

Initially, Audrey and Doreen were wary of this male newcomer into their mother's life. They showed an evident desire to monitor the couple's behavior and to slow down developments:

> Our second date the kids were supposed to go visit their dad, and they didn't want to. So it ended up that Lloyd and I went bike riding with the kids. We'd stop the bikes and walk along the shore and sit down on rocks or a bench. Whenever we'd stop the bikes and walk and Lloyd and I would sit down, one of them would sit between us. We had just met a week before, and we were laughing, because if I sat here, one of them would run quickly to sit beside me, Lloyd with his rear end in midair, and one would sit down between us. They were clearly protecting their mom or making sure one of them was between Lloyd and myself at the beginning.

After dating for a year, Lloyd and Heather decided to live together, and he moved into the house in Poquott. His divorce from Rhoda was final, and she had gone to live in Manhattan with a man named Warner, whom she was to marry. Laura had gone with her, and came to visit the stepfamily in Poquott on alternate weekends and in the summer. After another year, living in Poquott, Lloyd and Heather decided on two further important steps. The first was to get married and the second was to move to a town much closer to Queens, where Lloyd works. The three girls were happy their parents were going to wed.

> Audrey and Doreen wanted us to get married. In fact they were calling up friends of ours and trying to plan a surprise engagement party. I think Laura wanted us to get married—she was in on the surprise engagement party with Audrey and Doreen. The three of them were planning that.

The girls' reactions to moving from Poquott were more mixed. It was much better for Laura, who consequently had much less traveling time when she came to visit her father, and since in the old house there were only three bedrooms, when she visited she had to share a room with Doreen.

> She was upset that she felt she didn't have a place of her own. She was upset that the day bed had to be pulled out for her in Doreen's room instead of having her own place there. She didn't like it. It was important to have four bedrooms so that each girl could have her own room. There's a permanent place for her here, where she leaves her things and when she comes back she finds them. It's her room.

Audrey and Doreen, however, were very unhappy about moving. They were used to Poquott, they had all their friends there, and they knew the school there. They objected to the new house on the grounds that it was messy and ugly—Heather admits that at the beginning it was—but its saving grace was a swimming pool, which induced the girls to give it a try.

After the initial hesitation about Lloyd, and even in spite of the move, Audrey and Doreen began to settle into the new stepfamily. Their struggles at the beginning had less to do with their new stepfather than with their feelings about their father.

> They went through a period of upset questioning their own loyalty to their father—they would make slips and call Lloyd "Dad" and then tell me later, in tears, "I wish Lloyd were my dad." Audrey in particular was very ambivalent about wanting her dad or Lloyd to be her dad and at times she's come out and call him "Dad," and then would get mortified that she had committed the crime of calling him "Dad" by mistake.

Eventually, though, Audrey and Doreen came to realize that their affection for their stepfather did not contradict their love for their father.

Audrey and Doreen's feelings about their father further complicated the adjustment at the beginning. While Heather and Jacob were married, she had been a traditional housewife and mother, at home full time with the girls, while he had been away working long hours. Even though he had seldom seen his daughters Jacob initially attempted to obtain custody. Heather thinks, "it was just a harassment because he never had spent time with them, he was just harassing me. He had the money to pay for the legal fees to harass us, and I had to take them for psychiatric tests." Lloyd's much more participatory style of parenting showed Jacob in a comparatively bad light, which must have exacerbated their conflicted feelings about the men. After a while, the girls accepted the obligation to visit their father, while he accepted a more limited visiting schedule. As they have gotten older, he has had to accept the restrictions imposed by their school and social lives and they can decide when and if they do visit him.

Heather's stepmother-stepdaughter relations with Laura took more effort to resolve, partly because Laura did not live with her father. And before her father's divorce, he had done most of the child care, so she had previously had him essentially to herself. In the early days, she was angry and confused, but had few outlets for her emotions.

> I remember Laura one morning taking magic markers or crayons or lipsticks and she had been destructive along the walls of the house. I think she clearly was angry and was acting out. She was angry, but she was not used to talking as much as Audrey and Doreen. She was very closed with regard to her feelings. At that time if she was angry or upset, her body would become rigid, her knees tighten, with her legs stiff. If you said to her, "Come on, let's sit down and talk about this," she would run away to the bathroom and lock herself in the bathroom.

Laura wanted very much to visit her father, but it was hard for her to share him with another woman and two other girls, particularly since during the first year or so she had no place of her own during visits.

Laura's relationship with Heather began as "a lot of fun — going to the beach, swimming, laughing . . . it was a novelty, it was a kind of honeymoon." But when her father and Heather seriously began talking of marriage, "she became very tense, very uncomfortable with me, very nervous and skittish, in particular in my company. That made me feel like an ogre. That made me feel awful. And I was uncomfortable as well. I became tense as well." She constantly interrupted Lloyd and Heather, directing attention to herself. Sharing her father became more and more painful.

> Audrey and Doreen had some time off from school, and Lloyd took them to the college where he teaches for the day. [Laura] was very upset, and told him how could he take them and introduce them to the secretaries and other professors, because she felt displaced. She had always gone to the college with Lloyd once a term. The fact that he brought Audrey and Doreen was an intrusion into her turf.

Around the same time as her father and stepmother were getting married, her mother and Warner were getting married, as well. While she had gotten to know both of her parents' prospective spouses, their respective relationships were solidifying. In Heather's perceptive words,

> The relationships that were ongoing in her life were becoming permanent and fixed. Whatever fantasies she might have entertained of reuniting her parents, it would be hard to maintain the fantasies because now there were going to be two marriages.

But she had no easy way to express the emotions that flowed from these changes. On top of the family difficulties, Laura's performance in school also began to suffer. Consequently the adults agreed on some counseling for her.

> The psychotherapy was very significant. The three of us went for a session together, and at one point toward the end, Lloyd got up and went to the therapist's desk. We had been talking about some very heavy stuff, about Laura's feelings about what's going on, my feelings, Lloyd's. When he got up to pay the therapist, [Laura] broke down. He had been sitting in between the two of us—which was interesting, showing how he was trying to juggle—she lunged over and held onto me and started crying and saying that she loved me, that she wanted very much to be held. There really was a major breakthrough.

Ever since then, Heather feels, she and Laura have been able to communicate openly with each other. Indeed, Heather thinks that she is closer to Laura in some ways than the girl's mother is, because she is treated differently in the Norris household. Rather than a sophisticated urbanite, Laura is treated as a suburban child when she is with Heather in the suburbs.

> She said at the therapist that she feels like a ball being bounced back and forth, because she doesn't know what's expected of her. Here things are one way, there things are another way. In Manhattan, she doesn't have too much independence. She can't just go out on her bike. Her mom is concerned for her safety. Appropriately so. Here she has a lot more freedom and can be a lot more independent. I think in this household a lot more is expected of her in terms of neatness.

The contrasting styles of life in the different households were confusing for Laura at first, but with the help of time and some therapy Laura has accepted them.

Audrey and Doreen have had a similar experience with their father's household.

> Much more is expected of them here. When they go to stay with their dad he has a need to be much more adolescent with them, so they'll talk about Bruce Springsteen, they'll hang out, he'll watch television, wear clothes more adolescent-like. When he's with them he tries to be like a teenager with them. When they're here, we are not teenager-like, we are the adults in the household, and they are expected to participate and do certain chores, things like that. I'm not going to talk cool or hip with them as if I was a teenager.

Many more chores are expected of them by Heather and Lloyd, including vacuuming their own rooms and helping out. There are major differences in terms of values as well. In Jacob's house, by Heather's account, money is highly significant, and a person is respected in direct proportion to his material possessions, while she and Lloyd emphasize the quality of people's caring for one another.

Laura and Heather's relations are close, but not intimate. As an illustration of the latter, Heather tells of Laura's experiences with the initial stages of puberty.

> She is starting puberty. We just had an incident, because she is concerned when she perspires. I think she thinks maybe she's menstruating through the armpits or something, some terrible symptom of growing up. I saw her taking some facial cream or some kind of moisturizing cream and putting it in her armpits. So I talked to Lloyd about it, I said, "I think Laura's concerned about perspiring and I saw her putting moisturizer in her armpits, and maybe we ought to get her some deodorant for her if she wants. And he happened to be going shopping with me. I said, "Listen, when the two of you are together, maybe you should talk to her to find out if it's so." And it was so.

But the closeness means a great deal to Heather, in the things that she does do with her stepdaughter:

> I know that there's been heartache and upset, but I know that it's very good when Laura wants to swim laps in the pool with me. We have a deal, every day we'll swim five more laps; there's a bond. It was very important, we did it together. We built up the number of laps we did, and it was as if we were building something up between ourselves.

Although things have now stabilized, Heather concedes that at times it is difficult living with other people's children, and even more difficult if Lloyd criticizes her children. At the same time, she sees that "sometimes, as a parent, you see your child through rose-colored glasses," and that a stepparent's observations may be more honest and astute. But as an emotionally more neutral adult, a stepparent is freer to provide guidance and criticism that would ordinarily be rejected by a child:

> Lloyd and I noticed something very special. My oldest daughter, Audrey, had some papers to do, some research to do, and she needed some help with something. Now if I were to sit down to help her, she would have been at my throat in three minutes. She would have been resistant, in fact, downright hostile. Whereas when Lloyd goes over it with her she's much more open. If Lloyd tries to go over Laura's work with her, she gets downright ornery. "It's fine the way it is!" But if I sit with her, some of the charge is gone, because I'm not her parent, I'm not her mom or dad.

The same pattern developed when Audrey recently learned to drive. When Jacob or Heather tried to teach her, the tension was so great that little learning was done. But Lloyd had more patience and was tolerated more, and could be her driving teacher because he was a stepparent.

Heather explains what she sees as the success of her stepfamily as stemming from two key factors, both resulting from the adults' relations with each other. The first is the closeness of her relationship with her husband.

> I think the key to a marriage or a remarriage or a family is really the togetherness of the man and woman involved. I feel very much as a team with Lloyd. We clearly set up our household, him being the man of the household and my being the woman of the household, and we are very much a couple in this house. Which I think gives the kids a lot of security, and they don't have to worry that this world will blow up again.

The other factor results from the decision by all the adults to accommodate their lives to the emotional needs of the children. For Heather, this was symbolized in a stepfamily get-together on visiting day at a camp that Audrey, Doreen, and Laura all attended together one summer.

> Maybe this could be in the Guinness book of stepfamily records or something. Jacob and Matilda, Rhoda and Warner, Lloyd and myself were involved in visiting. So what we did was coordinate a picnic together. "We'll bring sandwiches, do you want to bring drinks, etc." In fact it was two summers we did it that way. It certainly would not be my choice of the best way to spend a summer day, nor is it anyone else's, I'm sure. We were setting up a picnic, and Rhoda and Warner arrived, and we set out vegetables and dip and immediately asked them if they wanted some. This year Laura's mom had made sandwiches, too. Laura has a terrific appetite, God bless her, she ate one and I had said something like, "Do you want a turkey breast sandwich as well?" And she said, "Sure, I'd like that," and Lloyd said, "That's what happens with stepfamilies — you have to eat a half a sandwich from that side and a half from that side.!" The children have to take potato chips from this adult but also remember to take pretzels from that adult, to take half a sandwich from this one and that one. So it's kind of funny, you can enjoy some of the humor in it.

From Outsider to Intimate

Heather Norris successfully traversed the rocky ground of becoming a successful mother and stepmother in a stepfamily, from the early days of dating Lloyd to the present stable role as both an active mother, a coequal wife, and a significant person in her stepdaughter's life. One study describes this as the journey from *outsider* to *intimate*, one that requires overcoming substantial but predictable obstacles.[6]

The stepparent begins as an outsider because of the intense parent-child relations that predate the stepfamily. This is partly because of the amount of time parents have previously spent with their children, and because of the ways in which children evoke intimacy from their biological parents. Even a hostile relationship, or a manipulative one such as we saw in the previous case, has a greater presumptive legitimacy than the stepparent-stepchild relation. Stepparents must also deal with the obstacle of loyalty conflicts suffered by the children, who initially resist being close to a stepparent because it seems like a betrayal of a biological parent. Though the biological parent is committed to the remarriage, the temptation persists to rely on the easy "middle ground" of parent-child relations rather than the newer ground of husband-wife relations. In the face of this initial resistance, a stepparent must establish a place for herself. Developing the stepparent role requires going through distinct stages.

The first stage is *fantasy*, in which all the members of the family have unrealistic ideas of what the future holds. Stepparents have fantasies about what good parents they will be, healing the hurts of divorce. Parents dream of how the new family will succeed where the old one did not. Children, however, fantasize that the marriage will end and their parents will reunite. The next stage is *immersion*, in which the contrast between the lovely visions of the previous stage and the gritty reality of stepfamily life cannot be denied. The children are not angels, they are hostile and unappreciative; there is no honeymoon, intimacy is often interrupted by children; the relationship is not a pristine beginning, ex-spouses are a constant and irritating presence. The next stage is called *awareness*, in which a stepparent moves from the thought "Something's wrong here and it must be me" to "Something's uncomfortable here and it's not just me, and furthermore I can tell you what it is." The realization that the feelings of exclusion are not purely subjective lead to the stepparent's understanding that something can be done about them, which in turn leads to the next stage, *mobilization*. It is in this phase that the stepparent sets about asserting herself as autonomous actor with her own needs and agenda in the family. If this phase is successfully negotiated, it is the one during which the biological parent must shift his priority from a parent-child solidarity to a marital one, looking at the parent-stepparent relation as that of a team. The following *action* phase is one in which relationships move from "triangles" to "pairs." Where previously the stepfamily had seemed to be made up of three-way relations in which the stepparent was always the unwelcome third, two-way relationships now appear: husband-wife, parent-child, sibling-sibling, stepsibling-stepsibling, and especially stepparent-stepchild relations from which the biological parents are excluded. This makes possible the emergence of a *contact* phase, in which stepparent and stepchild deepen their communication with and understanding of each other. It is at this stage that actual details of the relationship are worked out, that the stepparent and the stepchild write their script with a minimum of outside interference. In the final *resolution* phase, a sense of solidity and confidence pervades the stepparent role, tinged with sadness at a recognition that the biological relationship will always have priority in the end, no matter how close and loving the steprelationship has become.[7]

Heather Norris's description of the evolution of her role as a stepmother illustrates each one of these stages, sometimes dramatically so. (Lloyd undoubtedly went through the same process, but we only get glimpses of his adaptation.) Heather and Laura started in the fantasy phase with activities that both enjoyed, and Heather describes as fun—going to the beach, swimming, biking, laughing with each other. "It was a honeymoon," particularly because Heather felt that Laura's mother was not particularly close to her, and she could be a more pleasant adult companion.

Then things changed "when Laura realized this was serious stuff," at the onset of the immersion stage. Both stepmother and stepdaughter felt nervous, tense, skittish, and Heather "felt like an ogre." Laura defaced the walls, interposed herself between Lloyd and Heather, refused to talk and locked herself in the bathroom, showed jealousy and possessiveness of her father in relation to her stepsisters, and was doing badly in school. Immersion was particularly difficult for her because it was around this time that her mother remarried, to a man whom she had known for some time. After that Laura could no longer hold onto the dream that the stepfamily was going to go away and her father was going to get back together with her mother. There is no clear indication of what led Heather to the awareness stage, but what is very clear is how Heather went about mobilization. She and Lloyd talked the issue over with Rhoda, and decided that psychotherapy was indicated. Most important, the therapy involved the three of them, as the therapist doubtless perceived that a relationship had been set up that was painful for all. And the dramatic moment when action became possible was when Laura let herself go and hugged Heather, telling her how she loved her. From then on, it was possible for the three-way relationship to begin to become distinct two-person relationships where nobody was in the middle.

Although Heather says little about it, Lloyd's cooperation with her in dealing with Laura's maladjustment was an important step in cementing their relation as a couple. It is particularly interesting in this connection that Heather describes how her household differs from the ones where her daughters visit and her stepdaughter lives. As regards the latter, Heather says "In this home she's safe to be a child, with her feelings," while in Rhoda and Warner's home she is in a quasi-adult, sophisticated role. In Heather's ex-husband's home, the generational lines are blurred by Jacob's trying to act like Audrey and Doreen's peer.

In the action stage Heather is firmly in a coequal team with her husband, with the children and stepchild on a definitely subordinate level. "I feel very much as a team with Lloyd," she proudly says.

When Heather and Laura moved into the contact stage, it became possible for them to develop their specific relations with each other. Both love swimming in the backyard pool, and their summer contract to swim five more laps with each other every day describes an activity they have just between them. Heather is gratified that she can communicate on an emotional level with Laura, while Laura's mother and stepfather are more intellectual. For all of the stability and confidence of the resolution stage that Heather has reached with Laura, though, she realizes that it has boundaries. When Laura was showing a pubescent concern with her body, Heather asked Lloyd to suggest to her that it would be better to put deodorant rather than moisturizer in her armpits; she did not do this herself. There are definite limits to a stepmother's intimacy, and Heather realizes this.

Heather Norris's success in creating a visited stepmother role for herself took place in the overall context of a stable, functioning stepfamily. Remember her description of the tradition of visiting days at the childrens' summer camp, where biological parents, ex-spouses, remarried spouses, and in-laws all cooperate as adults in making the youngsters the focus of family care. There is no pretense that all the grown-ups love each other; Heather is frank that she can think of better ways of spending the day. But this annual event bespeaks an extended stepfamily unit in which old hostilities and resentments seem to have been worked through or set aside so that it can be thought of as a stable structure.

Eugene Brown and Heather Norris have "allies" in their biological children, whose presence either as residents or visitors gives them leverage in their stepfamilies. In the next chapter, we look at stepparents who started out in the relatively marginal position in which Maynard Howard and Bonnie Roberts began, but whose role in the family was transformed by their having a mutual child with their new spouse. These are the "yours and ours" stepparents.

Notes

1. See p. 367 of D. Mills (1984), "A Model for Stepfamily Development," *Family Relations* 33, 365–72.
2. L. White, D. Brinkerhoff, and A. Booth (1985). "The Effect of Marital Disruption on Child's Attachment to Parents," *Journal of Family Issues* 6, 5–22.
3. D. Mills, "A Model for Stepfamily Development."
4. P. 39 of J. Ransom, S. Schlesinger, A. Derdeyn (1979), "A Stepfamily in Formation," *American Journal of Orthopsychiatry* 49, 1, 36–43; see also E. Einstein (1973), *The Stepfamily: Living, Loving, Learning* (New York: Macmillan), 72.
5. A. Dahl, K. Cowgill, and R. Asmundsson (1987), "Life in Remarriage Families," *Social Work* 32 40–44; see also pp. 310–11 in K. Pasley and M. Ihinger-Tallman (1987), "The Evolution of A field of Investigation; Issues and Concerns," in K. Pasley and M. Ihinger-Tallman, (eds.), *Remarriage and Stepparenting: Current Research and Theory*, (New York: Guilford, Perspectives on Marriage and Family Services).
6. Patricia Papernow (1988), "Stepparent Role Development: From Outsider to Intimate," in W. Beer (ed.), *Relative Strangers: Studies of Stepfamily Processes* (Totowa: Littlefield Adams), 54–82.
7. This excellent model of stepparent role development is based on a more comprehensive model of stepfamily development in Patricia Papernow (1984), "The Stepfamily Cycle: An Experiential Model of Stepfamily Development," *Family Relations* 33, 355–63.

5

"Yours and Ours" Stepparents: Rookie and Veteran Parents

Many people who remarry have a "mutual child." There are almost three million mutual children in the United States at latest count; slightly less than one-third of the minor children in stepfamilies were born to remarried parents who brought one or more children into the new marriage.[1] Almost a third of stepparents, then, are in "yours and ours" or "yours, mine, and ours" stepfamilies.

Before the mutual child's birth, a stepfamily is an aggregate of persons kept together by the tenuous bonds of adult love and matrimonial law. Just how tenuous these bonds are is obvious to all, since divorce of one or both of the grown-ups ordinarily preceded the remarriage. But as a result of the birth, everyone in the stepfamily is related directly or indirectly by blood. In addition to the actual parents, the children and stepchildren are related to the baby as half-siblings. The stepsiblings in the family become related indirectly to each other by blood, since every stepsibling is a half-sibling's half-sibling. Even noncustodial parents are related to each other, because their children are half-siblings of the new baby.

Although social scientists tend to de-emphasize such factors, blood has great visceral importance to people, and heredity plays a very large role in personality. A child who shares genetic material with his half-sibling may very well see facial features and behavioral characteristics of his father or mother in the new baby. When this kind of relationship is present in a family, its internal workings are likely to be quite different from those where it is not.

The most fundamental change that takes place is in the nature of the relationships. Peoples' roles change from being reversible to being irreversible. To illustrate, the role of being a husband or a wife is reversible, while that of being a parent is irreversible. Divorce can terminate a marital relationship, while only death can terminate a parental relationship, and even then it is not really over. Similarly, in a stepfamily without a mutual child, aside from the parent-child relations that preceded the remarriage, all the roles are reversible—husband, wife, stepparent, stepchild, stepsibling. But when a mutual child is born, these same roles become irreversible. While a divorce can dissolve the former types of stepfamily, it cannot erase the latter type. The people involved may not be called by precisely the same term—the parent of my half-sibling is no longer my stepparent if he divorces my mother—but the tie is still there. The consequence of people's roles being irreversible is that they regard them differently, requiring more and different kinds of commitment.[2] This is not to say that stepfamilies with mutual children necessarily function "better," however that term is defined. A recent report said that there was no evidence of better adjustment in mutual-child stepfamilies compared to non-mutual-child stepfamilies.[3]

In regard to parent and stepparent roles, families are transformed in four fundamental areas: the balance of power between the spouses, the degree of teamwork between the spouses, the relations between stepparent and stepchild, and the relations with people—particularly ex-spouses and stepgrandparents—outside the stepfamily.[4]

There is an imbalance of power in a stepfamily in which one partner is parent and the other is not. The adult with the biological children has a presumptive authority over them not possessed by the stepparent. The children, at least at the beginning, tend to resist the stepparent. The biological parent may subtly and/or overtly abet this resistance, by overruling the stepparent or by neglecting to consult the stepparent when making parenting decisions. The imbalance is exacerbated by the fact that the noncustodial parent further dilutes the power of the stepparent, because of different rules and values emphasized during visitation, and by financial and practical decisions that can disrupt the stepfamily's functioning.

This is a particularly acute problem for men, who make up the large majority of stepparents, because their self-image as a source of authority is seriously undermined by the greater power of their wives and their wives' ex-husbands. Being a childless stepparent, conversely, may be a particularly acute problem for women, who as adults generally desire to validate themselves by becoming mothers. Thus both sexes suffer, in their own particular ways, from the imbalance of being childless stepparents.

When a mutual child is born, the balance within the couple shifts because both are equally parents of, responsible for, and authorities over the same child. The previously childless adult thereby achieves full membership in the stepfamily. This is why the birth of a mutual child has much less of an effect in those families where both remarried parents were already parents.[5] In our terminology, this would lead us to expect that a mutual child that creates a "yours and ours" family will have a more profound effect than one who creates a "yours, mine, and ours" family.

A birth that leads to a "yours and ours" stepfamily is likely to get much of the credit for welcome changes, and much of the blame for unwelcome changes. In the shift of parental balance, one of the less desirable effects is the heightened differentiation between a stepparent's children and stepchildren. These different degrees of attachment also exist in nuclear families, where in spite of ideals, parents frequently show bias for one child over another, but are greater in stepfamilies of this type.

The distinction between biological and stepchild is greater for stepmothers than for stepfathers, and the effect of the mutual child is thus greater in stepmother families than in stepfather families. In addition to lacking the physical tie of gestation and childbirth, stepfathers, like fathers, are usually more preoccupied with breadwinning concerns outside the family than with child-rearing inside it. The relative remoteness of adult males in families means that the balance of power is shifted more when a previously childless stepmother gives birth.

Another aspect of gender differences is that the sexual division of labor is altered in complex ways. Part of the "deal" for stepmothers is that they will serve as mother substitutes for the absent mother; this leads them to be more conventionally maternal. Part of the "deal" for stepfathers is to be more egalitarian, to help out an overburdened single mother; while some of this help is certainly financial, at least part of it concerns domestic tasks. Though stepfathers are more distant than biological fathers with the children, therefore, they tend to be more active in family affairs when they become fathers. Stepmothers who become mothers are doubly maternal.[6]

When the balance is altered by the birth, the social structure of the family is altered in another important way: the couple is put in the "middle" of the family. Prior to the stepparent becoming a parent, the central preoccupation tends to be between parent and child and between stepparent and stepchild, which in turn affects the relationship between the adults. Like the proverbial tail wagging the dog, this represents a misalignment; when both adults in the family are parents in their own right, priority can be restored to the relationship between them.

Parenting is difficult at any time; it is made easier when a "rookie" has a "veteran" around to provide advice. The parental team is thus made even tighter by the interdependence that comes from one "knowing the ropes." Becoming a parent, by the same token, gives a stepparent an insight into his or her partner's role as a parent; behavior that puzzles a nonparent is more understandable to a parent. Being better understood, at the same time, gives the biological parent better appreciation for his partner. The end result is greater empathy between the adults.

Parenting teams are made tighter by the stepfather being more involved when a new child comes along. In addition to the factors just cited, stepfathers who become fathers are likely to have more time and energy for parenting, if only because in their previous marriages the struggles early in their careers seriously cut into their family time. When they are older, men tend to be more established in their occupations and have less need to sacrifice attention to their children. And they are more likely to have altered priorities as a result of looking back at a disintegrated family and deciding that this time it would be better to pay more attention to home than to a profession.

A stepparent gains legitimacy with stepchildren by becoming a parent. A mutual child is a "ticket of admission" to the family. No longer just somebody that dad or mom is married to, the stepparent becomes a more acceptable adult to the stepchildren. Although it means relinquishing the dream of reuniting one's divorced parents, a stepparent's having a child with one's biological parent suggests that this marriage is not going to break up. It also means that one is related indirectly by blood through the half-sibling to the stepparent. Some evidence, however, suggests that the existence of a common gene pool in the half-sibling is less significant than the parity all have with regard to the baby. Remarried parents with adopted children report feelings of integration stemming from the fact that the child is related to nobody, equally, and therefore cannot be claimed by anyone more than anyone else.[7]

A mutual child rectifies the adult-child authority structure of the family because it makes the stepparent less vulnerable to the stepchild. Before becoming a parent, the stepparent can be easily wounded and rejected by a stepchild. As is often the case with stepchildren, this gies a youngster inordinate power that children in conventional families do not have. But children do not always enjoy this age-inappropriate power; while it may be somewhat gratifying to be able to manipulate a grown-up, it is also a source of anxiety. When a stepparent becomes a parent, a stepchild's frightening power is reduced.

The other side of this restoration of authority is the diminished resentment by the stepparent over the time stepchildren spend with his or her spouse. Prior to the appearance of the mutual child, competition for the biological parent's attention exacerbates tension between stepparent and stepchild. Because it is a three-way rivalry, it is a zero-sum contest in which one side's gain becomes another side's loss. When the adults have a child in common, the stepparent-parent, with his own child competing for his attention, is less likely to be jealous of the stepchildren.

Of the adults outside the family, ex-spouses are most likely to be affected by the birth of a mutual child. Ex-wives are particularly likely to be in competition with stepmothers, even in the most amicable divorces. Particularly when they do not have custody, ex-wives are more likely to be accused of unwarranted intrusion into their children's upbringing, while ex-husbands are more likely to be accused of the opposite—neglect and abandonment.

Thus when mutual children are born in a stepfamily while the ex-spouse is still childless and/or unmarried, the likelihood is that the "ex" will be uncomfortable and may retaliate. Conversely, the ex-spouse will be more accepting if he or she has successfully adjusted to the divorce, either by finding a satisfying relationship, by remarrying, or by having a mutual child in his or her own new marriage. The important factor is symmetry; just as the mutual child produces less changes if both remarrying parents are already parents, the maladjustment is lessened if ex-spouses have achieved satisfactory postdivorce relationships, and if there are mutual children in both houses. Even well-adjusted ex-spouses are not free of ambivalence, though. One ex-wife presented a beautiful needlepoint tapestry to her former husband and his new wife when they had a baby, and then immediately demanded an increase in child support from him.[8]

Finally, children outside the stepfamily are affected by the birth of a mutual child. Sometimes children in the household will want to leave when presented with a half-sibling, but more often children who were previously living with the ex-spouse want to move in. For older children, a "family-centered" home with a new baby has great attractions.

Both of the stories presented in this chapter illustrate this model of mutual child effects. They differ in important ways, though. Brenda Campbell, who speaks first, had her first mutual child after she had become a resident stepmother, whereas Monica Morrison had her first mutual child before. These differences affected the internal dynamics of their families and explain different ways in which "yours and ours" stepparents can behave.

Brenda Campbell

Brenda Campbell married her husband, Albert, nine years ago. Albert was divorced; he and his ex-wife, Harriet, had been married for fifteen years and had had two children: Cal, fourteen at the time of the remarriage, and Elizabeth, eleven. The children were living with their mother and her new husband, Irving, in Florida. Some four months after the wedding, Cal moved in with Brenda and Albert, and Elizabeth followed a year later. This had not been foreseen by Brenda. As she put it, "My stepchildren were not part of the package, but they both ended up coming here to live with us, one at a time." Elizabeth's arrival coincided with Brenda's pregnancy with Freddy, the first of her and Albert's two mutual children. Five years after Freddy's birth, they had another mutual son, Gilbert. Although Cal has since moved out, he lived in the stepfamily for four-and-a-half years; Elizabeth still lives there.

The return of Cal and Elizabeth to their father's home was unusual and was caused by the children's unhappiness at their mother's having moved to Florida when she remarried.

> It was hard, partly because they had to pick up and move to Florida and partly because they had to leave their father, whom they were very close to. It was worse for Cal, it seemed, than for Elizabeth. Elizabeth seemed like she was curious enough that she wanted to try it. But Cal couldn't accept the situation. From the start he wanted to stay here in New York.

Cal seemed so unhappy that Brenda and Albert consented to have him live with them, and Harriet offered no objection, although she retained legal custody.

Brenda initially accepted Cal's coming to live with them because she imagined he would be so little trouble. She was twenty-five at the time, and thought that since he wasn't a baby it would be easy. "I didn't feel like I was going to have to cater to him, cut his meat for him." But it turned out to be much more difficult than she imagined.

Unexpectedly, she felt as if she was competing with her stepson for her husband's attention.

> I'm a piano teacher and when I'd come home from work, I'd see them outside playing catch. And that used to bother me to death, that I should be out working and he should be playing catch.

Never having been married before, let alone having no experience as a parent, Brenda encountered great difficulty in obtaining obedience to her ways of doing things.

> There were the rules in my home—he didn't understand them, like that he should wipe his feet when he came in. And that I wanted him to pick up his clothing and put them in the hamper. And it was difficult because he didn't have to do that in his mother's house, so this was all new to him. Whatever it was that I wanted, that's not what he did at home, and he couldn't understand why he had to do it here. I didn't understand why I didn't have to just say it once and that was it.

Even this conflict of rules would not have been so hard, if Albert had not shown some ambivalence about siding with his wife in imposing discipline on his son.

> In front of Cal he might say, "She asked you to do it, so do it." But then he'd say to me in private, "Why does he have to? What's the big deal?" To the point where I began to feel that I had come to live with them.

Brenda soon came to have the feeling that her husband and stepson were a team, while she was on the outside looking in.

Compounding the feelings of being excluded, Brenda felt that Cal's presence was a serious invasion of her privacy. As a newlywed, she expected a certain amount of casual domestic dalliance with her husband, but found herself under such scrutiny by her teenage stepson that she felt inhibited by his presence:

> I am not very modest. I would clean the house naked if I wanted to, but of course he changed everything. I don't think he ever had a crush on me, I just felt he was always looking. Not with a sexual interest. Just looking.

And it was not just her stepson's infringement on her own privacy that disturbed her.

> I know when I had my first son I breast-fed him and all my friends were free to do it any way they wanted, but now Cal was fifteen going on sixteen, and I couldn't do that. I tried, once. We went to a drive-in and I figured he was in the back seat with his sister, and I was in the front, with the baby. I figured he might not even know, but then there was suddenly a lot of chuckling from the back. And it made me uncomfortable.

Further increasing the strain, Brenda had not yet accommodated to Cal's presence when her stepdaughter arrived. Brenda believes that Elizabeth had been unable to adjust to being in a new state, with a new stepfather and a mother who was engrossed in her new marriage. Her brother had left to go back to her father, so that "she felt like a tag-along," in Brenda's words, while her father's home seemed "more like a family," especially since a new baby was due to arrive there soon. Harriet was opposed to the girl's return, but "Elizabeth was beginning to do strange things, like sitting in closets." The summer she was eleven, as per the divorce decree, she went to stay with her father, but when it came time for her to go back to Florida, she said, "I'm not going."

Brenda's feelings of exclusion were augmented when Elizabeth came to live with them. Here were three biologically related people who had all lived together for a long time, confronting her, an interloper in her own home. "They all did things the same way. They all seemed to understand each other, and they all seemed to know how to communicate with each other. Then there was me."

Two things saved the marriage and the stepfamily, in Brenda's opinion. First, at her insistence, she and Albert went for marital therapy.

> The counselor helped us to realize that we needed a common front, that we had to make them understand that this was not their old house, that this was their new house. In a new house with new people there were new rules and if we decided on these rules beforehand, we could come to an agreement on them — those are the rules we'd give to the children. And that helped a lot.

Not only did Brenda feel that she was now part of a team with Albert, she felt that he subsequently was less inclined to question or subtly sabotage her authority.

The more important factor in helping to resolve the painful contradictions was Brenda's becoming a mother.

> Having a baby of my own is what saved me. That child was treated like MY child. I didn't want anyone doing anything for him; that was MY child. I did everything for him.

Brenda says that being a mother is such a unique thing that all other relations were put in a different perspective.

> Being a biological mother means love at first sight. When I saw my baby, I just loved it. He didn't have to do or say a thing.

Brenda not only had a child that was unequivocally hers, she became so busy that many of the issues that had seemed so important as a "pure" stepmother faded into irrelevance.

> The fact that Albert was playing catch with Cal — I became happy about it because I didn't have time to sit and talk with him and I didn't have time to cater to Cal.

The reactions of the stepchildren to their half-brother's birth were different.

> Cal wanted to know why we didn't just get a dog! Elizabeth was tickled to death. For Elizabeth it was like a little toy. I think with Cal it helped that the baby was a boy. Later on, Cal became very close with that child.

From the moment of Freddy's birth, Brenda feels, everything changed.

> It seemed to tie us all together. That baby seemed to make us all a family. 'Cause we all now had something in common. He was something to everybody.

Although some serious conflicts subsequently erupted, Brenda thereafter felt secure enough to be able to do a good job as a stepmother, especially with the stepchild who was younger and seemed to need her more. For example, Elizabeth was interested in music at school, and when the chorus needed an accompanist, her stepmother served in that role, which made the girl feel proud and special. Brenda also became intensely involved in remedial teaching with Elizabeth.

> When she came here she was a very poor student, with D's and C's mostly. She practically walked through the door saying, "Look, I know you're very strict about school, and I'm letting you know right now that all I get are D's and C's. So don't expect anything from me because I have dyslexia."And I said, "If that's true, if you put everything you've got into it and you get D's and C's then that's perfectly okay. First you're gonna have to prove it to me."

Every night, Brenda sat with Elizabeth and carefully pointed out new ways to study. By the end of the year, her stepdaughter was an honor-roll student and remained so until her graduation.

> I'll never forget when she came home after having had a test that day. And she said it was the best test that she ever took. And I said, "I take it that you got 100." And she said, "Well, I don't know, but do you believe that somebody cheated off of me?" She was so thrilled that somebody thought she was so smart that they would actually cheat off her paper!

At present, Elizabeth is doing well at college as a premedical student. Brenda is proud of having helped the girl improve her intellect and self-image, and for the friendship that flowered amid the toil. "We became very close. We've come to be best friends."

Her subsequent relations with Cal were warmer than at the beginning, because of her solidarity with Albert, her assumption of a parental role in her own right, and her attempts to make friends with him.

> There were times when I felt I needed to make more time for Cal. Not that there was anything I could do with him because he liked sports and I didn't know anything. I would even try and sit down and watch a basketball game.

There was also the fact that Cal became very close with Freddy.

> Cal and Freddy became inseparable. My little one adored him so, the sun rose and set on Cal. And at the end, before he left, my stepson couldn't bear to be without Freddy.

She talks with a certain sadness of the friendship that grew between the half-brothers, because since he moved out, Cal has cut himself off from most of the family. The rift has caused her much pain.

When Cal was to graduate from high school he applied to a college in Florida. He attended school there for a year or so, living with his mother and stepfather. He met a woman, Emma, on one of his part-time jobs and decided to marry her. Brenda and Albert were against their getting married, partly because they thought Cal too young and partly because Emma is seven years older than Cal. She is thus only four years younger than Brenda herself, a proximity of age that might explain much of the subsequent animosity between the two women. Albert grew to resent Emma too, because when he visited Florida to try to dissuade the two from marrying quite yet, he learned that Cal had bought a very expensive engagement ring for her with the money Albert had provided to pay for Cal's college.

As plans for the wedding solidified, more and more irritating incidents cropped up. Most important was that Brenda learned that her sons were not going to be invited to the wedding—this in spite of the closeness between Freddy and Cal. Brenda perceived this as Emma's doing.

> I felt comfortable enough to phone my stepson, and say, "You know, have you considered this?" And he said my children were not going to be invited, that no children were going to be invited. I said, "Well, I guess I can understand that, but these children don't fall into the category of just children. He's your brother." And she grabbed the phone from him and said to me, "I've had

enough of your shit! You've been trouble since the day I met you. If you showed up at my wedding, I'd have you thrown out!" I in turn expected my stepson to say, "Wait a minute!" We had had our problems, but we had tried very hard to be a family in this house. Or so I thought. But he didn't do anything about it.

The outcome was that only Albert attended the wedding, and avoided the reception. There are deep feelings of hurt all around, which continue to this day. For Brenda, they are exacerbated by her having shortened her honeymoon for Cal, while being repaid so shabbily.

> I'll never forgive him for doing that, because I sacrificed a lot for my stepchildren, especially him, because he was the first one. He took from me what none of my children took from me. That was my private time with my husband. I was four months married; even normal people who just get married and have a child, they have nine months. I only had four months. If I had it to do all over again, he wouldn't have come so soon. I don't mind having done it, but I do expect him to care about me, so I feel very gypped.

Her feelings about stepmothering are far from entirely negative, though. She is particularly pleased that she and Elizabeth continue to have warm relations. Like Bonnie Roberts and Heather Norris, she was able to acquire a distinct role in her stepchild's life, one that was more emotionally neutral than a parent, which made her as much a confidante as an adult:

> There are things I could tell her that her mother couldn't tell her. When it came to the birds and the bees, her mother was too embarrassed to discuss things like that with her, and I wasn't embarrassed at all. If she has problems, she comes to me, not to her mother.

Although she refuses to keep from Albert any confessions Elizabeth may make to her, her role is to be a kind of relay between child and parent, softening the blow of potentially upsetting communications in both directions. This makes her feel very important in her stepdaughter's life.

> On Mother's Day she never forgets me. She sent me a wonderful Mother's Day Card last Mother's Day saying how much she appreciated all that I had been for her and done for her. That's very rewarding because I know that's not automatic.

Parental Parity

Brenda had no expectations of stepmotherhood. Her marriage with Albert began as a straightforward remarriage of a noncustodial father; in her words, "the stepchildren were not part of the package." For four months she was in a role that might have turned out to be like that of Bonnie Roberts, except that her stepchildren lived in Florida, rather than around the corner. Then, without knowing what she was getting into, Brenda became a resident stepmother.

What are the differences between a resident stepmother and a visited stepmother? A resident stepmother is relatively rare, and when she is present in the family structure, it is likely to be because in one way or another the biological mother is unfit, either in the eyes of the law or one or more of her children. A home life with a mother must be seriously disturbed for a father to be given custody, while even a kind and loving father is unlikely to be awarded care of his children in a divorce settlement. The stepchildren of a resident stepmother are thus more likely to be difficult to deal with than the children of a resident stepfather. A resident stepmother therefore has a real challenge before her right from the start. It is compounded because a noncustodial mother is likely to visit and be visited by the children more frequently than a noncustodial father, or at least to have more influence. The result is greater loyalty conflicts for children who have a noncustodial mother and a custodial stepmother.[9]

Our cultural norm is that a mother is primary in the lives of children in a family. As long as she was not a mother, Brenda felt like an outsider in her own home. but as soon as she became a parent, she had parental parity with Albert; she was strengthened in comparison to Harriet, Albert's ex-wife and mother of her two resident stepchildren; she had legitimacy as a real adult with her stepchildren; and her children themselves gave her allies. Parenthood thus reinforced her position in the overall stepfamily structure.

At first, Brenda felt excluded by the emotional closeness between her husband and Cal. To come home and see Albert and Cal playing catch together, which to another might have been a heartwarming scene of father-son togetherness, was a source of pain to Brenda. The feeling of exclusion was compounded by several other frustrations, some of which had nothing to do with stepfamily life. Cal was a teenage boy, a species not known for their excessive neatness, and he was hard to handle. His father had been used to living with him, and they did things the same way. Brenda, who had no experience as a mother, had standards of cleanliness and neatness that were difficult to impose on Cal. She could not, at the beginning, understand why she did not have to tell him to do something once and receive instant compliance. Albert, as both a male and a veteran parent, was not only less conscious of housekeeping standards, but had trouble understanding Brenda's discomfort. Brenda points out that he overtly went along with her, but later, in private, would ask what the big deal was all about. His solidarity with his son made Brenda double unsure of herself.

On top of all this, Brenda felt she was sacrificing part of her marriage for the sake of her stepson. She mentions it frequently enough that it obviously pained her. Instead of a honeymoon of romance and intimacy with her husband, she shared a home with a grubby adolescent who seemed to steal her husband away. Instead of being able to walk around nude or in her nightgown, she had to be discreet and modest. Brenda's profession as a music teacher and Cal's avid taste for sports kept them from having things in common. He was a constant, irritating, obtrusive presence that, in her recollection, made her early married years a trial rather than a joy, as she imagines they should have been. This is a particularly apt illustration of one of the stepfamily features mentioned in chapter 1, that family members must adapt instantly to each other, rather than gradually over the years, as the family experiences new additions by birth.

Like Heather Norris, Brenda realized that an impasse had been reached from which the stepfamily could not extricate itself alone. With professional help, she and Albert came to operate more as a "common front." The therapist saw that it was necessary to change the locus of the family from the father-son relationship to that between husband and wife.

What really changed things, though, was the birth of Freddy, whose birth may have saved the marriage. The possessiveness and sense of power that Brenda derived from becoming a mother comes through strongly. The predicted changes took place. She no longer felt jealous of Cal's time with Albert. She became busy with her maternal tasks. Her standards of cleanliness became more flexible. She mellowed.

When Brenda became a mother, the couple was definitively restored to the focal point in the family. As soon as she thereby became a validated adult with greater authority, she could develop a closer stepparent-stepchild relationship. Besides being related indirectly through Freddy to the stepchildren, she became more acceptable to them as a figure of authority. Her relations with Cal were never as close as with Elizabeth, partly because of gender, and partly because Elizabeth was younger and more flexible. Brenda sparkles with pride when she describes how hard she worked with her stepdaughter. By any standards, it is an extraordinary accomplishment to have started with a youngster whose first words were that she was dyslexic and an underachiever, and to end with an honor roll pupil and premed college student. For a stepparent to have done this while carrying on the tasks of her profession and motherhood is praiseworthy indeed. And the closeness between stepmother and stepdaughter was such that Elizabeth was overjoyed to have another half-sibling, and was honored by being made godmother. The warmth that still glows between Brenda and Elizabeth would probably not have been possible unless Brenda had acquired the self-confidence she did from being a mother in her own right.

Brenda's situation was slightly different from that of the ordinary resident stepmother, because Harriet did not lose legal custody. Cal and Elizabeth's mother was not so incompetent that the courts assigned custody to Albert. But the family situation in Florida obviously had its problems. Cal had called frequently to tell his father he had to get out of the house, and Elizabeth was developing strange habits like hiding in closets. It appears that Harriet's remarriage to Irving was so engrossing that the children felt like "tag-alongs." Harriet's apparent satisfaction in her postdivorce life in general and her remarriage in particular were probably among the reasons why she accepted her children's going to live with their father with a minimum of fuss.

Cal came to live with Brenda before Freddy was born, but Elizabeth came to stay just before the birth of the mutual child. Elizabeth's feelings of exclusion during the previous year had been compounded. She already felt like an outsider with her mother and her new stepfather; meanwhile Cal was reporting back about family life on Long Island, which Elizabeth still remembered. Harriet showed no signs of having another baby, while at the same time Elizabeth was hearing news that her father's new wife and brother's stepmother was expecting. The contrast between the adult-centered home in Florida and the seemingly strong family atmosphere at Brenda's house became too much, and she opted to move north, a dramatic act of self-assertion for an eleven-year-old girl.

The fact that Cal's arrival preceded the birth of the mutual child and Elizabeth's arrival coincided with it explains their differing reactions. At first, Cal was indifferent, and "wanted to know why we didn't just get a dog," since his primary interest in the family had been his father. But Elizabeth "was tickled to death" and the baby "was like a little toy," because the baby was part of the reason she had wanted to come there in the first place. Subsequently Cal and Freddy became inseparable, partly because they were both boys and fondly knocked each other around and partly because the little one adored his older half-brother so.

The account of Brenda's rift with Cal is important because it is a sign of the emotional investment Brenda felt she had made in stepmotherhood. We already know that she felt that Cal seriously detracted from her early married time. She resolved the resentment by perceiving that the sacrifice and effort were worth it, for the sake of forging a successful stepfamily. Now that Emma and Cal have alienated everyone in both households, Brenda feels "gypped," because it seems to her that all this sacrifice was for naught. The feeling of having invested unwisely points out some of the difference between stepparenthood and biological parenthood. While biological parents sometimes feel that their children are ungrateful, they tend to see that the attention they pay to their children as part of the role of parent. With a stepparent, love is more conditional, in the sense that an investment of effort is more of an option than a requirement, and that it is reasonable to expect some reward in return. Brenda's splendid accomplishments in stepmothering Elizabeth are testimony to her investment, while Elizabeth's reciprocal loyalty and love represent the return. How much more galling is the contrast with Cal, who caused much more pain but who gave much less back. Brenda's anger at Cal goes beyond the kind of squabble that happens all too often in any type of family. She feels that Cal cheated her and the stepfamily by taking too much and giving too little in return in the way of loyalty.

Brenda Campbell's story presents an important comparison to that of Monica Morrison because of its similarities and differences. Like Brenda, Monica was the new (and younger) wife of a noncustodial divorced father, and for some time was a visited stepmother. She became a mother *before* her stepson came to live with her, and the birth of her first child had profound effects on her own household, on that of her husband's ex-wife, and on her subsequent stint as a resident stepmother.

Monica Morrison

Monica Morrison met her husband Daniel in 1973, two years after he had divorced his first wife, Clara. Daniel and Clara had had two children; Luke was six and Felicity was two. Clara had initiated the divorce, which had become final two years before, had obtained the house and custody of the youngsters. Daniel had strongly resisted the breakup. Monica believes that it was because he is a Roman Catholic and greatly values family life, and because of his love for his children. Even after the divorce and remarriage to Monica, he took great pains to remain in close contact with them. They lived nearby and visited the newlyweds in their apartment with little objection from their mother.

Soon after the remarriage, Daniel changed careers. Before the divorce he had been in an academic career whose financial prospects were so poor that, he and Monica suspect, part of Clara's reason for getting rid of him was a desire for a more prosperous mate. In his new line of work, financial and estate planning, Daniel was extraordinarily successful.

It was at that point where I could see a vast change in her attitude toward us. I think she became very jealous and envious that all of a sudden her ex-husband was content and happy and he was becoming successful in his business, and we were able to buy a home and all these things were flowing very nicely. And where was she? She was a single parent and she was now working full time, had to struggle a little, even though to this day she gets alimony and child support. Her attitude toward me changed and she started asking for more money from him.

Monica and Daniel had their first child, Jenny, in 1978. Immediately after Jenny was born, Luke let it be known that he wanted to move in with them. At that time the boy was twelve years old. Clara offered no objection at that time, because "she felt like a bit of a failure, not a successful parent," so Luke came to live with the couple and their newborn. Says Monica:

That was very, very tough on me, because all of a sudden not only was I going to have a brand new baby, when I knew nothing about child rearing, but I was going to have this stepson come and live with us. What annoyed me most was that he expected that he would be moving into this house where I would be picking up after him. I kept saying, "I don't have to pick up after you or clean the bathroom for you. You're a big kid, you can do it yourself."

Part of the problem also stemmed from Luke's having lived so long in a household headed by a single working mother. There was no regulation of the children, because "at the end of the day Clara was exhausted; she just closed her eyes" to what the children did. Luke was simply not used to discipline and order.

More important, though, was that at first he did not see Monica as a legitimate source of orders. Daniel moved swiftly to show the teenager that his father and stepmother were a team.

Daniel said to him right off, "Look, I can't be home all the time to tell you what to do. If Monica tells you to do something, you've got to do it. You can't argue with her. If she asks you to pick up or help set the table for dinner, you've got to do it. Monica is my wife and I love her and that's the way it is. If you want to stay here with us, these are the rules."

Luke continued to resist, and one of the weapons he used was dirt.

There was a time during that pubescent period when he decided he wasn't going to shower every day. I would say, "Oh my God, I can't handle the smell!" and I'd say "Go take a shower!" and he'd say, "I don't have to!" and I'd say "Yes you do, yes you do!" I didn't want to clean up after him. I didn't want to clean up his dirty wet towels or his stinking socks.

The impasse continued until Monica went with Daniel for some counseling.

> I was tired, and I had a year old baby, and I had this teenage kid and I said "I need to get some answers. I need some guidelines and help." The counselor said I should set a chart for Luke, saying "You've got to do these things on Monday, this on Tuesday . . . " The counselor was in a stepfamily himself. He used to chuckle at the things I used to say, and say, "Oh, God, I know what you mean."

At length, after at least a year of struggle, Luke learned to conform to the order of things in his stepmother's household. He also learned to enjoy taking care of his half-sister, which gave him a feeling of being important to the family. But after four years of living with father and stepmother, Luke decided he wanted to move back with his mother again, since she and his sister had moved to a suburb close to New York City. At that point he was about to begin tenth grade.

> He thought he was going to be painting the town red, but then he got there and he realized it wasn't all peaches and cream and very expensive to do all these things. And his grades in tenth grade weren't too terrific. So he decided to go to military school. He said, "I need to be disciplined"—on Monday do laundry, on Tuesday strip his bed; at 6:00 A.M. he wakes up, at 6:30 eats breakfast. He does very well being organized like that.

The military school turned out to be ideal for him. It gave him the discipline he needed, that he had found with his father and stepmother but his mother had been unable to provide. He has recently completed college in the air force and is continuing his military career with further technical training. Monica is pleased at his achievements, but does not see them as something in which she necessarily takes pride. "He's a clean cut, preppy guy. He's very intelligent. He really did quite well for himself."

Aside from regular visits and summer stays, Felicity never lived with Monica, Daniel, Natalie, and Jenny. She is closer to her mother than Luke, yet feels deprived when she sees the stability and security of the Morrison home.

I think she suffered more from the divorce than Luke. She has her tale of woe about her mother. She'll talk about it at this point in her life. "In those years, if my father had been home . . . " She sees the two little girls and the things he does with them and she feels she really missed those things.

But Felicity was never more than a fairly peripheral player in the stepfamily household.

The present state of affairs, from Monica's point of view, is that she has a conventional household with Daniel and their two daughters. She did her stint as a resident stepmother, and may even have made some positive contribution to Luke's maturation and successes. At present, Luke and Felicity visit, are very fond of their half-siblings — whom they refer to as "sisters" — but are old enough for their roles as stepchildren not to be obtrusive. But Monica is not free of stepfamily entanglements, since Clara continues to be an irritating, if usually unseen, presence.

In the background of Luke and Felicity's feelings about, and comings and goings to and from, the Morrison household, are Clara's machinations about money. As Daniel and Monica thrived, Clara became more hostile.

> The divorce was amicable and everyone was as cordial as they could be, but she later kept getting more and more spiteful and vindictive. Once or twice Daniel had to go to court and explain to the judge, saying, "I can't pay any more." Both times he won. She gets very angry.

Even though she works full time and is well paid, she continues to receive alimony as well as child support, since the divorce decree did not stipulate that either would cease or be reduced if she went back to work. Clara also enlists Luke and Felicity in her sniping.

> She says to them, "Oh, your father's a millionaire, he doesn't send me any money, look at the house he buys." They'd tell Daniel, "Mom's angry that you're a millionaire and you don't send her any money." Now what can Daniel possibly say, that I'm not a millionaire, I work a million hours a week, and I pay your college tuition and your mother alimony and put food on the table.

Monica therefore wishes ardently that Clara would remarry, but Daniel's first wife shows no inclination to do so.

> I think she has never remarried for several reasons, and I think one of them is the financial part of it. She's very well taken care of. She would have to be willing to give up a lot financially if she were to get married. She gets child support and alimony and a lot else. Daniel pays for college and all their

medical expenses. This is a big chunk of money that she doesn't have to shell out every year. It's like she just doesn't want to let go, she doesn't want to give him that peace of mind.

Nor, it would appear, does Clara want to give Monica peace of mind, either.

A Secure Base

Monica had her first child with Daniel just before Luke moved in with her. She had been married to Daniel for several years and had settled into a comfortable visited stepmother role with Luke and Felicity in upstate New York. Her situation during this time was a stable one as the wife of a remarried noncustodial father, similar to that of Bonnie Roberts. At that point the stepfamily structure was in a state of equilibrium, with Clara obtaining substantial support from Daniel while she had custody of the children, Monica in the marginal but relatively rewarding role of visited childless stepmother.

When she and Daniel had a mutual child, the equilibrium was altered. The birth of Jenny coincided with Luke's deciding he wanted to come to live with Monica and Daniel Morrison. The parental power balance was less affected because Monica had been a visited stepparent and her marriage to Daniel had had a long time to jell, so that the more disruptive changes in parent teamwork did not occur. Consequently, her legitimacy as a source of adult authority predated the birth of their mutual child. When the Morrison family became a "yours and ours" stepfamily, its major effects were on the children and the behavior of the ex-spouse.

Luke loves his father, by Monica's account, but the timing of his decision to come and visit cannot have been a coincidence. The Morrison household was becoming a "real family," in contrast to the truncated household in which he had been living. Luke probably also was feeling the same contradictory desires for order and freedom that subsequently guided many of his decisions — to return to his mother in search of greater freedom but then to enroll in military academy and, later, the armed forces in search of the discipline he craved. When he was in prepuberty, his mother was doubtless less able than he would have liked to impose on him the order he more or less consciously felt he needed; besides being more of a complete family, the Morrison household offered him the kind of structure that did not exist at home.

Clara had not remarried, and so neither Luke nor Felicity felt excluded from their mother's life the way Cal and Elizabeth Campbell had. This may explain why in the former case both children left their mother to return to their father, while in the latter only Luke did. Felicity remained with her mother, not only because of the gender similarities but because she had her mother all to herself.

Monica did not seek from the beginning to impose standards of cleanliness that were based on the criteria of a nonparent; she became a parent at almost the same time as she became a stepparent. There had been no time during which she failed to understand Daniel's perspective as a parent because of her own lack of parental experience. Monica was therefore more self-assured in her battles against pubescent dirt. She could also experience the typical second wife's feeling of rescuing superiority over the single-parent first wife whose household is usually more chaotic. Part of the reason why Luke came to live with her was because there was less order in the household where his mother alone was in charge. Monica's high standards were reinforced by her husband, which gave her yet more confidence.

Monica too made use of a counselor when it appeared that the situation with Luke was insoluble. But, importantly, the counselor's diagnosis was not that the parents had to form into a team, breaking up the biological parent-child relationship for the sake of the marital one, as had been the case with Brenda Campbell. Daniel had already transferred his solidarity from his children to his wife. What the therapy consisted of was advising the stepmother on specific techniques for getting Luke to conform to a structured schedule. Most important, though, was that the priority in the family was already concentrated on the adult couple, and the problem was thus relatively easier to solve.

Monica does not say much about the early time as far as taking care of the baby goes, and this is significant. Although certainly loving, it is a conventional mother-child relationship. It does not have added onto it the child's role as a mother's ally in breaking up a daunting father-son team. It is likely to be less intense as a result.

The principal person affected by the birth of the mutual child was Clara, whose envy of her ex-husband's remarried happiness was compounded by his becoming a father with his second wife. The equilibrium was disturbed in that she was not in a satisfactory postdivorce relationship to begin with, although this was compensated for by her being the custodial mother and her household the "center of gravity." Her principal ammunition at that time consisted of demands for greater child support, and although it appears that she lost the two skirmishes she initiated, such demands have great harassment value. When the mutual child was born, her son decided he wanted to live in the newly formed family, which excluded her yet further. From this perspective, the equilibrium has not yet been restored, but because Luke and Felicity are legally adults, Clara's weaponry has been reduced to periodic complaints to her children that Daniel is a millionaire who forces his ex-wife to live in poverty.

When Luke decided that he wanted to go back to live with his mother, therefore, Monica did not feel cheated. She had not given up her early marital intimacy for the sake of her stepson, disruptive though he was. With great firmness she had given her stepson what love and guidance he wanted from her, but was able to detach from him. Because she had invested less, had acknowledged a marginal role with him, and did not feel jealous that he was taking her husband away from her, Monica was able to carry out the stepmother role with less discomfort than Brenda had.

A shift in equilibrium followed the birth of the mutual child in both the Campbell and the Morrison families. In the former case, the principal balance change took place inside the family, because it led to greater legitimacy and confidence for Brenda in her household. In the latter case, the principal shift took place between the households, where Clara lost and Monica gained. Thus, although two children moved into Brenda's house, and for a longer time, the main effects of Freddy Campbell's birth were internal to that household. While only one child moved into the Morrison household as a result, the birth of Jenny Morrison had the greatest change on the equilibrium between the two households, because Clara has still not established a stable, satisfactory postdivorce relationship. Even though many years have passed, her eyes are still on her ex-husband and his wife and their children.

Changes in equilibrium are thus the principal result of a "pure stepparent" household becoming a "yours and ours" household. They are also the key consequence of mutual children in "yours, mine, and ours" families, but in such cases there are considerably more players on the scene. The balance is thus much more intricate, as the stories of Brad Henderson and Andrew Stewart attest.

Notes

1. P. 29 of P. Glick (1989), "Remarried Families, Stepfamilies and Stepchildren: A Brief Demographic Profile," *Family Relations* 38, 24–27.
2. With regard to reversible and irreversible status, see L. Schnore (1961), "Social Mobility in Demographic Perspective," *American Sociological Review* 26, 1, 411–14.
3. L. Ganong and M. Coleman (1988), "Do Mutual Children Cement Bonds in Stepfamilies?" *Journal of Marriage and the Family* 50, 687–98.
4. A. Bernstein (1989), *Yours, Mine and Ours: How Families Change When Remarried Parents Have a Child Together* (New York: Scribners).
5. Ibid., 68.
6. Ibid., 58, 61.
7. Ibid., 115.
8. Ibid., 147.
9. See J. Keshet (1988), "The Remarried Couple," 49–50.

6

"Yours, Mine, and Ours" Stepparents: Delicate Balances

The next two cases describe a mutual child family in which the father is a noncustodial father and the mother has custody of her own children. They are more conventional than the cases of Brenda Campbell and Monica Morrison, in which a father's child or children lived with the family even though he did not have legal custody. It is more common that the father's children only visit, while the mother's children live in the household. When a mutual child is born to this type of household, different reactions occur. In general, there is greater prior equilibrium, and the consequences of "our" child's birth are not so pronounced.

Things are more balanced before the birth, because both spouses are already parents; they have the experience, self-confidence, and legitimacy that accrue to parents. To be sure, both have their own approaches to parenting, which can become particularly engrained if the mother has been a single parent for an extended period of time. But the desire to remarry is likely to lead the parents—if not the children—to be flexible enough to adapt.

Some imbalance results from the fact that the male does not have custody of his children and the female does have custody of hers. Yet this is a more settled arrangement, if only because a father-custody family is probable evidence of a less-than-competent mother. It is also more settled in that it is regarded as "more normal" that a mother keep her children. The ex-wife of the stepfather in the usual "yours, mine, and ours" stepfamily is therefore less likely to feel bitter and deprived. Moreover, she will be that much more content if she is also in a satisfactory postdivorce relationship or marriage.

For the same reason, more balance is likely in the present type of family than in the previous type, because in the former the father was the biological parent of all the children in the household, whereas in the present type the mother is biological parent of all the children. A stepfather more easily replaces a father than a stepmother replaces a mother; because of the greater closeness that mothers have with their offspring, this is likely to be a more stable situation than when the wife is parent to only some of the children.

Visiting stepchildren in this sort of household are particularly disruptive, because they are not biologically related to the mother. She is a visited stepmother, and the household routines are her routines, which the visitors are almost certain to question. They also are a physical embodiment of her husband's first wife, and an unpleasant reminder of a previous life. They are primarily interested in their relationship with their father, and tend to regard their stepmother and her children as a necessity that accompanies time with him. A rivalry over time with father is therefore likely to grow between stepmother and visiting stepchildren.

Overall, then, the stability of the households described by Brad Henderson and Andrew Stewart means that the birth of the mutual child did not affect family equilibrium as much as in the previous two cases. Instead, the birth further accentuated the settled aspect of these households, making them feel more solid and established. At the same time, though, important tensions persist. In both Andrew Stewart's and Brad Henderson's households, rivalries have sprung up that result from unresolved three-way relationships. Thus the idea that we will pursue in exploring the peculiar structure of "yours, mine and ours" stepfamilies is the idea of unstable three-way relationships, which are referred to as *triangles*.

Andrew Stewart

Andrew Stewart and his first wife, Martha, had a son named Ian in 1976, two years after they had married. They separated when the boy was three years old and the divorce became final two years after that. At length, she agreed to abide by some of the terms of visitation, and Ian visited his father during the summer and on certain holidays. Two years after the divorce, Andrew married his present wife, Amy, who had custody of a daughter named Sheila, from her previous marriage to Chad. Sheila is the same age as Ian, and her parents' divorce took place in the same year as his parents' divorce. Sheila's father has since married a woman named Wanda, and that couple has a son named Lyman. As for Ian, his mother has not remarried.

Prior to the remarriage, Amy had been a single parent in very difficult financial circumstances, as Chad provided no support. Thus Amy and Sheila moved into Andrew's home. In 1983 Amy and Andrew's mutual child, Brian, was born. Andrew sees theirs as a stable family, except that the equilibrium has been occasionally disturbed by people on the outside—his ex-wife and son on one side, and to a lesser extent by Amy's ex-husband, on the other.

The problems with his son began in the earliest stages of the divorce. True to the pattern sketched in chapter 3, Andrew's principal weapon was financial, while Martha's lay in manipulation of visitation.

> At the time we separated, he was about three and I got an apartment of my own. We ran into problems about visitation. I would be pulling one arm and she would be pulling another when it came time for me to pick him up for visitation on the weekends. The kid was caught up in the middle.

But the fights between Andrew and Martha only used Ian as a bargaining chip. Once Ian was in his company, Andrew was not sure what to do with him. Andrew now acknowledges this.

> Although he enjoyed coming with me, we had that typical father-son visitation type of weekend when we don't know what the hell to do with each other, looking at each other—well, here we are, and we'd rather be rid of each other. It was a relief when I got rid of him. Much as I loved him.

Andrew, who is a car salesman, repossessed a car on which his ex-wife was not making payments.

> He watched it get towed out of the driveway at my house. He held it against me. I think he was developing an attitude that I was a bad guy. I used to get there at one o'clock and nobody would be there. At four o'clock they'd show up and she'd go 'Oh, I'm late, but here he is.' One day I went to her apartment to pick him up for the weekend, knowing I was in for the usual fight. And I knocked on the door and a stranger answered the door; she wasn't there, and he said she doesn't live here any more. And from that point on, it was a battle all the way.

Eventually, Andrew found that his ex-wife had taken their son to the West Coast on the pretext that since she was not receiving enough money from Andrew, she needed to move to a less expensive part of the country.

At length, the legal system put an end to both parents' schenanigans. Andrew was required to make his support payments to the county, which in turn paid Martha; Martha was warned that if she did not stick to the summer and holiday visitation schedule, she could be found in criminal contempt.

Ian thus began his summer visitations. The first summer, he stayed with Andrew and went to camp. By the following summer Andrew had married Amy, and Ian stayed with his father, stepmother, and stepsister.

> He didn't like Amy. We knew that from the first day when she tried to discipline him. She said, "If you're going to live in my house for two months, you're going to do things our way. You're going to get along with your stepsister." "Clean up your room," or "Be careful of Brian," or "Don't kick me in the back of the seat in the car."

Andrew believes that much of Ian's behavioral problems stemmed from the fact that he got little discipline in his mother's home; and that when Ian had visited with him as a single father, he had tried to buy the boy's affection. He says he "mistakenly" thought that since their time was so brief together, disciplining him would tarnish the experience. Unfortunately, the consequence was that Ian was not used to submitting to anyone's authority. When Andrew was present, Ian obeyed, but at other times it was a different story.

If I wasn't there, he wasn't so cooperative. He just wouldn't listen. He used to say to Amy, "You're not my mother, you can't tell me that!" and he would only do it when I wasn't there. So I was unaware of it and when she told me I'd say, "You're full of shit."

This realization, for Andrew, is a retrospective one, because a crisis occurred at the end of the next visitation. It seemed like a vacation when the boy was adjusting to the visitation. He himself was learning not to try to buy Ian's love; he had decided to hire him to work for wages, rather than simply showering him with gifts.

Last summer he worked with me. He took the money he earned. For a little kid, he worked all right. He enjoyed going to work. He bought some nice things for himself. He bought a TV for himself. Little things that made him feel very proud. He even got along with Amy. He admitted it. He liked being disciplined. He liked being told what to do, being guided. He went home in tears last summer, saying to Amy and me that he would talk to his mother about the possibility that he could come on a trial basis and live with us, perhaps.

So it was a considerable shock that as soon as Ian returned to his mother, he phoned to tell Andrew that he no longer wanted to visit the stepfamily.

I then received a letter from him saying "I don't want to come because I can't express my true feelings and I don't get along with Amy." One line. No longer said "love, Ian." The letter was just signed "from Ian."

Andrew knows that he could use the family court to require Martha to send Ian to him, but he is not sure he wants to. First of all, there is the money it would cost to get custody.

I could try to get custody, try to prove that Martha is an addict or an unfit mother, but I'd have to spend another twenty-five to thirty thousand dollars like I did last time.

And then his family situation with Amy, Sheila, and Brian is going along nicely without Ian's presence.

> For him to come here right now the way things are is going to interfere with a very happy family we have here, and that's been something in my mind. That's not easy. Every now and then I get a twinge of guilt. It turns my stomach every now and then.

Andrew's guilt is exacerbated by his belief that Ian is not taken care of properly by Martha.

> She lives the typical West Coast divorced single-mother life-style, a waitress, she takes odd side jobs, besides selling fake jewelry. Out in a different bar and party every night, the kid's home alone. He's a real latchkey kid there.

Andrew's relations with his stepdaughter, however, were warm and close from the beginning.

> Sheila instantly adopted me as a father. She was the right age to need a father and want a father and see that I love her. She does call me Andrew most of the time, but sometimes calls me dad. I introduce her as my daughter. Always did.

Chad has apparently not chosen to stay in contact with his daughter. Even prior to his remarriage, he paid little support to Amy, and since he and Wanda wed and their son was born, he has little contact with Sheila. This seems to have increased Sheila's receptivity to her stepfather.

Sheila had also been deeply affected by her parents' breakup and by the difficulty her mother had had in making ends meet. She was "a bit of a discipline problem" when the stepfamily was first formed, but Andrew's principal memory of her at the time was that she was very depressed.

> She cried every day. She woke up crying and went to sleep crying every day; she thought that was the way to live. She just thought crying was the way to get along in life. She used to cry over every little thing.

Sheila has "turned around," to the extent that when her half-brother was born, she was thrilled.

> She loved it when Brian was born. She was nine and it made her feel like a little mother. She was always trying to emulate her mother. Still does. Brian was a like a living doll, a perfect play toy, and she loved every second of it.

The only potential problem that Andrew sees at present is the lack of a blood tie between himself and his pubescent stepdaughter.

> At her age she's turning on to boys and I'm not her blood father. I have to watch sometimes what I say, do, how I act with her. I think sometimes she'll be overly sexual with me. She used to say "Can I rub your back?" While we were watching TV. Now I have to watch these things. I think every father and daughter should at some point. You have to be a little more cautious when its a stepfather and daughter when shes getting to be that age, with physical contact, you have to be a little more cautious.

Amy, as a mother, is aware of the issues, but is evidently comfortable with how Andrew is treating them, as this anecdote shows:

> Yesterday Sheila went out and got her first couple of bras. She came in and showed me, she turned red, she was embarrassed, but Amy said, "Oh, I knew you'd want to see this. You'd be proud of her." That kind of thing. They feel like I'd want to be a part, like any father.

In the end, Andrew knows that the family he is in now represents a second chance for him.

> I get an awful lot of joy out of knowing that I'm parenting another child altogether through Brian from scratch, getting to do that all over again. Which I never thought I'd have an opportunity to do. And I got a lot of joy out of having a daughter now, even though I didn't know her until she was seven years old. I feel like I didn't miss a minute.

But at the same time he knows that there is a human cost that still bothers him.

> Being married to Amy, a relatively sane, rational person, has destroyed my relationship with Ian, because I can no longer let him get away with murder, and I can no longer turn blindly from his faults and his bad ways. He has to be raised like a human being, so I've lost him.

Triangular Trades

A "yours, mine, and ours" stepfamily like Andrew Stewart's illustrates emotional triangles with special clarity. Triangular relationships can appear anywhere, but are especially likely to appear in stepfamilies because of a pattern known as the problem of transitivity. If A and B love each other, and if B and C love each other, do C and A love each other? If C loves A and vice versa, then the three-way relationship is not triangular. It is balanced, because there is a symmetry of affection between all the members of the small group. But if C does not love A and A does not love C, then the group is fundamentally unstable. The bond between A and B excludes C and the bond between B and C excludes A.[1]

Not all three-way relationships are so unequal, of course. The best example of a healthy one is that of two parents and a child; in a healthy three-way relationship like this, each member has a distinct and rewarding tie to the others, and the overall result is one of balance: three people are involved, but the group is composed of satisfying one-on-one relationships. A triangle, by contrast, is a three-way relationship in which several types of pathological patterns emerge. Those that concern us in the present context are those in which coalitions appear between pairs of people that exclude the third, and when one person is the object of competition between the other two.

Triangulation is almost built into stepfamily relationships that follow bitter custody battles.[2] When an emotional divorce is incomplete, couples make children the pawns in their postmarital battles. A child's loyalty is sought by both parents, producing severe stress in the child, since he loses no matter which side he chooses, and if he refuses to choose he risks alienating both parents.

Such obviously was the case with Ian Stewart. Andrew and Martha's animosity against one another is still strong today, ten years after they split up. A sure sign of unresolved postdivorce resentments is the regular recourse to family court instead of private negotiations to resolve problems. That Andrew has had to make his child support payments by court order, that a judgment has reiterated Martha's obligation regarding visitation, that Andrew refers to Martha's taking Ian to Oregon as a "kidnapping" is also ample testimony to the lack of civility between the two parents.

Andrew loves Ian and Martha loves Ian, but Andrew and Martha detest each other. Because of this triangle, Ian's chances of merging with Andrew's new family may have been doomed from the start due to the threat this would have posed to Martha. The remarkable transformation that the boy underwent after a particularly enjoyable summer with his father, stepmother, stepsister, and half-brother suggests the extent to which his mother was disturbed by the possibility that Andrew might "win" him. It appears that she must have made some serious and passionate appeals to his loyalty. Andrew, for the moment, is the excluded person in the triangle. His anger stems equally from his love for his son, who says he does not want to see him and will not explain why, and his rage over his ex-wife's power to manipulate the situation. Although he could, in theory, force his ex-wife to send Ian to visit, he has not done so, and the reasons for this reveal some other triangular relationships in the Stewart stepfamily.

Ian and Andrew love each other, Andrew and Amy love each other, but Ian and Amy's feelings toward each other are not warm. When Ian came to visit at first, the triangle between Andrew, Amy, and Ian was one in which Ian regarded Andrew as the only legitimate authority, Andrew had long been overindulgent and tried to purchase Ian's love, and Amy was the one trying to impose order and discipline. Ian tried vainly to subvert Amy by only being good when Andrew was around, and resisting when he was not. But Amy's position in the triangle was strong, because she had Andrew's tacit support, and was already a mother, twice.

Two stable three-way relationships have also appeared. One is the biologically based one between Brian and Amy and Andrew. Andrew is overjoyed at the opportunity to have a new chance to raise a son, and perhaps to do it better this time. Andrew and Amy's relationship is secure, and their parenthood is testimony to their renewed commitment to each other. Although Amy does not speak directly in the story, Andrew's concern for family relationships is in contrast to her first husband's neglect. The relation between Amy and Andrew and Sheila is also symmetrical. Andrew and Amy love each other as spouses and Amy and Sheila love each other as mother and daughter. And even though it raises a number of thorny sexual issues as Sheila matures into a young woman, Andrew and Sheila love each other as stepfather and stepdaughter. These stable three-way relationships bring into relief the instability of those between Ian, Andrew, and Amy, and between Ian, Andrew and Martha.

They bring us back to the persistent problem of Ian. Andrew knows that if he wanted to, he could force Martha to send Ian East to visit. He knows, though, that Ian is an obnoxious presence to Amy, and that it would take much struggle and pain to bring Ian into the stepfamily, even temporarily. At present, without Ian around, their home is a calm and relatively happy place. Andrew thus knows that Martha's emotional kidnapping of their son may be a blessing in disguise. Because of the triangle between Andrew, Ian, and his visited stepmother, it would probably be best for the family's sake if Ian did stay away. Andrew is in the midst of carrying out an emotional triage reminiscent of the extrusion of Randy Maxwell's son and Eugene Brown's stepson. It is very painful, but it seems necessary for the sake of the stepfamily.

Brad Henderson

Brad and Anne Henderson were both married previously, and both had children from those marriages. Brad's are Holly and Cheryl, aged sixteen and thirteen respectively; Anne's is Carol, aged twelve. Two years ago, Brad and Anne had a mutual child, Roger. Holly and Cheryl live in Florida with their mother, Edith, and her new husband, Harvey. Carol lives with her mother, with whom she lived for over two years before the remarriage, and with Brad. Anne's ex-husband, Lee, has remarried, and he and his new wife Justine have two young children, Irene, age two and Gary, who is less than one year old.

Although at present the stepfamily is relatively stable, the hostility of Anne's ex-spouse was and continues to be intense. Brad and Anne bought a house in Berkeley, and were about to move because they were under the impression that Lee had given his consent.

> We wound up staying for less than six months and Anne ended up practically not living there at all. We got into a tremendous financial hole. Lee wound up going to court and forcing Carol to be returned to New York and of course Anne had come back with her. He met Anne at Kennedy Airport with police and literally tearing Carol from Anne's arms, with Carol hysterically screaming, and then having to show up in court the next day for a hearing to determine custody and so on. Carol has nightmares about that to this day.

Brad does not believe that Lee seriously cared about seeing Carol. Justine and he do not get along well, and Brad believes he was made jealous by the happiness enjoyed by his ex-wife and her new husband.

> Here we were moving to a new house in Berkeley, we were happily married, nice-nice and he was miserable.

The confirmation of this suspicion is that Lee tended to ignore Carol when she visited his household.

> Carol's visitation used to be Wednesday evenings, and it's supposed to be that she sleeps over every other weekend. But in the last year or so she has cut that down tremendously. A lot of that has to do with her relationship with her stepmother, which is very poor. From very early on, Justine was very resistant to Carol being included in any of the activities, because she was very jealous. And Lee allows himself to be manipulated so that when he finally does stand up to Justine there's a big conflict. Storming out of the house, to the point where he leaves Carol with Justine rather than taking Carol with him, and then he'll come back hours later.

Brad feels that the difficulties experienced by Carol in the divorce and visitation have made the girl closer to her mother, but not to him, and this disturbs him. Before he and Anne wed, Carol adored him, because he made her mother happy, was a source of affection and gifts, but made no attempt to control or discipline her. As soon as he became a constant presence in her life, she was aloof and inaccessible. Her cool autonomy jars with what Brad feels is an appropriate mutual dependency such as he and his daughters have. He has numerous explanations for it.

> Her problems with her father and stepmother have not made her closer to me; they've made her closer to her friends because she's reached that preteen time when friends have become more important to her sooner than I think they might have otherwise. And I think she's always been extremely close to Anne. Anne had always been the anchor to which she was tied, and she felt secure thereby. Carol was almost out of the textbook as far as being as close to the perfect child as you can find, very overadaptive, superpleasing, and kind, I mean she would do anything to get approval; diligent, responsible far beyond her years. Recently, she's started to become fresh and disrespectful. Not anything that's age-inappropriate, but is such a vast change from the way she was before.

Brad also thinks that his frustrating lack of rapport with his stepdaughter is linked to some unresolved conflicts between Anne and himself.

> I'm the disciplinary force, and she's a pushover, but I'm like a kind of paper tiger. Because Anne will frequently countermand or reduce my effectiveness. For example, if I say to Carol something like, "If you use the phone when you're not supposed to, you can't use the phone tomorrow," Anne will then say, "Well, she wasn't abusing the phone, so there is no punishment," or she'll say, "I ended the punishment early because I felt that it wasn't necessary."

Brad understands that part of Anne's efforts to subvert his authority result from her guilt over the pain the child suffered during the divorce. But he believes that if the three of them are to work as a family, he must be allowed to impose discipline as an adult. Compounding the conflict is Carol's knowledge that her mother is an ally against Brad's authority.

> Carol's taking advantage of my impotence in imposing punishment, because she knows that implicit in what Anne's doing is saying, "Listen, bozo, the bottom line is that she's my daughter—she's not your daughter. I'll make the decision as to whether she's punished or can go to the movies or whatever the case may be."

Brad knows that children try to play adults off against each other in intact families, too. But he believes that when Roger is Carol's age, there will be, or there is supposed to be, an agreement between the parents that they will check with one another before imposing discipline. Brad's optimistic idea of how unbroken families function makes the contrast of Carol's alliance with Anne particularly galling.

The tension between Brad and the two females in the household is in interesting contrast to his relations with his daughters. Holly and Cheryl did not want to move to Florida, because it meant leaving all their friends and their school. But their mother insisted, since life in Florida promised to be much more leisurely. After selling the house that she obtained in the divorce, she could buy a home in Florida for one third the price and live on the investment of the rest. Plus, Brad sends $250 a week in child care, and Edith's new husband also has a comfortable income of his own.

Apparently the girls are particularly unhappy because Harvey has no experience in dealing with children. He is consequently "unreasonable" with them.

> This guy is mister macho. He's now forty or so, he's the type of guy who's very egocentric, his raison d'etre is to make sure he has a new outfit to go out dancing every Saturday night, go to a bar they frequent. He wants Edith to be the earth around his sun. His way of dealing with the girls is extremely harsh, rigid, old-fashioned. A lot of it is punitive rather than what he really believes. For example, he won't allow Cheryl to talk on the phone unless he or Edith is in the room. It doesn't matter who she's talking to, she's not allowed. She's not allowed to receive any phone calls from boys whatsoever. I mean I'm her natural father, and I think that's ridiculous.

Although one can detect a tinge of jealousy in Brad's description of Harvey, the essential aspect of the account is that he sees his ex-wife's new husband as contributing to his daughters' unhappiness. It appears to Brad that Harvey's aim is more or less deliberately to drive the girls away so that he can have Edith all to himself.

> Holly can't wait to leave. And Cheryl can't wait to leave, she just has a longer sentence to serve. Cheryl said, "How would you feel if I came and lived with you?"

This suggestion was met with a flat refusal by Anne. The relations between her and the girls have apparently always been delicate. Even though Brad had not met Anne when he and Edith divorced, Cheryl and Holly's mother told them that Anne was the reason why the marriage broke up. As a result, when the girls first were introduced to their stepmother, their preconceptions made them extremely hostile.

> As time went on they relaxed and became very good friends. Except that Anne, I think, was the one who held back more than the girls did. She made it very clear she doesn't want them living with us, and I think the girls sensed that Anne didn't like their sharing time with me.

Anne senses the same kind of solidarity between Brad and his daughters that she has with her own daughter. Of course, it is not as threatening as it might be, because Holly and Cheryl are only visitors. But it is still hard for her.

> When I'm going to be seeing the girls for a very limited amount of time a few times a year, there are going to be times when I'm going to want to be alone with them or something that isn't necessarily a fun activity but is designed to give me an opportunity to be connected with them, to make up for the time when we're apart. Anne has a very hard time dealing with that.

Holly and Cheryl are not unaware of their stepmother's competitiveness.

> They said to me, "What's the point of us coming to visit you dad, if you're not going to spend any time with us alone and if Anne doesn't want us there?" Cause they were able to read her.

Brad says that the previous summer the visit went better than before, because he carefully arranged things so that when he was seeing his daughters alone, Anne had something interesting to do so that she would not be brooding about how excluded she felt.

Brad sees that there is a contrast between Anne's systematic exclusion of him from too much closeness with Carol, while at the same time resenting any exclusion of herself from his relations with his daughters, even during their relatively infrequent visits. He sees it as the single most disruptive force in the family. He is not sure why this contradiction persists, besides ascribing it to a certain childishness on his wife's part.

> When I try to reason with her, Anne will reply to me, "I don't want to be mature. I don't want to know anything except that I want to be holding your hand and be sitting next to you." She goes into a kid head and acts just like the kid.

Balance and Checks

In Brad Henderson's stepfamily, there is more symmetry than in Andrew Stewart's because both of the ex-spouses have remarried. Even though Lee may not be as happily married as he might like, and even though Edith has no children in her new relationship with Harvey, both seem sufficiently contented to avoid sniping at Brad and Anne. Even though there is much evidence of past struggles, at present a balance has been achieved between the three households.

The main consequence of this is that the birth of Roger to Brad and Anne did not bring about any fundamental change in the stepfamily's functioning. Though Brad is appropriately fatherly and proud, his account does not dwell very much on the changes wrought by his son's birth. This is, of course, very different from the important results that flowed from the birth of a mutual child or children in the previous case studies. The greater symmetry reduced the impact of the child's birth, and, even more than in Andrew Stewart's account, what emerges is a greater emphasis on past and present triangular relationships.

The first of these resulted from the bitter divorce dispute between Lee and Anne over Carol, who was a prize to be fought over and a weapon to be used. When Lee perceived that Brad and Anne had achieved a measure of happiness and contentment, he was impelled (at least in Brad's account) to use heavy legal artillery in an attempt to wrest control of his daughter away from his ex-wife in as dramatic a way as possible. Evidently Carol was less the issue than Lee's postdivorce resentments over Anne's apparent happiness and his own less-than-blissful marriage. As in typical triangular relationships, Lee saw himself losing to the extent that Carol was close to her mother. With such a zero-sum perception, Lee's "victory" was Anne's loss.

At the same time, though, Lee is witnessing anther type of triangular relationship between himself, his wife, and his daughter Carol. Justine is the visited stepmother, and unenthusiastic about the periodic sojourns of her stepdaughter. Justine is twice a mother, and has no need to try to integrate her stepdaughter into the household. Carol was therefore the center of conflict between her stepmother and father, and as a result would now prefer not to visit. Lee, for his part, is probably going through the kind of emotional transfer of loyalty that Andrew Stewart is struggling with. The visits of his daughter are so resented by his wife that to preserve the peace of his household he is having to cut himself off from his daughter. The difference is that Andrew Stewart is happily married, while Brad Henderson described Lee's marriage as unsatisfactory at best.

Although this triangle seems to have resolved itself to a certain extent, several other conflicting relationships persist. Brad is at the center of all of them. Brad is in competition with both Edith and Harvey over Holly and Cheryl. His strife with his ex-wife has faded somewhat, since legal machinations resulted in his daughter's being moved to another state and his visitation curtailed. And in spite of his contempt for Harvey as a man and a father, he is not actively disputing control over the girls. His acceptance of Edith's "victory" is a function of the settled nature of his household with Anne and Carol and his new fatherhood with Roger, though it is not clear whether the birth of the mutual child produced this acceptance or was a result of it.

Anne, as visited stepmother, shows an attitude to Holly and Cheryl that is similar to Justine's attitude toward Carol. She does not try to conceal that she does not want the girls living with them, although she does not apparently make them feel as unwelcome as Carol's stepmother does with her. Particularly strong is her feeling of competition with her stepdaughters; Anne feels rivalry with Holly and Cheryl over time spent with Brad when they visit. Here again is a zero-sum competition typical of an unhealthy three-way relationship; what one side gains, the other side perceives as a loss. Brad is trying as hard as he can to reduce the tension resulting from the contest between his daughters and his wife, but the contest itself remains.

The most important and disruptive triangle persists between Anne, Brad, and Carol. For Carol, Brad was "fun" at the beginning, when he was dating her mother, but now "I try to treat her more like a natural child," and "she thinks I'm too rigid and inflexible and so on." This illustrates the common sequence between stepparents and stepchildren, in which during the dating phase children are happy with the new adult with whom the resident parent has a relationship. He is like a "play parent" who is all the more enjoyable because he not only makes the parent happy but goes away after a while and does not contest the child's monopoly over the parent's attention. But Carol's attitude changed radically when she realized that Brad was not going to go away and he was not so much "fun" any more.

Another leg of the triangle is constituted by the close and possessive relationship between Anne and Carol. Anne was a single mother for two years, long enough to develop emotional dependence on her daughter. The legal struggles with Lee make Carol even more highly prized, since she was the pretended object of contention between the ex-spouses. Carol's resistance to Brad feeds the proprietary relation between her and her mother. In spite of the loving parental and marital relationship between Brad and Anne, Anne does not regard Brad as a legitimate source of authority over Carol, either. The parent-child dyad is so strong here that Anne has not succeeded in relinquishing it in favor of her relationship with her husband. The result is that it is a grievous bone of contention between them.

Brad Henderson's story illustrates the major conclusions of a study that contrasted people's expectations about, with actual behavior in, stepparent roles. About one third of the respondents in that survey expected that a husband should take care of his children from a previous marriage more than his wife, while about the same proportion thought that a wife should take care of her children from a previous marriage more than her husband. More than half thought that the husband and wife should be equally responsible for one another's children from a previous marriage. Yet when they were asked about how people actually behaved in their stepfamily relationships, the results were much more extreme in the direction of biological links. In almost one third of the cases the husband "always" made decisions about his biological children, and more than a third reported that the husband "more than the wife" made decisions about his children. Only one-fifth of the respondents reported that the husband and wife actually made decisions about "his" children mutually. The results of questions about the real responsibility for a wife's children from a previous marriage were very similar.[3]

In sum, when it came to "yours" and "mine," the biological tie was much more important in practice than it was in theory. The biological tie between Anne and Carol is supplemented by the triangular tensions we have looked at in-depth, and the result is a persistent and abrasive type of solidarity. This mother-daughter alliance is a very sore spot in an otherwise symmetrical extended stepfamily, in which the birth of Roger, the mutual child, has had a consolidating, rather than a disruptive effect.

Brad Henderson's story not only completes our discussion of the "yours and ours" and "yours, mine, and ours" stepparents. It finishes our discussion of the different stepparent types. But the discussion of adults in stepfamilies is not yet finished, because Brad's and Andrew's stories raise an issue, the tie between biological parent and child, that will be dealt with in the next chapter. Like other stepfamily patterns, the blood parent-child tie has been touched on in passing but now deserves our full attention. How is it that a remarried parent manages to transfer loyalty from a biological child to a spouse? Michelle Martin tells how and why it happened in her case.

Notes

1. See J. Davis and S. Leinhardt (1972), "The Structure of Positive Interpersonal Relations in Small Groups," in J. Berger (ed.), *Sociological Theories in Progress* (Boston: Houghton Mifflin).
2. D. Mills (1988), "Stepfamilies in Context," 21–27 and passim.
3. J. Giles-Sims (1984), "The Stepparent Role: Expectations, Behavior and Sanctions," *Journal of Family Issues* 5, 1, 116–30.

7

Centrifugal Children: Parent-Child Relations

A remarried couple needs to give priority to its relationship over the tie between parent and child. This axiom is the same in nuclear families, where solidarity between parents is expected and the strength of the married couples' relationship is central to the family.[1] Successful stepfamilies, too, are those in which the couple consider their relationship more fundamental than that between parent and child. This is not always an easy task.[2] For a remarrying husband or wife, the couple's relationship is always in potential competition with the relationship one or both of the spouses have with their residential or visiting children. There is often an initial temptation for children to exert a centrifugal force on a remarriage. The biological parent-child tie is a heavy counterweight to the legal and emotional tie between spouses, for several reasons.

The tie between parent and child is of longer duration than that between remarrying parent and his or her new spouse; time and habituation give it a strong edge over the newlyweds' love. Moreover, it is based on blood, and while social forces can alter such a link, it is of great significance to both parties, if only because parent and child usually resemble one another in habits or appearance, in obvious or subtle ways. And as we saw at the beginning of the book, there is often a touch of guilt felt by a divorced parent over the pain a child has suffered as a result of the marital breakup, often leading to a feeling of obligation on the part of the parent and awareness of manipulative power on the part of the child. Finally, because of prevailing custody patterns, mothers are most often the remarrying parents in whose household the children live and who will have to accommodate the presence of a stepparent. Because mothers are ordinarily more intensively involved with their children than fathers are, they are the biological parents who most often must try to transfer their priority from their children to their spouses.

The success of the stepfamily requires that this transfer take place. A remarried couple's relationship cannot function well or even long endure when the children have the power to disrupt it by trumping marriage with biological loyalties. We saw in the chapter on remarried couple relations that emotional divorce from the ex-spouse is just as necessary as legal divorce; in the same way, children must be treated as children and not as co-equal partners in the marriage. But for a mother to loosen the ties that bind, and instead knot the relationship with her new husband, even over the vehement struggles and objections of one or more of her children, is painful and hard.

Michelle Martin

Michelle Martin lives with her new husband, Hugh, and with Gwen, her daughter by her ex-husband Miles. Miles and Michelle's other child, Eric, lives on his own. Hugh was also previously married; he and his ex-wife, Rose, had been divorced eight years when he and Michelle married. They have two children, Nathan and Esther, who live near their mother in Puerto Rico. At present, then, Michelle is a resident biological mother and a visited stepmother. The Martin stepfamily is stable and reasonably successful. How it got that way is depicted in the story of how Michelle and Hugh succeeded in adapting their relations with their children to the needs of their marriage.

Seventeen years ago, Michelle left her husband and children. Miles has a serious drinking problem, and Michelle felt that leaving was necessary for her own emotional survival. At the time, her son was away at college, but Gwen was still living with Miles. At first, Michelle was living in a tiny apartment and could not have Gwen live with her, and in any case her new residence was in another school district. During the school year and summer that Gwen was fourteen, she lived with her father, but Miles began to add physical violence to verbal and psychological abuse of his daughter:

> He used to follow her after school. He always instilled the fact that he did not trust her. She would go to school and she'd see him sitting in the car watching her get on the bus. She'd go to a party and he'd wait outside the party in his car. He was always accusing her of not acting properly. One day they had a violent argument and he had physically gone after her and she ran away for a day. She ended up at my apartment. And we had the police and everything. She came away very angry at him.

By this time Michelle had moved back to Gwen's school district, so that when it became clear that Miles and his daughter could not live in the same household, Gwen could easily move in with her mother.

Although he had gone away to school by the time the marriage broke up, Eric was even more deeply affected by the divorce than was Gwen. Michelle and Eric were very close, but the relationships in the family were full of conflict:

> Miles would take out his frustrations on me, I would take out my frustrations on Eric, Eric would take out his frustrations on Gwen and Gwen would take out her frustrations on the dog!

Eric perceived Michelle's leaving as an abandonment of himself and his father, arguing that his mother should have stayed and kept the family together. He became a caretaker for his alcoholic father, getting him out of scrapes and driving for him when his license was revoked. On the few occasions when he visited his mother, relations were very strained. He would only visit with his friends, and while physically present, there was little communication between son and mother. Already, then, Gwen had an inside track on the stepfamily, while her brother's siding with his father had put him on the outside. From then on, the two young people followed different roads, but both required that Michelle suppress her initial maternal instincts and let events take their course.

Gwen's adjustment was a more ordinary stepdaughter-to-stepfather accommodation. Michelle describes how the initial resistance was dealt with:

> She was quietly rebellious at the beginning here. I remember the day we were married, Hugh said something to her, and she turned around and said to him, "You're not my father!" It was as if she was putting a wall up between the two of them. It was that type of rebellion. But it was a very short-lived rebellion. Because then she and Hugh sat down and had a conversation and I stayed out of it. I had a lot of difficulty staying out of the middle because I was protecting her. And once I took myself out of the middle, then they were able to establish a relationship between the two of them. He reassured her that the reason we had rules and regulations was because we loved her and we had to establish guidelines for living together, and not as individuals. It was as if she was looking for a confrontation with him that they establish their own ground. And he grounded her for a period of time and she almost seemed to welcome that because it was like forcing her into the family.

After that initial period of testing, Gwen and her stepfather settled into a stable relationship of mutual affection and respect.

Eric's journey has been longer and bumpier. Before his mother remarried, one of the ways in which he showed his hostility to his mother over the divorce was to exploit her guilt for his financial gain. He began to borrow money from her that both knew would never be repaid. Even though her finances were poor, she says, "It was like he felt that I owed him. It was like he was going to get me." After Michelle and Hugh were married, Eric attempted to continue this pattern and accompany it by attempts to disrupt the harmony of the newly established stepfamily. Only now his mother was not as easily manipulated, because she was in an established home with a husband and her daughter. What ensued was a series of confrontations in which Eric's maneuvers were treated as unacceptable and met Michelle's increasingly firm resistance:

> He came here at one point for Christmas. And I was very surprised, because he never came to stay over. And he was really impossible—he refused to get up to come down to eat after he came home from work. And on our anniversary, which was around Christmastime, I went upstairs and said, "Come downstairs, Gwen's making dinner, and I want you to eat."
>
> And he said, "I'm too tired."

And I said, "Look, this is our anniversary and I want you to come and eat with us."

And he came down and he had on a gym outfit and he was sullen and nasty. Hugh went out later, and I said to Eric, "Look, you have to leave. You're disrupting our household. This is not the way we live, and you obviously don't want to be a part of it, and that's okay because we don't want to put up with this. You're choosing not to be part, you're choosing to break it up and you're going to have to go."

This was the first point at which Eric's attempts to pull apart his mother's remarriage failed, but it was not the last.

Eric may have begun to see that his passionate siding with his father against his mother was a mistake. While on the one hand, his only family was a father who needed him so much that he was able to give little support, his sister Gwen was receiving far more rewards from having joined the stepfamily. Eric began to understand that his proud exile cut him off from the Martin household, but left him with little in the way of kinship. So he found a temporary substitute.

He spent about a year living in a kind of familial "holding pattern," in another household, during which he began to reduce his ties to his father and began making stumbling, ambivalent attempts to join the Martin family:

> He was living with a friend of his and his family and he never really went back to his father after that Christmas. He lived with a family with a lot of children. They had known him since he was a little boy and they took him in and he became part of the family. . . . Then he started to show up for dinner but he would most often have a friend with him. One Sunday Eric and his friend came in and they looked like they had just come out of a gym someplace. After dinner was over, I told him that he would not be invited again until he could come to our table the way we expected him to come. And he was angry about that. And then he called about two weeks later and asked if he could come to dinner, and I told him no. After that he started to come around by himself, he started to show interest in being part of the family.

Michelle managed to communicate that her son was welcome in the family only as long as he did so on the family's terms, without attempts at malodorous disruption of meals. Her firmness paid off, because Eric then began to indicate that he wanted to be a member of the family. But he still was ambivalent, and persisted in his attempts at manipulation.

Eric got a job with a company in Rhode Island, and he needed a car. Because he did not have the money, he asked his mother for it. Only this time, Hugh and Michelle refused. Instead, Hugh said that he would consider cosigning for a loan, but that he would need to see the car first. Then Eric's attempted ploy was stymied:

> Eric came over one night and said, "My dad saw the car and he says it's a good car, and I have to do it tomorrow, so here are the papers. Please just sign it." And Hugh said "No." Eric went away in a really angry state.

This was the beginning of Eric's realization that not only could he no longer use his mother's guilt to his own ends, but that his attempts to use it to disrupt the remarriage would be futile.

> It was a turning point because he began to see that we were establishing guidelines that we were not going to cross over. Up to the point of the loan he was always borrowing money from me and I was always giving it to him, and he was always saying, "I'll pay you back in a month or so," which he never did. But it was the cosigning of the loan that was the end, and from that point on we never gave him money or anything. And that's when our relationship turned around, it got better. Now we have a wonderful relationship, Hugh and I and Eric. We really cut him off, which we had to do.

As a result, Eric has arrived at a kind of equilibrium that allows him to be as loyal to his father as he needs to be, but can acknowledge his obligations to his mother's remarriage at the same time. This maturity was reflected in the events surrounding Gwen's graduation from college. Much old animosity was revived at the time, because although Miles expressed a desire to go to his daughter's graduation, he had refused to pay her college expenses, arguing that she was not college material.

> Eric called me and said, "Look, Mom, we're all adults in this. At some point we're going to have to get together, because there will be weddings and things. And Gwen is just going to have to accept his going to her graduation, too." His father didn't have a car, and Eric's car was in the garage. So Eric had to rent a car to go up to Albany. He had to make the reservations, he paid for the room, he rented a car, and he took his father. We saw Eric at the graduation but we never saw his father. So Eric at that point was with his father and he was with us, because he would go back and forth during the ceremony.

Although still the caretaker and loyal to his childlike father, Eric literally went back and forth between the two poles of his new family configuration. Rather than showing sullen resistance or making petty attempts at manipulation, Eric has finally accommodated to the realities.

Michelle's success in constructing a stepfamily required that she get out of the way of Hugh's interaction with her daughter, and that she and Hugh both stand firm in resisting Eric's emotional guerrilla warfare. The story of her struggle to weaken maternal ties in favor of marital ones stands in interesting contrast to Hugh's parallel relations with his own children. Of course, the fact that as a male he was less intensely involved with his children, and the fact that they live far away, made this a relatively simpler job. But the contrasts do indicate how a father may go about coping with centrifugal children.

Hugh's son, Nathan, was furious with him for breaking up with his mother, to the point where there was either no communication or poison-pen letters from the young man. Nathan, predictably, refused to come to his father's wedding and sees his mother as wronged. In Michelle's words,

> Nathan wanted nothing to do with me. If he would call, and I would answer the phone, he would say, "May I speak with Mister Martin?"

Because of Rose's vilification of her ex-husband to his children, Hugh suspended alimony payments at one point. But this attempt backfired, since Nathan promptly phoned his father and accused him of impoverishing Rose. Clearly, Nathan will need much time to accommodate to the new situation, if indeed he ever does.

Because of this animosity, Hugh's break with him was much cleaner, and there was never any deliberate attempt to disrupt or control the remarriage as there was with Michelle's son. But with Hugh's daughter, Esther, it was a different story.

Esther was much more intrusive, not only because of her individual personality, but because she was always anxious to get her father's approval, and her father was much closer to her. This did not endear her to Michelle, whose eyes flash in description:

> She's a very rebellious person — when they were selling their house in Puerto Rico after the divorce, when someone would come and look at the house, Esther would empty the garbage cans in the middle of the living room rug. She's a very sensational person; she's a very insecure person in a very flashy body. She kind of looks like a hooker.

The point at which Michelle demanded that Hugh show more commitment to the marriage than to his daughter came at the very beginning, when plans were being made for their wedding. Esther telephoned her father to make arrangements to come. She needed money to fly in from Puerto Rico, and she needed money for new clothes since it was winter; Hugh consented even though they did not have that much money to spare. Michelle was irked:

> I'm listening from our end, and he's sending her tickets and letting her charge whatever she needs to wear, and, oh, that music would be great, and she'd tape all the music for our wedding and she wanted to be our best man.
>
> She said, "There's nothing that says that a female can't stand up for her father."
>
> Hugh said, "Of course you can be my best man. I would love it."
>
> And I'm sitting here steaming because all of a sudden a whirlwind is coming in and taking over my wedding. And so after she got off the phone, I said to Hugh, "It sounds like Esther's coming."
>
> And he said, "Yeah, she's getting the music and all that."
>
> And I said, "Well, when she gets around to sending out the invitations, I'll have to tell you I can't make it."
>
> So he said nothing. We went for the rest of the morning without saying anything and then he came back and he told Esther that she couldn't come, that he wasn't going to send her the money. She could come if she chose to come on her own terms, but that she was not going to come and crash our wedding. So she didn't come.

Three years passed before Esther came to visit Michelle and Hugh. Now Michelle knows that though she was jealous of her stepdaughter's closeness with her husband, Hugh passed this initial loyalty test well enough for her to accept regular visits from Esther in recent years. By Michelle's account, Hugh has evidently so successfully transferred his loyalty to the new marriage that he is attempting to shield his stepdaughter from his daughter's potentially bad influence:

> Yesterday when Gwen was going out, she was dressed in a very preppy outfit, and she went to Hugh and said, "Do you really think this looks okay?" And he said to me later, "I really appreciate that, because Esther would be going out looking like "I can catch anybody with this." He said she'd go out in the flashiest outfit—or nothing at all!

Michelle graphically sums up the lessons she learned that helped the family to be as successful as it has been:

> I think the detaching part was very good for me. It was very easy for me to get into the middle of things, and being able to detach and let the shit fly is really what I had to do.

But recent developments in the Martin household suggest that this is not a one-step task. It requires sustained effort to maintain loyalty to spouse over loyalty to children. Gwen had lived with her mother and stepfather for nine years, but after living on her own for a while and attending college, is back in the house until she gets on her feet. This is a source of some conflict today:

> We're having a disagreement on whether she should pay rent. Hugh wants her to pay rent. I don't want her to. I feel that at this point in her life I would be a little more lenient than Hugh is. A lot of the difficulty is that she's been away for five years and now she's back in the fold. Hugh's a very rigid person—everything is preplanned and set up that way and that's the way you do it. I'm a little more loose.

Granted, individual character must play some part in the present-day tension. But one suspects that Michelle's "looseness" in the matter of her adult daughter paying rent is a legacy of her maternal loyalties of the past.

Trading Bonding for Love

Michelle Martin's explanation for the success of her stepfamily emphasizes that the most important thing she did was cutting loose—whether it meant getting out of the way of her daughter's relationship with her husband, telling her son that he was not welcome when his behavior was not acceptable, or detaching herself from the residual problems between her stepchildren, their father, and his ex-wife. The first two of these required relinquishing her role as biological mother, a difficult task under any circumstances.

For a parent to change from parent-child to marital loyalty is difficult because of the nature of the biological bond. Bonding occurs between mother and child even before birth. A pregnant woman becomes aware of this bond as soon as she realizes she is pregnant. Atop this primitive "primary bonding" occurs "secondary bonding," in which a newborn baby cuddles against the smell of the mother, to feel her warmth and hear the same heartbeat that was audible in the womb. As soon as a baby is born, the attending personnel often place it directly on the mother's chest to encourage secondary bonding. Fathers are only capable of this second kind of bonding, because of the physical differences between the sexes, and often fathers do not bond with their children at all.

Later on, parents develop love for their children, but love follows and is distinct from bonding. Stepparents, too, can develop love for their stepchildren; we have already seen numerous instances of deep feelings of affection and care expressed by stepparents. But stepparents do not bond. Bonding is a psychobiological process of which only parents, particularly mothers, are capable, whereas love is an emotional or psychological tie. It is therefore inevitable that whatever the type of stepfamily structure, there will be a qualitatively different type of relationship between parent and child.[3] Its distinctiveness is apparent to those who share it, and a potential source of feelings of exclusion to those who do not share it. Only in "pure stepparent" situations does bonding fail to produce an imbalance between the children, because only one of the adults is a parent in such families.

Compounding these elemental relations are sociological factors that make for greater parent-child loyalty. They vary, depending on the gender of the biological parent. All other things being equal, a biological father will be likely to encourage his children to get close to their stepmother. Her closeness to the children frees him from child-rearing responsibilities, thus leaving him more time and energy for career and other extrafamilial pursuits. He may also feel that as a female, she is more adapted to nurturing children.

Conversely, a biological mother will tend, perhaps only unconsciously, to resist her children getting close to their stepfather. She tends to feel protective toward her children anyway, a feeling that will become deeper and more textured to the extent that she has lived with them for an extended period of time in a single-parent household. She will also seek a more disciplinary, and hence less intimate, role for the stepfather toward her children, not only because it is generally regarded as more appropriate for a male to have this function, but because single mothers are ordinarily less successful at getting their children, particularly their sons, to obey.[4] Finally, custodial parents, typically mothers, are inclined to be lenient with children because of guilt over the pain the youngsters have suffered as a result of divorce.

For all these reasons, the tie between mother and child in remarriage is a particularly close one. The tie must be weakened in favor of the marital tie, because otherwise it will weaken the marriage. Time and again, clinicians and sociologists alike have pointed out that children are the most common source of discord between remarried parents.[5] In stepfamilies, particularly in their earlier stages, the desires of children are likely to be disruptive. In nuclear families, the children ordinarily want to keep their parents together; in stepfamilies, they are more likely to want to drive them apart. And as we have seen, they have more power than other children to do just that. In short, children in nuclear families have a *centripetal* tendency, seeking to keep the family together, while in stepfamilies they tend to be *centrifugal*, attempting to pull the family apart.[6]

Growing up is more complicated for adolescent stepchildren. Ordinarily, adolescence is a time of tentative steps toward independence, when children play at being adults for brief periods of time, after which they retreat to a childlike role. This "pseudo-autonomy," in which a gradual growth of an independent and adult sense of self gradually emerges is almost always painful and halting, requiring a secure and stable family platform from which a young person launches himself. A step-adolescent, however, is faced with the job not only of gradually separating himself from his family but of trying as best he can to join the newly formed stepfamily. In sum, adolescent stepchildren need to move in two directions at once—away from the family and into the family. Normal adolescent mood swings may be much more acute because rage against parents is accentuated by feelings that one or both "failed," while parental feelings of failure may at least partially corroborate the teen's accusations.[7]

Eric's erratic hot and cold alternations are understandable from this perspective. The power that Eric had to manipulate his mother was, in the short run, an adolescent's dream, whereas what he really craved was limits and firmness that would give him a sense of being loved. While it had been financially useful for getting money out of Michelle, Eric's power was thus not gratifying in the long run, so that paradoxically he could join the family only after it was made clear to him that the biological and guilt-inspired nexus between him and his mother was broken.

His loyalty to his father explained his original siding against his mother, but as his mother's household came to seem more serene and attractive, his father's alcohol-related problems seemed worse. His normal developmental process of separation was inhibited by his solidarity with his father—and may now be "resolved" by his adopting a quasi-parental role where his father is childlike—and by his increasing desire to be accepted in the household composed of his mother, sister, and stepfather. He might have been even more disruptive if he had been living with the stepfamily, but his living elsewhere made him acutely resentful of the feeling of being "excluded" from all the good times he imagined his sister was having.

In normal adolescent development, there is usually a mildly erotic tie with the parent of the opposite sex, while for adolescents in stepfamilies, the new spouse can be seen as "usurping" that tie. Eric's resentment of Hugh was a response to this, and the fact that before Hugh came along, he was able to manipulate his guilt-ridden mother with ease. His hostility to his stepfather was also in direct proportion to his realization that Hugh was a considerably more competent male authority than Miles was. His recent coming to terms with Hugh was only possible when he managed to separate himself from the entangled relationship with his increasingly incompetent father. Significantly, Eric spent a period of time in another home, which helped him to reconcile his loyalty to his father and his attraction to Hugh and Michelle's household.

In many stepfamilies, the biological parent does not receive needed support from the stepparent, who has never seen the "good" side of the adolescent and may have no experience with adolescents at all. Michelle probably would have had much more trouble disconnecting from Eric's attempts to manipulate her if Hugh had not been so supportive. The marital relationship could take precedence over her motherhood largely because of Hugh's backing.

Michelle's own personal qualities were also an asset. She originally initiated the divorce by leaving the house because of her ex-husband's drinking. That she initially left both her children behind suggests that she was already able to loosen biological ties when it became absolutely necessary. The capacity to make that initial break for what she regarded as self-preservation reemerged when she had to be firm enough with her son to exclude him when the need became clear.

There was a more balanced three-way relation between Michelle, Hugh, and Gwen, so that no zero-sum situation arose and the biological tie did not have to be weakened. Michelle did not have to cut Gwen loose because Gwen posed little threat to her marriage and the stability of the household. Gwen's rebellion against Hugh was short-lived because she saw it in her interests to keep the marriage together. Her relationship with her father had been violent and stormy, while she had lived with her mother from time to time after the divorce. The contrast between Hugh's competence and her father's unreliability posed no conflict of loyalties as it had for her brother. Gwen had not been able to manipulate her mother the way her brother had, so that Hugh's backing for Michelle was not a threat to her. Her conservatism suggests a desire to be a good little girl to avoid being a bone of contention, unlike her brother. Michelle's staying out of the way made it possible for Hugh to arrive at a distanced, disciplinary stepfather role. His stepping into this role was aided by their gender difference and the fact that at this point Gwen needed a reliable authority figure of the opposite sex.

As regards Michelle's relations with her stepchildren, she shows some common visited stepmother feelings in her resentment of Esther's attempt to take over her wedding to Hugh, and in her characterization of the young woman as flashy, splashy, looking like a hooker, a bartender, and staying out all night until the sun comes up, in contrast to her own relatively demure daughter. Her feelings about Nathan are neutral because he really is not in the picture.

The problems with Eric worked themselves out partly because Eric got over some high developmental hurdles, partly because of Michelle's personal strengths, but primarily because Michelle was successful in loosening the knot that bound her to her son. This would have been harder or impossible for her if it had not been for a loving and supportive relationship between her and Hugh.

Notes

1. A. Goettig (1983), "The Relative Strength of Husband-Wife and Parent-Child Dyads in Remarriage: A Test of the Hsu Model," *Journal of Comparative Family Studies* 14, 1, 117–28.
2. T. Roberts and S. Price (1985), "A Systems Analysis of the Remarriage Process: Implications for the Clinician," *Journal of Divorce* 9, 2, 1–25.
3. Rosenbaum and Rosenbaum, *Step parenting*, 96–97.
4. J. Santrock (1979), "Father Custody and Social Development in Boys and Girls," *Journal of Social Issues* 35, 4, 112–25; A. Ambert (1982), "Differences in Children's Behavior toward Custodial Mothers and Custodial Fathers," *Journal of Marriage and the Family* 44, 1, 73–86.
5. See White and Booth *Quality and Stability of Remarriages* and E. Einstein (1973), *The Stepfamily: Living, Loving, Learning* (New York: Macmillan).
6. M. Nelson and G. Nelson (1982), "Problems of Equity in the Reconstituted Family: A Social Exchange Analysis," *Family Relations* 31, 223–31.
7. C. Sager et al. (1983), *Treating the Remarried Family* (New York: Brunner & Mazel), 249–72.

Part II

Inside the Stepfamily: Children

Introduction

To this point, we have been primarily concerned with life inside the stepfamily as it revolves around the parents. Since the existence of a stepparent relation defines a stepfamily, this priority is natural. Yet there is another domain of relations in stepfamilies that should not go unexamined, one inhabited by the children themselves. Abut half of all the children in remarriages have stepsiblings, but because of custody patterns they do not often life with them. Two-thirds of children in remarriage have half-siblings, usually when their stepfather has a child with their mother.[1] In terms of sheer numbers alone, then, stepsibling and half-sibling issues are important.[2]

Notes

1. Mills, "Stepfamilies in Context," 12; see also A. Cherlin and J. McCarthy (1985), "Remarried Couple Households: Data from the June 1980 Current Population Survey," *Journal of Marriage and the Family* 47, 1, 23-30.
2. Aside from my own book, *Strangers in the House: The World of Stepsiblings and Half-Siblings* (New Brunswick, N.J.: Transaction, 1989), only one article has appeared on the subject: E. Rosenberg and F. Hajal (1985), "Stepsibling Relationships in Remarried Families," *Social Casework* 66, 287-292.

8

Strangers in the House: Stepsibling Relations

Relations between stepsiblings have intriguing similarities and contrasts with those between siblings in conventional families. One of the most commonly recognized aspects of relations between brothers and sisters is that of *sibling rivalry*.[1] Rivalry is also an important issue between stepsiblings, but it is different in its nature and its outcomes. A second phenomenon that can be extremely important between stepsiblings is not ordinarily problematic for siblings, that of *sexual attraction*.

How these issues work out in general depends primarily on the age of the children when a stepfamily is formed. If children are very small, stepsibling relations will tend to approximate those of sibling relations in conventional families. If children are in their late teens or older, their relations will be remote enough for them to be like distant relatives. Thus at either extreme, stepsibling relations are less uncomfortable. In between, however, particularly if the stepfamily is formed when a child is in early adolescence, sexuality and competition are more problematic. In this chapter, then, we look at the cases of two people whose stepfamilies were formed at this more delicate stage in their lives.

Gender plays a critical role in determining the evolution of stepsibling relations. Same-sex stepsiblings tend to be rivals, a rivalry that, as in the case of conventional siblings, can be a healthy spur to a child's development. It opens new horizons, because it offers a wider range of people with whom a growing youngster can identify himself. Opposite-sex stepsibling relations are more complex and potentially more dangerous. Erotic attraction is the most salient issue, and it can be deeply disruptive. While rivalry is also present under the surface, it is not resolved in the same way, because a young person ordinarily does not use an opposite-sex peer as a positive or negative model. Let us therefore look at the simpler case first, and turn to opposite-sex stepsiblings later.

Stepsibling Rivalry

To understand stepsibling rivalry, briefly consider competition among biological brothers and sisters. Sibling rivalry revolves around children's belief that parental love is finite. If a brother or a sister gets parental love, to the sibling this means that there will be that much less left for him or her. This belief is, particularly in early childhood, impervious to repeated parental assurances that children are equally loved.

While originally love, in the form of attention, affection, and caresses, constitutes the stake in the competition, in later life rivalry can revolve around any number of things that symbolize it— such as food, time, gifts, approval, praise, money, and property. Thus siblings often insist on absolute equality in the distribution of everything from ice cream to hugs, because of the desire that every child receive comparable amounts of love and its symbols. While this competition starts out in early childhood, it does not necessarily fade with age; rivalry between siblings often persists far into adulthood. One study of older sibling relations revealed that almost three quarters of the people studied experienced adult sibling rivalry.[2]

Alongside rivalry over parental love arises "sibling generated" rivalry. Particularly likely between siblings of the same sex, this consists of competition over fulfillment of criteria that are generated by siblings themselves and their peers. Competition between brothers over athletic prowess, for example, might have parental approval as its background, but becomes an end in itself. It typically has two seemingly contradictory outcomes. One is that a boy will seek to imitate and surpass his brother; in the jargon of social psychology he is said to "identify" with his brother. The other outcome is that in competition with his brother a boy will take him as a negative example; rather than trying to surpass him in sports, he may denigrate him as a mindless jock, even as he himself seeks academic excellence. In such a case he is said to "de-identify" with his brother, by seeking to be everything his brother is not. The same applies, *mutatis mutandis*, to girls and their sisters. Although these reactions to sibling-generated rivalry seem contradictory, they are really part of the same process, in which children achieve their definitions of themselves by using competitive siblings as foils.[3]

Stepsibling rivalry's background is different from that of sibling rivalry. Aside from the circumstance in which children become stepsiblings at a very early age, the competition over parental affection is not the same. Particularly if the single-parent phase was long enough to give the children a feeling of interdependence with the custodial parent, a stepsibling is not usually a competitor for parental affection. Usually, stepsibling rivalry revolves around valued items that really are finite—having to share space, money, clothing, records, makeup, and so on. In this sense, the rivalry between stepsiblings is simpler than the rivalry between siblings. Between siblings, the competition is intractable, because even scrupulous parental equality cannot reassure a young child—and probably some older children too—that they are equally loved. For sibling rivalry, everything the children compete for is really a symbol of something else. In stepsibling rivalry, it is more straightforward because competition over space, for instance, is just that, rather than a covert form of competition for parental love.

Yet it is also more complicated, because neither stepsibling regards the other as equally entitled. In conventional families, parents typically cope with competition by trying to be equitable amongst the children. A stepparent who tries to be equitable among the biological and stepchildren in the family may well exacerbate tensions at first, even though he has little choice. A biological child who receives the same amount of attention as his stepsibling sees equity as unjust, since he is presumptively entitled to more because of his blood relation. But a stepparent who abandons attempts at equity exacerbates the situation, because this increases rivalry between the youngsters.

Stepsibling rivalry in some ways is thus not within the parents' power to alleviate. It is, however, within the power of the stepsiblings themselves to accommodate. As with sibling-generated rivalry, stepsiblings often use one another as positive or negative models as a way of finding out who they are. Just as sibling rivalry can be of great use to a young person in spurring his or her development as a person, stepsibling rivalry opens wider horizons to young persons than are available in nuclear families. Aubrey Larsen presents the case of a young man whose stepbrothers have presented him with challenging and stimulating examples.

Aubrey Larsen

Aubrey Larsen's mother died when he was about nine years old. His brother, Richard, had already moved out of the house to go to college. Richard's best friend, Amos, moved in immediately after the funeral. One year later, Aubrey's father remarried, to Rachel, a widow with two sons, Bill and Eli. Bill and Eli were married by that time, so for two years the household consisted of Aubrey, his father and stepmother, and Amos. For the rest of his adolescence, Aubrey lived with his father and stepmother. There is a finished apartment in the basement of their home, where Bill and his wife lived for a while. The whole stepfamily gathers every Sunday at the Larsen home, still staying in close and regular contact with each other.

Aubrey took to his stepmother so quickly and completely that he ordinarily refers to Rachel as his mother. He says that now, at age twenty-three, he does not remember clearly what it was like to be with his biological mother. He recalls events in his earlier childhood in which his stepmother was with him, but knows that this is impossible, and that his mind has replaced one with the other. He loves his stepmother, and acknowledges that she has made it easy for him to love her. His problems in growing up have revolved around deciding what kind of man he wants to be, and the different models offered him by the males to whom he was exposed.

One of the deepest, but most questionable, influences was Amos. Although ostensibly he had come to live in the Larsen household because Aubrey needed the companionship, it was not long until he was obliged to leave. Rachel was concerned about his influence on the impressionable young Aubrey:

> My mother—my stepmother—was not really crazy about Amos. He didn't pay any rent. He was bringing girls back. When my brother would come back from school he and Amos would take me to the beach to get high and they used to take me to all these weird places. All my friends loved Richard and Amos. They were the big boys, and they were really nice guys. Amos was a great athlete, so he used to play ball with all my friends and everything.

Little wonder that Aubrey adored Amos—he was older, he was an ambassador to the world of marijuana, he treated Aubrey as a peer, he was a great athlete, and he was admired by Aubrey's contemporaries. As it turns out, Rachel was quite right, and although Amos has ended up in a disastrous state, Aubrey's admiration for him persists:

> Amos became a cocaine addict. He's the ultimate wheeler-dealer. He is mister salesman, and he sells pharmaceuticals. He could sell you a pencil; he could sell you anything.

Amos was neither a brother nor a stepbrother—at most he could be described as a sort of foster brother—but his influence as a role model in Aubrey's life was crucial, particularly because he is such a sharp contrast to Aubrey's father.

Aubrey's father is a certified public accountant, but does not feel any intense desire for wealth. He is a relaxed and informal man who does not let work or ambition infringe too much on the contentments of home life.

> He's a CPA who doesn't earn a lot of money, and that's a rarity. My mother earns as much as he does, which doesn't say too much for him. He always went for a relaxed attitude.

Aubrey blames his father for not presenting him with an example of the kind of ambition and drive that he admires in Amos and others:

> Most of my life I've seen my dad, during the time when I should have been developing an instinct to go out there and earn money, my dad was working on his retirement. My dad made a seven-year calendar, and they both retired within a few weeks of each other; they had this calendar to count down the

days till their retirement. My introduction to the world of work was watching my dad retire!

Although Aubrey is only becoming conscious of it now, part of Amos's allure was that he offered such a polar opposite to the kind of man his father is. The other men in Aubrey's life, brother and stepbrothers, offer a similarly contrasting array of alternate male roles.

His brother, Richard, played with a rock band on the road for a few years, and then took a music degree at a college in New England. He abandoned that field when it proved to be less lucrative than he would have liked. After several years working for a pittance at a music company, he is now working for an investment firm. One suspects that Richard, too, was influenced by the contrast between his father and his best friend. The latter's example seems to have won out, at least for now, and the main reason is that their stepbrothers have tipped the balance.

Bill is a neurologist, and while not a businessman, is financially successful, as well as showing personality traits that Aubrey grudgingly admires. "He's a sponge type person. He just takes anything he can get his hands on." But Eli has by far the greater influence on him.

Eli is a millionaire. He started out as a hospital administrator, and started a company that sells specialized medical technology equipment for pets. He lives in his mother's old house, for which he paid most of the mortgage; there was a discrepancy in the balance of what he paid that is still a bone of contention between him and Aubrey's father. Eli's example is an attractive one, because he succeeded in becoming what Amos only promised. But he, too, has some less desirable aspects to his personality:

> Eli's personal life is a mystery and we all wonder what he's really doing. He's running the company, he's the president, but he's never, ever at home. We've heard there are orgies at the company and he laughs when my father says something, but he must be doing something on the side. I know he's tried cocaine. He's a real Type A person. I can see him working and stressed out and working on a heart attack. He's never with his kids.

Aubrey is thus aware that for both the people whose greed and ambition contrasted with his father's passivity, a high personal price had to be paid.

Doubt leads him to deliver a soliloquy not unlike that of Hamlet for its indecision:

> I think I have the capacity to be rich if I want to be, but I'm not so sure that I want to. I was always interested in art forms—music and video and makeup, making a person beautiful, things like that. Now I'm tending toward economics and finance. I'm headed toward investment banking, but I feel like just sitting back, and why can't I go to the beach, play my drums, and practice my music and weight lift and maybe work once or twice a week?

Aubrey's admiration for the entrepreneurial examples set by Amos and Richard and Eli is tempered by doubt about the personal price exacted, just as his manifest contempt for his father's example is touched with an admission of the appeal of the comforting warmth of family life is.

Stepsibling Sexuality

Stepfamilies require a rethinking of most issues related to families, and nowhere is this more necessary than in the area of sexuality. Sexual relations, and their regulation, are fundamental to the institution of the family. Within the family, sexual relations are strictly governed by a series of prohibitions commonly known as incest taboos, rules that prohibit sexual relations between blood relatives. It would be inconceivable to have a viable family system without them.

There are social and psychological reasons for prohibiting sexual relations between family members other than the parents, even aside from the emotional damage incest wreaks. One of the functions of the family is to rear youngsters in such a way that they will be able to become autonomous adults, independent of their family of origin, capable of social relationships and emotional intimacy with people they encounter after they have left home. The strict regulation of sexuality within the family has the function of encouraging its sons and daughters, at the appropriate time, to direct their search for partners outside the family. They cannot do this, or can only do so with difficulty, if they have become sexually entangled with a sibling or a parent.

Yet how do we adapt incest taboos to stepfamilies, in which several unrelated people of the opposite sex live in intimate conditions? Forbidding incest is simple when kinship relations are explicit and rules regarding daily life are unambiguous and universally enforced. But nowadays the rules of family life are often not clear. Stepfamilies dilute the boundaries between kin and nonkin, and the rules on incest are predictably weakened. Stepfamily sexuality fits uneasily into the framework of today's legal and social rules.

The issue of stepsibling sexuality, therefore, leaves us with a paradox. On the one hand, our society does not identify stepsibling sexual relations as incestuous, and has apparently held this view for at least four thousand years. On the other hand, we recognize that the everyday stability of a family requires prohibition of sexual relations between stepsiblings, at least those living under the same roof. If children are erotically enmeshed with each other, they will have trouble maturing, leaving the family, and succeeding in the search for emotional intimacy outside it. The stepfamily's sexual dilemma as regards opposite-sex stepsiblings is that it must manufacture its own stepsibling incest taboo in the absence of a societal stepsibling incest taboo.

Once again, as in the numerous other instances we have explored, the stepfamily is on its own when it comes to making up rules of operation. Since children are generally more powerful in stepfamilies, they tend to participate more in the establishment of rules than they might in a conventional family. A young woman describing her relationship with her stepbrother, when they were both adolescents, illustrates the way in which a stepfamily usually cooperates in establishing a stepsibling incest taboo.

> I don't think it [sexual relations] came into our minds, but I think that it was an idea in my father's head, and my stepmother's. *They* thought it might happen, but I don't think in *our* minds it would, because we knew that we were family now. My brother and I would always punch each other and fool around, and when my stepbrother saw my brother do it, he did it. You know, always beating them and punching them and joking around. I remember when he and I were just joking around and punching and everything, my father said, "Don't forget you guys are brother and sister." And I said, "Dad, what are you talking about? Of course I know that!" I definitely think it was in my dad's head. I would see it as something that was wrong because I consider my stepsiblings as family. I consider them brother and sister. I would never even consider dating my stepbrother or — I look at that as incest.

The woman quoted became a stepsibling when she was twelve years old, but had known her stepbrother previously and had often played with him in childhood. Her development of her own stepsibling incest taboo in these circumstances is not uncommon. If people become stepsiblings in infancy or early childhood, there is comparatively little chance that they will subsequently feel sexual attraction to each other.

This is part of a general rule; biologically unrelated children who are reared together since they were babies seldom feel any sexual magnetism between them when they become mature. The ancient Chinese practice of betrothing children who were then brought up as siblings often produced spouses with a strong aversion for one another.[4] A similar pattern emerges on Israeli collective farms, where children are reared together as if they were siblings from the time they are weaned. Until puberty these unrelated children live in close conditions with one another—sleeping, showering, playing in a single group. When they are adult, it is extremely rare that one person will marry another from his or her age cohort, even though there are absolutely no adult-generated rules prohibiting it. It appears that in such circumstances, at least, extended familiarity breeds not so much contempt as a lack of sexual curiosity.

When sexuality does become an issue, opposite-sex stepsiblings have three possible reactions to erotic attraction.[5] The first, and most rate, is that they actually will engage in sexual relations. It is rare partly because people in early adolescence are uncomfortable with and unaccustomed to their emerging sexual feelings, and because informal or explicit parental prohibitions would result in unbearable emotional pressure. What is much more common is the opposite outcome, where sexual attraction is so uncomfortable that it consciously emerges as hostility. Because a youngster feels so disturbed by an opposite-sex stepsibling, what he or she consciously feels is intense dislike, as a way of masking deeper emotions. Hostility between opposite-sex stepsiblings in prepuberty or early adolescence, therefore, is far more likely. The third outcome is one in which opposite-sex stepsiblings come to feel a deep, nonerotic tie between them, one that is often deeper and more affectionate than between brothers and sisters. Rather than turning it into dislike, such stepsiblings have successfully transformed their attraction into a warm, chaste affection.

This was the ultimate result of Colleen Macnamara's stepfamily development. But it was a rocky road getting there, because of the competition that accompanied the attraction, and she has still not managed to become an independent, functioning adult.

Colleen Macnamara

Colleen Macnamara lives in a small suburban community, where she has worked off and on for most of her adult life in a restaurant owned by her stepfather. Her mother and father separated when she was about two years old, and until she was eleven she lived alone with her mother. Then her mother married Simon, who was divorced and had three sons—Eddie, Dwight, and Ralph, who lived with Simon's ex-wife. While Simon was dating her mother, he used to bring his sons over to visit.

At the beginning, Colleen adored her stepfather, but when he moved in and took over as man of the house, things changed:

> I loved Simon. I thought he was great—until they got married and we lived together. Before they got married, anything I wanted to do was okay. He showered me with gifts. I was spoiled rotten. After they got married, all of a sudden there was this man who thought he was my father, or thought he was man of the house. I remember telling him, "You're not my father! You can't tell me what to do!" I greatly resented him. But it's changed over time to the point where my relationship with Simon is probably the best I have with anyone. Simon stuck by me, no matter what.

During her entire adolescence, Colleen lived with her stepfather and mother. Her stepbrothers, Eddie, Dwight, and Ralph, were living with their mother, who subsequently remarried, too. She enjoyed having them visit, because they were there often enough for her to enjoy their company, but were also at arm's length.

Throughout this time, Colleen's visiting stepbrothers had a very important influence on her, each in his own way, but distinctly as members of the opposite sex. All three of them were similar to brothers, in that they provided information and companionship of the sort a girl can get from male siblings. And they provided the kind of feelings of solidarity youth can get from banding together against the adults:

The boys had a lot of negative feelings toward their father, too, about what had gone on between their father and their mother. So when I went through the stage when I didn't like being with Simon, I could actually side with them against their father. It was not nice.

But they were also more than brothers, because from the beginning there was an erotic tone to their relations. It was not until later that feelings of stepsibling rivalry began to surface.

Until her mother remarried, Colleen had lived in an enclosed, exclusively female world that in a way was ideally suited to the asexual slumber of her latency period. She remembers that at the beginning, when the boys would come over, it was "scary," and she felt "mortified," because she wanted them to like her, and she did not know if they would, and "they were all good-looking, and Dwight used to say stuff like 'We can get married because we're not related.'"

Colleen regarded Ralph, the oldest, as a kind of older brother, since he was dating and soon got married. But he still awakened romantic feelings in her:

> I had a crush on Ralph, bad, bad. And that was very exciting. I still had a crush on Ralph after they were married.

Now, of course, she is out of the stage of having crushes, and he has two children, but "I still feel I could tell Ralph things. He's intelligent. There's something about Ralph I like."

Colleen developed a crush on Dwight for a while, too, although it did not last as long:

> I thought Dwight was the cutest. I was madly in love with Dwight. I just thought Dwight walked on water. He was Prince Charming. It was obvious. Simon used to tease me about it.

Colleen was intensely jealous of Dwight's girlfriend, because she was blond and blue-eyed, and "had a look I never had. Later on, "I think my taste grew up." And still later on, they grew hostile to one another.

Eddie is the stepbrother to whom Colleen felt the strongest attraction. Her gaining Eddie as a guide to the world of boys coincided with the onset of puberty and the awakening of romantic feelings:

> I felt closer to Eddie than I did to the other boys. I loved him. I never had a relationship like that before. We did things that kids at that age do, but I had had a sheltered childhood, and my mother was real restrictive and protective. But I was allowed to do things with Eddie. I learned about boys and how boys looked at girls. In a way he helped me grow up, because we would do things like smoke cigarettes together, or go trick-or-treating together in a big group. I was never allowed to do anything like that when I was with my mom, never, but now I was with Eddie, so it was okay. I think the first time I kissed was at Eddie's birthday party. I think we were playing drop the apple or spin the bottle or something.

At Ralph's wedding, Colleen was paired with Eddie for the party. She remembers, "I thought we were *the* couple." She also recollects when her feelings toward Eddie were strong enough to be disturbing:

> There was one time when I was aware of him as a member of the opposite sex, and I knew it wasn't quite right. We were coming back from Queens and it was late and we were tired. We were lying in the back seat and we were facing each other and I had my head on his thighs and he had his head on my thighs and I had a sexual feeling, and I didn't think it was quite kosher, but it was enjoyable, and I felt close, you know, it felt loving.

At the same time, though, the boys were stepsiblings as well as being boys, and there were issues of rivalry that underlay the romance and the flirting from the very beginning. From the start, Colleen was living with Simon, while Ralph, Dwight, and Eddie were not. He was the apple of her eye, and he showered her with gifts, a fact not lost on the boys.

Colleen remembers a specific incident when the rivalry between herself and her stepbrothers boiled to the surface.

> Ralph, Eddie, and myself were working at the restaurant. Dwight used to come in on Saturday and Sunday mornings and sit down and have breakfast. The rule had always been that when we came to the restaurant we didn't have to pay for our meals but we had to tip the girls. So here I am, waiting on tables and the son of a bitch isn't tipping. He would come in behind the counter and get his own juice and take coffee to go.
>
> So he went behind the counter, and I said, "Dwight, what are you getting?"
>
> And he said, 'I'll get it for myself, it's my father's restaurant.'
>
> I remember telling him, "You're too damned cheap to leave a buck on the counter!" I was being a real jerk.
>
> And he got off, he got real mad, and Eddie and Ralph of course defended their brother, because here's the issue of "It's my father."

And then he went and called me an asshole in front of the customers.

Even though Colleen was a girl and did not interfere with their home life with their mother, the boys' envy of her being doted on by their father must have been intense. Stepsibling rivalry for them revolved around the basic injustice that, although Simon was their father, Colleen was the center of his attention. They did not share a home with their stepsister but they did share the territory of the restaurant when they worked together there. They could not legitimately call into question Colleen's right to live where she did, but the restaurant was *their father's* restaurant, and finding ways to treat her as an interloper there was not difficult.

Looking back on the competition between her and her stepbrothers, Colleen says,

> There was a lot of jealousy involved. The other day, my stepfather said something—"Out of all my kids," meaning Ralph, Dwight, Eddie, and myself, "you're the best." And that made me feel so good.

Now that she is a mature adult, though, the stepsibling rivalry has faded somewhat, but there is a sad and disturbing residue to the sexual attraction that lurked along with it:

> Both Eddie and I have remained single. Eddie, I was sure he was gay. There was a girl he went out with off and on for years, but she's still waiting for him to pop the question. I don't want to get married, because I don't want to get divorced. It's a lot of responsibility, letting someone get close to you. And it's kind of distasteful. I don't want children. I don't think Eddie does. I was thinking, wouldn't it be nice if Eddie and I bought a house together and we lived together, like brother and sister, because to me that's a comfortable situation. It's not a spouse—you have the comfort and security and somebody there, but you don't have to be married.

Neither Colleen and Eddie, for so long flirtatious stepsiblings and tense rivals for the privilege of being Simon's chosen, seem able to escape their stepfamily.

Wider Horizons, Deeper Ambivalence

The stories of Colleen Macnamara and Aubrey Larsen illustrate how having stepsibling strangers in the house widen the horizons of family experience beyond that of children in conventional families. In Colleen's case, the wider horizons meant that during a formative time in her life, she was often in the company of a trio of young men who were closer than most boys but not as close as brothers. This meant that she could look at them, simultaneously, as males about whom she could weave romantic fantasies and quasi-siblings with whom she was in competition for their father. For Aubrey, having stepbrothers means that at an equally crucial period in his life, he was presented with alternative models of manhood that gave him a range of choices to imitate not normally available to young men.

Colleen's situation was ideally fitted for a pubescent girl to develop romantic attachments. She had been a sheltered only child living with her mother for many years. Then Simon arrived. She went through the familiar pattern of adoring him while he was dating her mother and then resenting him when he moved in and started taking some control over her life, but these resentments have been replaced by a very deep bond of affection and loyalty. The real asset in the situation at first was the visiting presence of Eddie, Dwight, and Ralph. Since they did not live with her, they did not contest her primacy in the household, but they visited often enough to be of great personal significance to her.

She had a crush on all of her stepbrothers. She had a crush on Ralph, even though he soon ceased frequent visitation, a crush that continued even after he was married. She was "madly in love with Dwight," who she thought was the cutest and used to tease her a lot. She learned all about boys from Eddie, in whose company she tasted the freedom of trick-or-treating in a group and kissing at parties, freedom she had not known as a young girl. All her girlfriends fell in love with Eddie, and rather than inspire jealousy in her, this confirmed how "adorable" he was. At Ralph's wedding—weddings are romantic episodes even for the guests—she was Eddie's partner, and "I thought we were *the* couple." She even remembers a distinctly sexual attraction to him, which was "not quite right." It is hard to imagine a situation in which a young woman could have her romantic feelings awakened more strongly, yet so safely, by boys who were not so close that they presented her with intimacy for which she was not prepared.

Yet her feelings of competition with her stepbrothers also come through. Her story of the dispute with them over the tip at the restaurant reveals a theme she admits recurred, that the man who owned the family restaurant was *their* father, not hers. The boys' feeling of possessiveness about their biological father was clearly a reaction to their feeling of being excluded by him; Colleen lived with Simon, and they did not. At the very end, Colleen points out that Simon told her that of all the children, he thought she was the best. Her competition with her stepbrothers was not the acute kind that arises between same-sex siblings and stepsiblings, because she was not competing with the boys as a male. Instead, she had the distinct advantage of being a girl, and being the only one in the home with her stepfather, who had always wanted a girl and who doted on her, spending what she thought were immense sums on her wardrobe. Because things were so stacked in her favor, the victory in the stepsibling rivalry was hers even before it had begun.

For both Colleen and Aubrey, though, wider horizons meant deeper ambivalence. Colleen sometimes cannot decide if her stepbrothers are creatures to be loathed or coveted. The fact that she was struggling to separate herself from her family as an adolescent at precisely the same time as she was seeking to find a place for herself in the wider stepfamily network meant that she was repeating a common trait of the adolescent in a stepfamily. At age thirty, she is still not ready to set up an autonomous adult life for herself. She is not married, she does not intend to get married, and her most active fantasy associated with marriage is to live in a chaste, nonmarital relationship in the same house with her effeminate stepbrother, who is also apparently reluctant to marry. The rich panoply of emotional experiences that stepfamily living opened up to her has not been without its snares. She is still trapped in the emotional entanglements of opposite-sex stepsibling attraction.

Aubrey Larsen, too, is suspended between step- and biological relations, because of the variety of models whom he can potentially emulate. His father represents a kind of antimodel for him, a man seemingly obsessed with security and routine, who, rather than seek riches or personal satisfaction from his career, was planning his retirement from the beginning. Aubrey has tentatively decided he wants to be everything his father is not, although another boy could equally have decided that he was an ideal to imitate. His brother, Richard, provides another model. Although Richard now has become a money-hungry young professional,

Aubrey remembers him as being wild, nonconforming, and interested in music. His stepbrothers seem to him to be aggressive, acquisitive, financially obsessed men with a "killer instinct," who are the diametrical opposites of his father. His description of them is a mixture of awe and misgivings, the first inspired by their wealth and ambition, the latter by their involvement with drugs, their secretiveness, and their lack of commitment to their families. The range of men available to Aubrey as models is even wider than in ordinary stepfamilies, because of the brief but extremely important time that Amos lived with the Larsens. Amos, to the objective eye a fast-talking con man, dazzled young Aubrey with his toughness and salesmanship, his easy way with drugs and his friends, and a nonconformity that matched Richard's. Aubrey is so conflicted about Amos that he avers that the man is a cocaine addict and a "wheeler-dealer in pharmaceuticals," in almost the same breath as he says that he loves him.

At present Aubrey has such an array of models whom he could emulate that he literally cannot decide. At times he feels as if he would like to play music, go to the beach, and work once in a while. At other times, he feels he would like to be rich, remembers that he always wanted to be, from the time of his childhood onward. He is suspended between types of people—a ritualist father, an artistically oriented brother, a charismatic drug addict, and two stepbrothers who are money-making machines—to the extent that the choices may be too numerous. In his words, "I'm trying to decide who I want to imitate. That is the problem. It's been a major problem." At present, he is paralyzed by the choices, rather than mobilized by them. One hopes that as he matures he will select his own identity from among these components.

Colleen and Aubrey illustrate attraction and competition, the two predominant stepsibling relations. They are characteristic mainly of "yours and mine" stepfamilies. In "yours and ours" and in "yours, mine, and ours" stepfamilies, though, the relations between the young people are complicated by the addition of a mutual child who is half-sibling to the other children. We have already had glimpses of how children react to the birth of a half-sibling, but their behavior and feelings were filtered through adult narration. So there again, a children's-eye view is needed to complement the parent's and stepparent's-eye view that we had earlier.

Notes

1. For a summary of research on sibling relations, see J. Schvaneveldt and M. Ihinger (1979), "Sibling Relationships in the Family," in W. R. Burr, R. Hill, F. I. Nye, and I. R. Reiss (eds.), *Contemporary Theories About the Family*, vol. 1 (New York: Free Press).
2. H. Ross and J. Milgram (1980), "Sibling Relationships: A Qualitative Study," in M. Lamb and B. Sutton-Smith (eds.), *Sibling Relationships: Their Nature and Significance Across the Lifespan* (Hillsdale, N.J.: Lawrence Erlbaum).
3. F. Schachter et al. (1976), "Sibling Deidentification," *Developmental Psychology* 12, 5, 418–27; J. Pfouts (1976), "The Sibling Relation: A Forgotten Dimension," *Social Work* 21, 200–4; B. Bryant (1980), "Sibling Relations in Middle Childhood," in Lamb and Sutton-Smith, *Sibling Relationships*.
4. R. Dinnage (1986), "All In The Family," *New York Review of Books*, 4 December, p. 39.
5. For an extended discussion of this, see Beer, *Strangers in the House*.

9

Outsiders and Insiders: Half-Siblings

The birth of a mutual child is an important event in the lives of the other children in a stepfamily. It can symbolize betrayal, because it means that a child has finally to relinquish the dream of reuniting his divorced parents. It can also, and at the same time, symbolize renewal, because it means that this remarriage is a "real" family now, in which the adults are committed enough to each other to become parents.[1] Different family configurations also affect how the other children will react—how long the single-parent phase lasted, how many siblings and stepsiblings preceded the mutual child's birth, their gender, their stages of development, and how much time has elapsed since the remarriage.[2] The mutual child itself is the center of attention—the "hub" of the family—but may well feel the pressure of symbolizing the stepfamily's hopes for rebirth and renewal.

The discussion of half-siblings underlines the problems of stepfamily vocabulary, because the same term purports to describe several different family roles. As we saw in the discussion of "yours and ours" and "yours, mine, and ours" stepparents, there is a basic imbalance built into the relationships of half-siblings because in any given household there are two distinct types. One has both biological parents in the household and the other has only one; the latter is, almost by definition, more marginal than the former. Such outsiders are doubly outside when they are visiting half-siblings, as contrasted with residential half-siblings. There is a built-in potential for half-sibling rivalry, just as there is for sibling and stepsibling rivalry. The difference is that it has a unique origin, the number of biological parents a child has in a given household. These three types of half-sibling can be termed "visiting outsiders," "resident outsiders," and "resident insiders."

To illustrate the difference between the attitude of resident outsiders and visiting outsiders, consider the following comments by Brad Henderson about the effects the birth of the mutual child, Roger, had to him and his new wife, Anne. First, the half-sibling rivalry displayed by Brad's stepdaughter Carol:

> I think there's very strong sibling rivalry that she's verbalized recently that she never acknowledged before. You have to understand that she was literally the center of everybody's universe in that family for about ten years. She was the only child of all of three children of the grandparents, all the grandparents on both sides, and the only child of the marriage even when they split up. So everyone was always saying, "Oh, look how cute she is!" Everybody fawned all over her. For the first ten years of her life, Carol lived the best of all possible lives for someone who was in that situation because she was showered with attention and affection and presents. She also was a professional model, she appeared on national TV, been in every national magazine. All of a sudden that came to an end. Everybody else started having children, and now she shares the spotlight. Roger gets so much more attention than Carol ever remembers getting, that now it's, "Hi, Carol, where's Roger?" It's made her resentful and bitter to a certain extent. The aging star has been replaced by the kid out of Tidewater, and now he's sitting on the bench.

To use the terminology coined above, Carol is a "resident outsider," whose antagonism to the "resident insider" is intensified because she was the center of attention for so many people for so long. Evidently, half-sibling rivalry can be at least as intense as sibling or stepsibling rivalry.

In comparison, let us look at Brad's description of the effects of Roger's birth on the "visiting outsiders," the two daughters of whom his ex-wife has custody and who visit the Hendersons:

> My ex-wife found out about Anne being pregnant in a very unusual way. Some court papers were served on her—the timing was bad, because I didn't expect

her to get the papers before I had a chance to talk to the girls. She called both girls down from their rooms as soon as she got these papers and said, "You see that? Your father's having a baby with Anne! He doesn't love you any more!" She really did a number on their head. So much so that Holly refused to talk to me for weeks on the phone, refused to come for visitation. But by the time we got down to the wire, the girls started to come around a little bit. And once the baby was born, they started to react very positively and now they're both crazy about him. And it grew geometrically as the baby got older.

Why such different reactions? For Carol, being a resident outsider is probably harder than for most, since in addition to having her mother all to herself after the divorce she had been an only child, had been doted on by her grandparents as the only grandchild, and had actually been a child model. It would be hard to imagine a more brutal fall from center stage than hers. Her stepsisters, the visiting outsiders, had a comparatively easy time. After they surmounted the prejudice with which their mother had tried to infuse them, they came to adore their half-brother, in part because he was much less of a threat. They have their mother full time, and being periodic visitors to the Henderson household, do not feel competitive with the baby because their home base is secure. Moreover, they are blood siblings, and get considerable support from one another in their journeys from household to household. Carol has no full-blood siblings to sustain her, and even though she has her mother, Anne is obviously preoccupied with Roger at present.

Visiting outsiders frequently come to see the stepfamily with mutual children as more desirable than the one in which they are currently living. The reasons vary, depending on the individual character of the child, and on the life stage and circumstances of the stepfamily in which he or she is living. In the story told by Karen Pappas that follows, we see a young woman who as a result of puberty and other awakenings came to see herself, her mother, her stepfather, her father, and her mother in such different terms than she had in her childhood that she made a brave and momentous leap into a new household. She made this move even though it meant moving into a home where her half-brother and half-sister already had an inside track. In a word, Karen Pappas is a visiting outsider who became a resident outsider.

Karen Pappas

Karen's mother and father, Edna and Matthew, broke up when she was about one year old and her sister, Alexis, was four. Almost immediately, Edna started living with Herbert, a very successful businessman. Although they were not married until eight years had elapsed, Herbert acted as stepfather to Karen and Alexis ever since. At first they lived in New York, but when Karen was twelve, Herbert was transferred to Tucson and the stepfamily moved there. In the meantime, Matthew settled down with and eventually married Pamela, whom he had met in graduate school while both were working on their degrees in social work. Four years later, they had their first mutual child, Shane, and four years after that they had Hope. Karen and Alexis regularly visited Matthew and Pamela right up until the time Karen decided to move in with them, at age fourteen. While the girls were living in New York visitation was frequent, but after the move to Tucson it was for the summers and once or twice during the year.

Matthew had become familiar with Pamela while he and Edna were still married. Edna still believes that Pamela deliberately set out to take her husband away. But her hostility to Pamela was based on more than the eternal triangle:

> My mother saw my stepmother as a totally alien creature, a hippy. She hated her and thought she was crazy and ridiculous.

As Karen got older, the contrast between Pamela and Edna became more and more evident, and eventually she made a choice. But this did not take place before her teens.

While she was living with her mother and stepfather, Karen's relations with Herbert were fairly typical of relations between a stepfather and a preadolescent stepdaughter who have been together since she was very young.

> When I was younger, I guess I thought of him as my father and living with him I identified more closely with him than with my father all during my childhood. I had a lot of respect for him.

Karen's unquestioning obedience and respect for Herbert was particularly important, because her stepfather was such a polar opposite from her father. Herbert was educated in military schools, had rigid views on nearly everything, evaluated people in terms of their bank accounts, and insisted on close scrutiny and management of Karen's life.

Edna deferred to Herbert in most matters of discipline, but Karen remembers that the three blood-related females had a kind of in-group from which Herbert was excluded. Their favorite activity was going to the malls and shopping, which they did three times a week. At first Karen went along, but as she got older she came to resent the activity, although it was not so much shopping *per se* that Karen resented. Rather, it was the kind of model to which her mother was trying to induce her to conform.

> I tried to look the way she wanted me to look, but it made me very unhappy to be shopping all the time and to be trying to look pretty when I really felt that I looked ridiculous in the clothing she wanted me to wear.

Her rebellion started in the malls, but soon spread to other areas in her life.

Meanwhile, Karen's feelings about her stepmother had gone through distinct phases. At first, when she and Alexis visited just their father and his wife, things were fairly harmonious, and the sisters felt they were having an adventure together:

> My sister and I went to visit and we always went together and it was always us feeling like we were in a foreign, strange place—although the visits were pleasant, they were fun, because we did things like go to the park or the library or a museum. My sister and I were very close with each other throughout, and very exclusive. We were like a team.

At first, Karen's feelings toward her stepmother were fairly warm. But she was disturbed when Shane was born.

> My stepmother tells me we were very close until I was about four. When I was four, my stepmother got pregnant with my little brother. And she tells me I got very, very upset because I was her baby.

Not only was Shane the new baby, but he lived with Pamela and Matthew full time, while Karen was just a visitor. This is when Karen's feelings about her stepmother changed.

> I think that was the point where I started picking up on my mother's feelings. I thought that their neighborhood in New York was just the most dangerous territory you could set foot in and that my stepmother and my father were just crazy barbarians.

When Karen started puberty, a series of factors came together that ushered in the next stage in her attitude toward her stepmother.

Much of her discontent, at least on the surface, had to do with the neighborhood to which the stepfamily had moved in Tucson. It was a "very upper middle class, rich, very snobby, very preppy community, and here I was from New York." Karen felt intimidated and excluded, a feeling that doubtless was accentuated by her being in early adolescence. It was then that her rebellion was generalized from resentment over her mother's desires for her to be a clotheshorse to a rejection of the whole style of life she felt was represented by the Tucson community. She thought, "I don't want to be anything like that, and I don't want to look like that, so I'll just dress in rags and wear jeans." At the same time, Alexis took a different course, and blended right into the new neighborhood. Karen felt jilted by her sister, who had been such a reliable companion on their visitation jaunts, because Alexis was adopting the very style of life from which she felt so alienated.

There was a specific incident, also, that tipped Karen's balance against Herbert and Edna and toward Matthew and Pamela:

> I was thirteen and I found out Herbert was having an affair, and not just one affair. I overheard them fighting and it was whether or not he should stop seeing this person. He was telling my mother, "Relax, it'll pass." So I realized he had been having affairs pretty much throughout their relationship. And that's when I got infuriated with both my mother and my stepfather. With my mother I felt really sorry for her and I felt she was really weak. And with him—when I found out about that I felt that I hate him. Entirely.

By this time, Karen had come to see Pamela as an attractive model to emulate:

> My stepmother became someone that I really, really wanted to be a lot more like. She's very independent. She's very strong-willed. And she's much more natural than my mother. She's more interesting. Her favorite pastime is working on her thesis. She gardens and she runs a lot.

Karen was especially voluble about her discontent with Tucson during the summer she spent in New York following these events. Pamela said, "You can come and live her if you're really not happy there." At first Karen hesitated, but she had such a good time, making friends with a more Bohemian crowd, that when she returned to Tucson, she told her mother she wanted to move in with her father and stepmother.

In short order, she was living with Matthew, Pamela, Shane, and Hope. But things did not go smoothly, since she had to get used to living with — as opposed to merely visiting — her stepmother. Much of her difficulty with Pamela stemmed from Karen's feelings of being an outsider, in comparison with Shane and Hope. The issues in the fights between her and her stepmother varied, but at the center was Karen's feeling of only having one parent in the family, while the other children had two.

> She seemed to think I wanted all kinds of special privileges, and I kind of felt like that I wasn't getting, that I was kind of an outsider, that my brother and sister were getting more attention and they were more loved by my stepmother and my father.

Money was a salient issue. Karen had an allowance at first, but after she got a job, Pamela argued that her allowance should be reduced because of the income from the employment. Karen now sees that this was a reasonable argument, and that its aim was benevolent, that she should become more self-sufficient.

> She wanted me to be independent and I took that as a threat. Because I felt that Shane and Hope were more part of the family and that I was being pushed out. Before I was even in.

Both Pamela and Karen tried to enlist Matthew's alliance in these early struggles, but partly because of his character and partly because it would be wise to let things take their course, he refused. It goes almost without saying that Karen perceived her father's staying out of the middle as a rejection of her.

Matthew and Pamela have values very different from Herbert and Edna. Among these differing values are a more laissez-faire attitude toward child rearing. Karen found herself with much more freedom than she had ever had when living with her mother and stepfather. But at the beginning, when she felt such an outsider in contrast to her half-siblings, even this tolerance was seen as a threat.

> I felt that they really didn't care about me because they let me do anything I wanted to do and they didn't ever really give me their opinion on anything. If I said, "Well, what do you think I should do about this?" They'd say, "Well,

what do you think? Whatever you do, you'll do what you're ready to do." And I would think, "Oh, so you really don't care what I do!"

Karen even felt shortchanged in the way her father and stepmother took care of her when she was ill:

> I used to get strep throat a lot. And they would say, "Oh, you're not feeling well? Okay, don't go to school." If after a few days I didn't feel better, they'd say, "Well, you should go see the doctor." And then they'd say, "Oh, the doctor gave you a prescription? Well, take your medicine and whenever you feel like you're ready to go back to school, go back to school." And I was feeling, like "Where's my chicken soup? Where's my mother hovering over my bed weeping because I have strep throat?" I felt that they didn't care if I lived or died.

Karen also had to cope directly with the rivalry her presence inspired in one of her half-siblings, and the well-known themes of sibling and stepsibling rivalry recurred here as well. One battleground was the common one of space:

> I got my little sister's room. It's at the top floor of the brownstone and it's the biggest and nicest room in the house and she was not at all pleased.

The rivalry over space was aggravated by age-order issues. Karen was put in charge of baby-sitting her half-sister. And Karen was particularly resented by Hope because she and Shane became friendly:

> We were doing a lot of the same things. He was listening to the same music I was, and he wanted to hang out with me and my friends, so we became closer. She felt very left out.

But for her part, at the time, Karen felt, "How could anyone in the family get the feeling that I'm taking away anything? I'm not even a part of this family!"

Today, Karen is nineteen and most of these issues have been resolved. Time is one reason why; after living long enough with the Pappas family, she got used to being there, and felt more secure about her place in her father and stepmother's eyes.

Growing up is another reason. Karen has a more certain understanding of what kind of person she is and wants to be, and acknowledges her debt to Pamela in showing her a kind of womanhood she had only heard about through her mother's disdain. She has come to terms with her mother, and when she goes back, "We shop and I let her buy me whatever she wants to buy me because I have no money." Malls have evidently lost their sting, because Karen knows that she has other ways to express herself than through buying clothing.

She does not feel excluded by her half-siblings now. Karen is in college, while Shane and Hope are still in high school, and "they spend a lot of time together and I'm not really there much and I don't spend a lot of time with either one of them." One issue is still very much alive, though. When Karen told Hope that she would be transferring to another college soon, her half-sister said, "Finally, you're getting out of my room."

From Visiting Outsider to Resident Outsider

Karen Pappas's saga of an adolescent discovering her identity is an account of how a girl chose between two radically different models of womanhood, one offered by her mother and the other by her stepmother. Yet underneath that is another story, in which sibling and half-sibling relations provide the essential background.

It would be difficult to imagine two women more different than Edna and Pamela. Edna is a wife who has quietly subordinated herself to a money-driven martinet, who is often absent and often unfaithful. What she values is appearances, both social and sartorial. One of her favorite pastimes is shopping, and finding the perfectly coordinated outfit for herself and her daughters is a source of real pleasure. She is willing to pay the price of a less than satisfactory marriage in exchange for the trappings of an upper-middle-class life-style. Pamela, by contrast, loves to garden, get dirty, and run. She lives in New York City, is a social worker, and is unconventional both in her views and in her way of life. Her favorite hobby is working on her doctoral thesis, a task with which she has been preoccupied for a long time. Her nondirective style of parenting was aimed at encouraging Karen's emotional development and personal autonomy, and entirely different from Edna's micromanagement of Karen's externals.

Also, the contrast between the adult males in Karen's life could hardly be more stark. Herbert is materialistic and authoritarian; Matthew is so relaxed that he seems hardly to be there much of the time. Herbert is an ambitious businessman; Matthew is a mellow social worker. Herbert was even more intrusive than Edna in Karen's live, while Matthew prefers to remain the background.

Karen's road to self-discovery began with her decision to cease identifying with her mother and to identify with her stepmother. This step also demanded that she actively reject her mother's model, to "de-identify" with her. It accounts for her present derogatory perception of her mother's style of life, one that she describes as plastic and artificial. Yet she protests too much, because it is clear that for much of her childhood she was very close to her mother, and has a deep reservoir of affection for what her mother represents. During much of her childhood, too, she rejected her stepmother, largely at her mother's inspiration, and only at puberty did she cease to see New York and her stepmother as symbolic of an alien, dirty, dangerous world.

For the background of Karen's childhood identifications consisted of her reaction to the birth of her half-brother, Shane. Previously, Karen had felt warm and affectionate toward Pamela, but when Shane was born, Karen felt betrayed and excluded, and it was then that she started sharing her mother's negative view of Pamela. This probably helped her to feel as close to Herbert as she did during her girlhood. Herbert had straight, simple answers for things, while her father was far away and seemed preoccupied with his son, Karen's competitor. In this background was her close and dependable sister Alexis, who was such a resource when they were visiting the strange world of Pamela's home.

Then a crisis occurred that led to Karen's decision to change her life. It began with the move to Tucson, to a part of the country and a neighborhood where she felt entirely alien. As soon as she got there, she began seeking out nonconformist peers, who solidified her sense of isolation. Her sister blended in better, began to imitate her mother more exactly than Karen wanted to, and then went away to college. Karen was thereby deprived of one of her main supports. Of course, one of the main changes took place within her body; Karen's entering puberty at this time exacerbated her rebelliousness. Her stepfather, as with many stepfathers of adolescent girls, reacted against her physical maturity by becoming even more rigid and harsh than he had been before. One precipitating event was the discovery that her stepfather had been committing adultery, and that her mother had seemingly accepted, or at least submitted. It was at that time that her stepmother began to emerge as another type of woman Karen could emulate, one who was diametrically opposed to a mother she felt she could no longer respect.

Once she made the move to New York, though, she still was engaged in struggles in which her half-sibling conflicts provided the backdrop. Her relations with Hope were decidedly distant. She did succeed in displacing her half-sister, who still resents Karen's having taken over her room. She also managed to establish a quasi-peer relationship with her half-brother. Ironically, Hope thought that Karen had displaced her with Shane, while Karen herself did not feel as if she was really part of the family. She also felt she needed to gain a place along with the half-siblings in her stepmother's attention. The fights with her stepmother used money as a substitute for love, and Karen looks back now with a rueful maturity at the intensity of her attempts to gain a place for herself.

Her ambivalence at the beginning was intense. On the one hand, she had much more freedom than she had had in Tucson. On the other, her father and stepmother's permissive parenting meant that her ploys at getting attention through illness did not work. Although she frequently got sick, the result was not Pamela or Matthew hovering over her with chicken soup, it was rather the businesslike directive to go to the doctor and to go back to school when she felt better. At present, she has arrived at a kind of reconciliation. While she still rejects her mother as a model, her rejection is less vehement; she has come to accept her mother as a person even as she rejects what her mother stands for. Karen has grown up, and is contented with the kind of person she has become, with the help of the parents, stepparents, siblings, and half-siblings who provided her with foils.

The Variety of Half-siblinghood

There is no single role for a half-sibling in a stepfamily. At one extreme, a lone mutual child has both parents in the home and no recollection of a family that preceded it. Brad Henderson believes that the birth of his son, Roger, has brought the extended stepfamily together, in spite of Carol's envy and the fury of his ex-wife. It is likely that as Roger grows up, he will become aware to what extent he is the focus of everyone's attention, even though Carol's is hostile. Being the "hub" of the family for some children is a risky situation, since in the event that the family breaks up, he or she could be blamed, even as his or her birth was credited for all the good things that subsequently happened.

At the other extreme is Karen Pappas, who illustrates one of the most precarious types of half-sibling relation. Her daring move from Tucson to New York was more than geographical, and her leap from a materialistic upper-middle-class world to a semi-Bohemian home headed by laid-back social workers was more than social. In pursuit of her self, and because of her attraction to an alternative model of womanhood offered by her stepmother, she undertook to carve out for herself a niche in an already-established nuclear family. It is little wonder that at first she was struggling with her half-sister. From Hope's point of view she was an interloper with little legitimacy, who not only pushed her way into the family but took her room away from her. Shane was more welcoming, because she was closer to him in age, was of the opposite sex, accepted him more as a peer, and probably taught him teenage lore. And little wonder that she struggled with her stepmother, since even though she respected Pamela, she had the residual memory of feeling excluded when Shane was born. Karen had to find a place in her stepmother's world before she could learn to imitate her. That she succeeded in leaving her mother and joining a stepfamily along with her half-siblings is testimony to her strength and courage. The expanded opportunities of stepfamily life for her had greater dangers but ultimately their own rewards.

Notes

1. See Beer, *Strangers in the House*, 93–125.
2. A. Bernstein, "The Politics of (Half) Brother-and Sisterhood: Sibling Relations in Families with a Mutual Child" (Paper presented at the Annual Meeting of the American Orthopsychiatric Association, New York, April 1989).

Part III

The Stepfamily in Society

Introduction

American stepfamilies today are unlike those that were prevalent in the past. Formerly, stepfamilies resulted mainly from bereavement and remarriage, while today they are mostly the products of remarriage following divorce. Because of their novelty, they present a challenge to stepfamily members themselves and to society at large. In conducting their lives, stepfamilies create units whose internal workings are different from those of conventional families, as described in the foregoing chapters. Adults and children struggle as best they can to devise families that are emotionally satisfying for themselves, supportive of one another, and faithful to the central mission of all families—raising children to be happy, autonomous, mature, and socially responsible people. That not all stepfamilies stay together should not be surprising, considering the extraordinary internal pressures to which they are subject. The members of those that do stay together experience stresses and opportunities unknown to people in other types of families. Some stepfamilies, in short, meet the challenge and others do not.

Stepfamilies also pose a potential problem to society at large. The fact that there are so many of them, and that their numbers are increasing, raises the question of whether and how they fit into the larger society of the United States. This really is a twofold question. What social and historical forces lie behind today's stepfamily explosion? Do stepfamilies represent a threat because they spawn misfits, or do they produce children and adults who can be productive members of society? These two questions are answered in chapters 10 and 11.

10

Challenge to Society: Where Do Stepfamilies Fit In?

The contemporary American stepfamily is the result of social changes that have long been at work. The historical background of today's stepfamilies consists of the emergence of divorce as a common pattern of behavior, which in turn stems from a series of economic, technological, political, and cultural changes that are sketched below. The stepfamily has characteristics that make it uniquely adapted to the conditions of contemporary America.

The Stepfamily in History

Edward Shorter has provided a composite picture of the typical farming household in premodern Europe:

> First of all, there was the rural couple. . . . Wed in their late twenties, the couple could look forward to perhaps five or ten years before death would carry one of them away. Widowers were quick to remarry, widows a little less so. . . . Any given marriage might well not be the first for one of the partners, and . . . some of the children in the household would stem from previous unions.[1]

In the past, stepfamilies proliferated because of the appalling mortality rate. The history of the stepfamily is thus an account of the change from bereavement to divorce as its primary generating event. In tracing this change, let us start half a millenium ago.

Emmanuel Leroy Ladurie provided a rich portrait of village life in southern France in the fourteenth century in his book, *Montaillou: the Promised Land of Error* (New York: Braziller, 1978). Bereavement resulted in the creation of numerous stepfamilies then. Divorce was not unknown, however, because the hold of the Catholic church was relatively weak in this land of the Albigensian heretics.

One of the main reasons why bereavement and stepfamilies were relatively frequent was because men often did not marry until comparatively late in life. Accumulation of sufficient property was a precondition for matrimony, but this took time, and one consequence was that "the girls were beginners; the men were settling down. This difference in age in a world where people died young soon produced a crop of young widows. With one husband in the grave, women prepared to go through one or even two more marriages."[2] Stepfather, rather than stepmother, families were thus the predominant form of stepfamilies.

When divorce occurred, it was usually initiated by the husband rather than the wife, since the system of family land-holding gave priority to male heads of household. As Ladurie described it,

> Fabrisse Rives was one of those turned out. To begin with, she lived with her husband, Pons Rives the farmer and . . . his father and mother, Bernard and Alzais Rives. The husband and mother-in-law soon saw that the young wife was going to interfere with their [religious observance]. "It was the devil who brought you into our house," said Pons to Fabrisse. So he drove her out of the [household]. She simply carried on as an independent woman, the wine-seller of the village. She brought up her daughter Grazide as best she could.[3]

Ladurie's words demonstrate that in some ways, a late medieval divorce in southern France was probably not that different from today's. And the precarious subsequent life of a single mother was not dissimilar, since Fabrisse and her daughter eventually joined another man's household, though not through marriage. He also described several cases in which women took the initiative in divorces, but in these cases she was obliged to leave, rather than expel her husband. The only single women in charge of households were widows, and they usually remarried.

In Renaissance Italy, a different pattern prevailed. Bereavement was as common, but remarriage did not usually result in stepfather families. Children belonged to the lineage of their fathers. If a mother died, no major displacement accompanied a father's remarriage. But if a father died, and a mother remarried, she did not take the children with her. The result was that "although the stepmother was a very familiar figure in Florentine households, the stepfather was practically unknown."[4]

As the legal system became increasingly codified and sophisticated, provisions were made for the consequences of remarriage. Robert Wheaton, in studying the families of Bordeaux in the seventeenth century, was struck by the frequency with which marriage contracts contained provisions for kin that we would call stepfamily members. The background of high mortality rates made every parent likely to be concerned about the welfare of surviving children and of stepchildren in remarriage. A remarrying widow, for instance, would frequently stipulate in her marriage contract that her new husband undertake to support children she may have had from a previous marriage. Widowers, too, required such commitments from their new brides. These contractual obligations, concluded Wheaton, were actually honored. "That step-relatives actually performed these obligations is reflected both in apprenticeship contracts for step-children, and in the marriage contracts, in which they constituted [dowries] for their daughters."[5]

Wheaton's depiction of what was considered family in Bordeaux at that time included most of the roles we would include today, and stepparents and stepchildren were among their number.

> When Bernard de Faux, a peasant in the Entre-deux-Mers, and Marie Drouilhard, widow of a cooper in Cenon, across the Garonne from Bordeaux, contracted marriage, the bride brought with her a [dowry] of fifteen livres. The household into which they envisaged settling was to consist of themselves, the bride's two children by her first marriage, the groom's widowed father, the groom's brother, the latter's wife and their children, in all a household of nine people.[6]

Even in the seventeenth and eighteenth centuries, death intervened at every turn. Families at that time still comprised a relatively short-lived tie between husband and wife, since it was so common that one should die not long after the marriage. The family was a relatively brief link between parents and children, too, since a married couple had a less than even chance of living more than a year or two after their children left home. At least one out of three children had lost a parent by the time they reached adolescence. And parents often saw children die; infant mortality in some cases exceeded 50 percent. For these reasons, among others, relationships between spouses and between parents and children tended to be cool and distant, because the likelihood of death made substantial emotional investments in family members a losing proposition.

Yet members of premodern stepfamilies were not unmoved by the process of death and remarriage. John Angier wrote in his diary in 1657,

> My wife died. . . . One night after her death, the children were in the parlor praying together; and, hearing a noise, I went to the door, and hearing my son at prayer with his sister; he acknowledged to God that they had despised father and mother, contrary to God's command, and therefore God had taken away mother; he desired God that they might not provoke him by their sin to take away father also; which did much affect me.[7]

The diaries of Sir Thomas More also attest to intense bonds and resentments. More's mother died when he was six years old. His father was unmarried for the next fifteen years, but then remarried three times in succession. Perhaps because of the long period of time when he had his father all to himself, More wrote of his stepmothers with great hostility. "Even a loving stepmother," he wrote, "is a misfortune to her stepson."[8]

In France, in the 1700s and 1800s, the mortality rates of spouses were such that marriages generally lasted only twelve to seventeen years, and the bereaved frequently remarried. Historian Lawrence Stone estimates that in the late sixteenth and seventeenth century, one quarter of widows and widowers among the upper classes in England remarried. This figure declined subsequently with the increase in adult longevity, but it was still about 15 percent in the 1700s, and about 5 percent married three or more times.[9]

So it was in the New World, too. In the Plymouth colony of New England, John Demos has documented that 40 percent of the married men over fifty and 25 percent of the married women over fifty were remarried. By age seventy, the percentage rose to 45 percent for men and 31 percent for women.[10] In the seventeenth and eighteenth centuries, about 20 to 30 percent of all marriages in the colonies were remarriages. One estimate is that of married persons in Newburyport, Massachusetts, in the nineteenth century, 50 percent of the men and 20 percent of the women were remarried.[11]

The history of the stepfamily is thus very long, but today's American stepfamily is different from its predecessors because divorce has replaced death as the causal event that leads to parental remarriage. It was not until 1940 that for the first time, the number of divorced men exceeded the number of widowers in the United States.[12] This raises the question of why divorce seems, in the past few decades, to have become so common.

The Rise of Divorce as an Institution

"Divorce probably dates from the same time as marriage, though I think that marriage is a few weeks older," is a remark attributed to Voltaire. His cynical wisdom notwithstanding, divorce has only recently become common. Today, divorce is a *social institution*, which sociologists define as a pattern of behavior that in all probability will continue over time. Using this definition, and reviewing the statistics cited at the beginning of the book, we can see that divorce has become institutionalized.

The history of divorce in Euro-American culture coincides with the gradual abandonment of its prohibition, which had been maintained by the medieval Catholic church. Before the sixteenth century, it was all but impossible to obtain, although annulments were not unknown. The real impetus was given by the Protestant reformers, who based their liberalization of the grounds for divorce on the famous "escape clause" provided by Matthew 5:32. Under Zwingli in Switzerland, a number of grounds for divorce were added to that described in the Bible, including abandonment, illness, promiscuity, and insanity.

Because of the influence of Calvinism in the United States, divorce was therefore obtainable from the earliest days of the Colonies. In Puritan New England, civil courts allowed separations, annulments, and divorces. A declaration of pastors in Cambridge, for instance, allowed the latter on grounds of adultery, desertion, and prolonged absence. In Connecticut, "total neglect of duty," which meant a husband's nonsupport was additional grounds for divorce. Divorce was also sought in situations that today would be described as those of physical and psychological abuse.

A Puritan mother asked for a divorce for her daughter because her daughter's husband

> carried it so wickedly to my daughter, and so Infidel like, that instead of providing for her tooke from her, her wearing apparrell, And left her almost naked more like an Indian than A Christian swearing abominably threatening to split her open, calling my Daughter Mary Dam'd whore, commanding her to give him his hatt, and several Times beating and abusing her, Since which Time he hath never come nigh to my Daughter nor provided for her, neither for meate, Drink Cloathing nor Lodging, neither hath my daughter any way to subsist but what she earned for a considerable time by hard working.[13]

Massachusetts permitted twenty-seven divorces between 1639 and 1692. Divorce was more difficult to obtain in the South because there was a stronger Anglican tradition that was less receptive to divorce—the Church of England did not permit divorce except by Act of Parliament before 1857. South Carolina did not definitively legalize divorce until 1949. But for the most part, divorce was always relatively more common in the New World than the Old.[14] In the course of the nineteenth century, it increased, from 1.62 per 1,000 families in 1870 to 4.00 in 1900, a figure that itself doubled by 1920.[15]

These historical preconditions provide a backdrop, but the appearance of divorce as an institution is due to the confluence of a series of long-gestating sociological factors that explain the decline in importance of kinship in general and of the nuclear family in particular.

To begin with, divorce has proliferated as the importance of family cohesion has diminished. Across the span of Western history, there has occurred a general decline in the importance of kinship in social organization. In primitive society, virtually all social structures are an extension of kinship relations: around the nuclear family of parents and children are accretions of extended family, clan, and tribe. With the growth of civilization comes the increasing strength of nonfamilial institutions—such as organized religion, armies, educational institutions, and the administrative apparatus of the state. Kinship declines as other social categories (caste, class, community, nation, for instance) become more salient, and people rely more on nonkin for their needs.

The state has an inverse relation to the power of kin. Historian Georges Duby put it eloquently: "In fact, the family is the first refuge in which the threatened individual takes refuge when the authority of the state weakens. But as soon as political institutions afford him adequate guarantees, he shakes off the constraint of the family and the ties of blood are loosened."[16] This trend was explicitly recognized in American history by John Demos, who said, "[B]roadly speaking, the history of the family in America has been a history of contraction and withdrawal; its central theme is the gradual surrender to other institutions of functions that once lay very much within the realm of family responsibility."[17]

In modern society, we rely far less on family members than at any previous time in our history. The young are almost entirely educated by hired professionals, and at an earlier and earlier age are left in the care of unrelated adults. The state today replaces parents' moral authority over children as, for example, in the provision of state-subsidized birth control to minors without parents' permission or knowledge. Mental health professionals are empowered to intervene in relations between parents and children when they deem it necessary. The state authorizes the police to intervene in relations between parents and children (as with child abuse) and in the personal and sexual relations between spouses (as with spouse abuse and marital rape). The elderly are no longer cared for primarily by their children but are supported by public and private pensions and, when they are infirm, by nonfamily members in residential homes. Most religious denominations worship outside the home, although the Jewish practice of welcoming the Sabbath within the family is a reminder of earlier times. But nowhere has the eclipse of family relations been more important than in economic activity, largely as a result of the advent of industrial society.

The effect of the industrial revolution upon the family was profound. The predominance of a small, mobile, nuclear family in Western Europe and the New World colonies encouraged the development of capitalism and, later, industrialism. The cumbersome extended families typical in Eastern Europe, by the same token, had an inhibiting effect on capitalist development.[18] The family does not simply change its form as economic structures change; family forms themselves can have powerful determining effects on the shape of economic history. However, although the nuclear family predated the industrial revolution, the latter in turn fundamentally transformed the social function of the family.

Before the advent of industrial production, virtually all goods and services were produced in and by families. The family was the basic economic unit in preindustrial society—farm families produced food, artisans and craftsmen produced goods in their homes, and their families were workers in the joint enterprise. Home and workshop were one, and partly as a result, the emotional content of family life was relatively absent. Functional, rather than affective relations, were the norm. We saw above that death was so common that emotional investments in spouses or offspring were not profitable; in addition, the economic cooperation of families meant that the grounds for marriage were primarily practical, rather than romantic. Husbands and wives seldom married for love, and sought significant social relationships from peers of the same sex rather than one another. So also were parent-child relations rigid and harsh.

Among many other things, the industrial revolution meant that work became centralized, rationalized, and mechanized. People no longer worked where they lived. The family ceased to be an economic institution, and its function became concentrated on child rearing. Home was a place people (primarily males) retreated to after a day of work, and the focus of families became interpersonal relations rather than economic production. The nuclear family, composed of two adults and their dependent children, became a child-centered institution.

Husbands and wives consequently concentrated less on marrying out of economic motives and more on romantic ones. Love as a basis for marriage became paramount following the rise of the nuclear family.[19] Since the family became child centered, the affective content of parent-child relations also became important. A sexual division of labor was established that matched the emphasis on emotional fulfillment. Males, as breadwinners, provided the economic wherewithal for their dependents and served as legal representatives of the family to the broader society. Although men were the ultimate authority, females were in charge of internal family life. This included housework and child care, looking after the material and emotional dimension of the interior life of the family. Although disparaged by many today, the conventional specialization of jobs by sex in this type of family was and is efficient.

Like all specialization, it fostered interdependence. Because men concentrated on the world of work outside the family, they were essentially incapable of taking care of their domestic needs and the needs of their children, and required the services of their wives in this regard. Household technology was until recently so primitive that keeping a home well run required a long apprenticeship that was given not to boys but to girls in anticipation of their biological reproductive function. Males could not have performed these tasks even if they had wanted to, because they were not prepared for them. Wives were also excluded from much work outside the home because it required physical strength most women do not have, and in any case they had not been trained in these masculine specialities.

This dependence between males and females was the last functional basis for the biological family, because almost every other task had come to be carried out by extrafamilial agents. To put it a little differently, the only glue that held the nuclear family together was the love of parents for each other and their children, and the domestic division of labor whereby women stayed at home and men worked outside the home. Over the last century, the adhesive has become weaker and weaker, since women have become progressively freer to participate in work outside the home and less encumbered by obligations of family and matrimony.

One set of reasons stems from technology. Labor-saving devices steadily freed males from the backbreaking toil to which nonindustrial societies are condemned, but also resulted in women's ability to do the same work outside the home that men could do. This transformation became even more profound when automation changed the nature of work from blue-collar manual labor to white-collar service and management. The distinction between men's work and women's work outside the home became increasingly artificial.

Household technology also changed the nature of work inside the home. Gas and electric stoves and ovens, canning, central heating, refrigeration, freezing, vacuum cleaners, washing machines, dryers, dishwashers, detergents, drip-dry clothing, no-iron sheets, no-wax floors, frozen dinners, disposable diapers, prepared baby foods—the list of innovations that have eased the drudgery of housework could go on and on. They meant that the amount of time spent on the less rewarding aspects of housework was reduced, and that men could be called upon to do more of it, since it was relatively easy to learn to do. The line between men's and women's work inside the home thus also became difficult to draw.

Birth control and abortion technology was made more effective and safe. Women's sexual activity had, of course, always carried with it the danger of pregnancy. Without marriage, the result of crude or no birth control was illegitimacy and its companion, infanticide. Female sexuality was normally conditioned upon matrimony, because a male was required to support his offspring and their mother. The delay of sexual activity until marriage may well have contributed to the obsession with romantic love that was its precondition in the heyday of the nuclear family; much of what passed for love may simply have been sexual frustration. But reliable birth control and safe abortion meant that, whatever moral objections either may inspire, women could have active sex lives prior to or even without the necessity of marriage.

These three technological changes erased much of the practical basis upon which the nuclear family had rested. If women no longer depended upon men to support them, and if men could fend for themselves when it came to preparing food and running a household (and, if necessary, taking care of children), and if sexual activity was not predicated upon marriage, what reason remained for marriage besides the emotional attachments of husband and wife?

Such technological changes are sociological preconditions that can be added to the historical preconditions sketched above. But these factors were present before the divorce explosion of postwar

America, which had more immediate causes, some social and some political, centered around the new social role of women.

During World War II, millions of American women had the practical experience of working outside the home—not, as had been necessary during the preceding decade of the depression, out of financial need, or as had long been the practice, preparatory to finding a husband and settling down to motherhood, but as a routine activity. Although most wartime working women returned to housework and child care, many did not. Even more important, the image of an economically self-sufficient woman who was still feminine became accepted in the public consciousness.

After World War II, the United States embarked on a breathtaking period of economic expansion; between 1950 and 1985 the real income of the average American family doubled. One by-product of the first decades of this enormous increase in prosperity was the so-called baby boom, in which the birthrate jumped between 1946 and 1964, and as a consequence of which there was a massive influx of young people into higher education in the late 1950s and the 1960s.

Economic expansion was accompanied by changes in the nature of the economy that reduced the demand for unskilled labor and increased the educational requirements of workers. A predominantly white-collar working class was needed, one with substantial post-high school education. Whereas before World War II a college education had been a luxury, and one not needed for most employment, with the evolution of a postindustrial economy, higher education became the condition for much employment. In recognition of this need, the same postwar decades saw the expansion of public higher education, with the public subsidies of universities so massive that state universities came to be the peers, and in some cases the superiors, of the old, private, elite universities.

All these factors came together to produce a hugh influx of young women into higher education, on a scale never dreamed of before. Prosperity meant that families could afford to send their sons and daughters to college rather than making them work and living on their income, and they no longer needed to hurry to marry off daughters because of financial pressure. Public subsidies of higher education made it yet more affordable to more and more families. A college education was more needed for employment anyway, and the changing nature of work made it possible for women to be employed outside the home as a career, rather than as a temporary phase prior to matrimony or as a stopgap for family finances. And the baby boom meant that the sheer numbers of young men and women obtaining this education became a torrent. American universities reeled under the demographic shock.

With the vast increase in college educated women, though, women themselves, their families, and society were faced with a dilemma. On the one hand, there were masses of women prepared, by dint of their education, for public life—in business, the professions, government. Yet on the other hand, women had expectations of themselves that did not sit easily with these new possibilities. Matrimony and child care were still seen as the essential roles for women, roles apparently contradictory to those for which education was preparing them. That these roles had been imparted by other women—mothers—did not make them any less confining. In a phrase, American women were faced with the contradiction between outdated sex roles and the modern possibilities available to them.

The feminist movement reappeared to try to fill this gap. In the nineteenth century it had been the outgrowth of three interrelated demands—temperance, female suffrage, and emancipation of slaves. They succeeded so well that feminism slumbered for another fifty years. Betty Friedan's publication of *The Feminine Mystique* in 1964 announced a reinvigorated American feminism, which tried to solve the dilemma that confronted these increasingly educated women. Its own claims notwithstanding, feminism thus did not *cause* the emancipation of American women, it was the *consequence* of the emancipation of a certain class of American women.

The class it appealed to, obviously, was that group of women who had benefitted from university and professional education—upper middle class, white women. (*The Feminine Mystique* was based on a questionnaire filled out by Friedan's fellow alumnae of exclusive Smith College.)[20] But the fact that feminists are of the elite does not mean that they have been without influence. Indeed, the fact that they are primarily of the upper middle class has given them a public voice that made it possible for them to successfully spread their message, redefining womanhood in line with its new possibilities.

This new message was broadcast to the population by the means of communication to which these new women had access. Its impact was vast. The message, first, required demeaning of housewifery as a form of slavery. For example, *Sisterhood is Powerful*, an early handbook of feminist ideology, poured contempt upon the female functions associated with the nuclear family. Being independent of men was the second component of this message; "A woman needs a man like a fish needs a bicycle" was a phrase made popular by Gloria Steinem. Publishers drew up rules of language that were supposed to convey the new feminist message and editors everywhere were urged to require writers to conform to them. Even the mode of address of women was changed. "Ms." took the place of "Miss" or "Mrs." because the old appellations were a function of a woman's relation to a man, while "Ms." asserted that a woman's relation to a man was irrelevant.

Feminist hostility to nuclear family roles for women extended to marriage itself, and it was broadcast that a woman could and, if she felt like it, should have a child without encumbering herself with a male. The new woman did not need men, she did not need marriage, and the idea of family responsibility was decidedly less important than career development. This message was, and is still, enunciated so widely and so loudly that it greatly legitimated divorce for women.

Economic, technological, and political changes thus led to an increase in, and increased acceptance of, working wives and mothers. The proportion of working women went from 38 percent in 1960 to 54 percent in 1984. The percentage of married working mothers went up even more rapidly; 19 percent of mothers with children under six were employed in 1960, compared to 53 percent in 1985. There were drastic unanticipated consequences of these changes, though. The rapid rise of working wives is directly related to an increase in marital instability.[21] Educator Mary Jo Bane claims this is because working wives make their husbands feel insecure.[22] The reason is actually much simpler: employment means economic independence, and when the emotional ties of matrimony have faded, an employed woman is much better prepared to forge out on her own.

Finally, divorces have been increasing simply because they are easier to get. "No-fault" divorce has steadily replaced the older grounds for divorce, in which one party had to be accused by the other of committing adultery, cruelty, desertion, or some other wrong. As of 1985, no-fault divorce could be obtained in some form in all states except South Dakota.[23] In a review of the effects of no-fault divorce, Lenore Weitzman points out that juridical change was more than merely technical. It marked a fundamental shift by the state from a position safeguarding marriage to one facilitating divorce. In her words, "The new divorce laws no longer assume that marriage is a lifelong partnership. Rather it is now seen as a union that remains tenable only so long as it proves satisfying to both partners."[24]

Our values about marriage and divorce have correspondingly shifted. A study of Americans' psychological adjustment from 1957 to 1976 showed that by the latter date, more was expected of marriage in the way of emotional satisfaction, and that it was more acceptable to recognize marital problems. In 1957, if people were having difficulties in their marriages, they were inclined to blame their own inadequacy as a spouse, but in 1976, it was more commonly attributed to some interpersonal problem. The responsibility for a successful marriage was thus shifted from oneself to the quality of the relationship between the spouses.[25] If a marriage did not work, it was less likely to be seen as somebody's shortcoming than as a failure in the relationship.

All these factors have culminated in the institutionalization of divorce. Of course, not everybody gets divorced, and the growth of divorce has not been steady. Sociologist Alex Inkeles has shown that when economic prosperity increases, birth and marriage rates, as well as divorce rates, tend to rise, while people tend to hold back on these decisions when there is an economic downturn.[26] There is no realistic expectation that the rate of divorce will substantially decline; divorce will remain an established social institution in the United States for the foreseeable future.

Although seriously weakened, the nuclear family has not been destroyed. It still hangs on in a substantial portion of the population. Rather, what has happened is that married, lifelong, monogamous family life is only one of a wide variety of options available to men and women. And other family forms—single parent, divorced parent, stepfamilies—are supplanting and competing with it. Even though they are now common, remarried families following divorce are a sufficiently recent phenomenon for some social scientists to talk of them as "incomplete institutions"[27] or "non-institutions."[28] These analyses seek to ascribe instability in stepfamilies to a lack of clear expectations among their participants. Our analysis suggests, however, that instability in stepfamilies is primarily a result of the contemporary emphasis on adult gratification.

As historian Edward Shorter says, the center of the family today is increasingly the "eroticized couple," which marries for a while and stays together only as long as is emotionally comfortable for both. The children have decidedly been relegated to secondary importance. There was some hesitation in the 1950s over whether divorce was damaging to children, so discontented couples stayed together "for the sake of the children." Soon, however, some social scientists leaped to the fore to reassure divorcing spouses that they were doing the right thing, since children suffered more from an unhappy marriage than from a divorce.[29] Some mental health professionals nowadays are having second thoughts, and suspect that the emotional damage to children from divorce may be much more severe than previously thought.[30] But this does not prevent over a million minor children a year from being involved in parental divorce.

The paradox is that even as more and more Americans get divorced, many still say they believe that divorce is too easy to get. Our public ideology disapproves divorce in theory, even as more and more people do it in practice. This contradiction results from our ideology having its roots in tradition, while our actual behavior is responding to present-day realities. As sociologist Daniel Bell has pointed out, capitalist society has produced its own contradiction: the self-denial, hard work, and frugality that was necessary for the accumulation of wealth has produced a society so full of riches and possibilities that these same values seem pointless.[31] What is more, traditional values have strong cultural challengers: the messages of mass media, liberal theologians, and many mental health professionals are that self-gratification is seen as coextensive with happiness, self-restraint as outdated and puritanical. Adult fulfillment is displacing responsibility as the paramount value in our family life.

The study of American psychological traits from 1957 to 1976, referred to above, illustrates how quickly and how much our attitudes toward children in marriages have changed. In that nineteen year period, the percent of Americans expressing positive feelings about parenthood declined from 58 to 44; the drop was almost as sharp for parents as for nonparents. The most important reason for Americans' negative feelings about having children was that parenthood was too "restrictive." Evidently, with the development of postindustrial society, values increasingly emphasize adult freedom and self-centeredness.[32] Our society evidently fosters adult-centered families.

In contemporary postindustrial society, virtually all of the functions that previously had been carried out by kin are now carried out by nonkin. Marriage is ideally thought of as a lifelong commitment, but in fact is more often than not a temporary arrangement that depends on emotional compatibility. Divorce is not just a possibility, but regarded as preferable to remaining in an unsatisfactory relationship. As we know, though, most divorced people do not remain so. The result is that American adults today tend to marry, divorce, remarry, and redivorce. Since, occasional adultery excepted, these relationships are with one person at a time, contemporary marriages are properly called monogamous. But they take place in a series, in what social scientists call "serial monogamy." Serial monogamy is a growing marriage pattern, and the stepfamily is the result.

Stepfamilies and Postindustrial Society

Stepfamilies are thus not simply the by-products of a recent breakdown in the nuclear family, but of a long historical process. The rise of the nuclear family coincided with the rise of the bourgeoisie, reinforced by patriarchal authority, emotional cohesion, and a sexual division of labor.[33] It has been increasingly undermined by a series of economic, technological, and political forces that have eclipsed the bourgeoisie, virtually abolished patriarchal authority, and erased the division of labor by gender. The stepfamily is one logical consequence of the processes traced above. But it would be a mistake to think that the stepfamily was simply a passive reflection of other changes. The stepfamily matches the needs of postindustrial society (and vice versa), just as the nuclear family and industrial society fit one another.

In its internal power relationships, the stepfamily is the latest stage in a decline of patriarchal power that has continued since the industrial revolution. A stepfather often shares financial and parental power with a noncustodial father and with the children's biological mother. Biological fathers, as illustrated in the pattern of custody awards, have much less power over their children, compared to mothers. This familial decline in patriarchy is accompanied by a societal decline in male authority and the commensurate rise of women in public, business, and professional life.[34]

Postindustrial society consists of a largely service-oriented, white-collar work force that is highly educated, often professionally. The importance of intellectual capital contributes to great individual social mobility. Women and men do largely the same types of work, particularly among the more educated, and increasingly work in large, impersonal public or private bureaucracies, where relationships are impersonal. It is a consumer society, where much wealth is expended on items, the demand for which is largely the creation of advertising in the print and electronic media. Families are typically small, and planned around careers. Moreover, they are not child-centered, in that the emotional and professional needs of the adults usually take precedence over the needs of the children. Extensive sexual experimentation is the norm. Public morality stresses instant gratification. Public responsibility is increasingly restricted to payment of taxes, and paid professionals— counselors, social workers, special educators—take over (largely at taxpayers' expense) the care of the deranged, the addicted, the delinquent, and the diseased. Community life is, consequently, minimal, and self-fulfillment is all. Indeed, happiness is defined in terms of fulfillment of the self.[35]

Serial monogamy and stepfamilies match the needs of such a society. Remarriage, like first marriage, is undertaken with the personal fulfillment of the adults its basic aim. Stepfamilies come into being, not so much with the happiness or unhappiness of the children in mind, as that of the parent. Children may adjust or not adjust, but the stepfamily's raison d'être is elsewhere. This is, of course, a fundamental change away from the nuclear family, which was quintessentially child-centered. Divorce and redivorce can be contemplated by females as well as males because of the lack of interdependence between the sexes and the availability of paid personnel to make up for a missing spouse. Flimsy family structure is ideally suited to a society in which rapid social and geographical change is common.

There is an even deeper match between stepfamilies and postindustrial society. Impersonal relationships are increasingly the norm, so that the importance of kin approaches a vanishing point. Personnel can be replaced easily because what they do is more important than who they are. This includes teachers, care givers, co-workers — and even sexual partners. Stepfamilies represent the latest stage in the proliferation of such replaceable relationships, because in them nonkin are admitted to the very heart of the family and asked to carry out functions conventionally performed by blood relations. A stepparent is called upon to be a replacement parent, at least in terms of his or her family function if not in emotional terms. The interchangeability of people in postindustrial society at large therefore achieves its apogee in the interchangeability of parents and children in stepfamilies.

While serial monogamy and stepfamilies fit the needs of postindustrial society, a very large question looms unresolved. What about the children? For all the sociological insight we have as to why families are the way they are, the question remains: How is children's development affected by the changes that have taken place? The final chapter of the book, therefore, focuses on the question: To what extent do stepfamilies succeed in rearing children who are emotionally and socially competent? Stepfamilies fit the needs of postindustrial society because they match the needs of adults, but we need to find out if they ultimately sabotage society by rearing social and emotional cripples, or if they fulfill society's long-term needs by producing children and adults who are well adjusted.

Notes

1. E. Shorter (1977), *The Making of the Modern Family* (New York: Basic Books), 25–26.
2. Emmanuel Leroy Ladurie (1978), *Montaillou: the Promised Land of Error* (New York: Braziller, 191.
3. Ibid., 201.
4. C. Klapisch-Zuber (1985), *Women, Family and Ritual in Renaissance Italy* (Chicago: University of Chicago Press), 125.
5. R. Wheaton (1980), "Affinity and Descent in Seventeenth Century Bordeaux," in R. Wheaton and T. Hareven (eds.), *Family and Sexuality in French History* (Philadelphia: University of Pennsylvania Press), 117.
6. Ibid., 114.
7. Quoted in W. Saffady (1973), "The Effects of Childhood Bereavement and Parent Remarriage in Sixteenth century England: The Case of Sir Thomas More," *History of Childhood Quarterly* 1, 2, 310–36.
8. Ibid.
9. L. Stone (1977), *The Family, Sex and Marriage in England, 1500–1800* (New York: Harper & Row), 56.
10. J. Demos (1970), *A Little Commonwealth: Family Life in the Plymouth Colony* (New York: Oxford University Press), 194.
11. Pasley, K., and Ihinger-Tallman (1987), "Evolution of a Field of Investigation: Issues and Concerns," in K. Pasley and M. Ihinger-Tallman (eds.), *Remarriage and Stepparenting* (New York: Guilford Press).
12. Ibid.
13. E. Morgan (1966), *The Puritan Family* (New York: Harper & Row), 34–36, 36n.
14. See R. Phillips (1989), *Putting Asunder: A History of Divorce in Western Society* (Cambridge: Cambridge University Press).
15. P. 9 of A. Inkeles (1984), "The Responsiveness of Family Patterns to Economic Change in the United States," *Tocqueville Review* 6, 1, 5–50.
16. Quoted in P. Aries (1962), *Centuries of Childhood: A Social History of Family Life* (New York: Alfred A. Knopf), 355.
17. Demos, *A Little Commonwealth*, 183.
18. W. Goode (1970), *World Revolution and Family Patterns* (New York: Free Press), esp. 10–26; J. Hajnal (1983), "Two Kinds of Pre-industrial Household Formation System," in R. Wall, J. Robin and P. Laslett (1983), *Family Forms in Historic Europe* (Cambridge: Cambridge University Press).
19. Morgan, *The Puritan Family*, 59.
20. Feminist causes have consistently been supported more by men than by women, yet among women are far more warmly endorsed by the highly educated than by the less educated.
21. A. Booth, D. Johnson, and L. White (1984), "Women, Outside Employment, and Marital Instability," *American Journal of Sociology* 90, 3, 567–83, esp. 581.
22. M. Bane (1978), *Here To Stay: American Families in the Twentieth Century* (New York: Basic Books), 33.
23. Weitzman, *The Divorce Revolution*, 41.
24. Ibid., 368.

25. J. Veroff, E. Douvan, and R. Kulka (1981), *The Inner American: A Self-Portrait from 1957 to 1976* (New York: Basic Books), 162–64.
26. Inkeles, *Responsiveness of Family Patterns*.
27. A. Cherlin (1978), "Remarriage as an Incomplete Institution," *American Journal of Sociology* 84, 634–50.
28. S. Price-Bonham and J. Balswick (1980), "The Non-Institutions: Divorce, Desertion and Remarriage," *Journal of Marriage and the Family* 42, 4, 959–72.
29. See, for example, I. Nye (1957), "Child Adjustment in Broken and in Unhappy Unbroken Homes," *Marriage and Family Living* 19, 356–61; and J. Landis (1962), "A Comparison of Children from Divorced and Nondivorced Unhappy Marriages," *Family Life Coordinator* 11, 3, 61–65.
30. E.g., E. Kinard and H. Reinharz (1984), "Marital Disruption: Effects on Behavioral and Emotional Functioning in Children," *Journal of Family Issues* 5, 1, 90–115; and R. Kulka and H. Weingarten (1979), "The Long-Term Effects of Divorce in Childhood," *Journal of Social Issues* 35, 4, 50–78.
31. Daniel Bell (1978), *The Cultural Contradictions of Capitalism* (New York: Basic Books).
32. Veroff, Douvan, and Kulka, *The Inner American*, 200.
33. P. Aries (1962), *Centuries of Childhood: A Social History of Family Life* (New York: Knopf), 405–7.
34. See F. Weinstein and G. Platt (1969), *The Wish to be Free: Society, Psyche and Value Change*, (Berkeley: University of California Press); see also Tamara K. Hareven (1976), "The History of the Family as an Interdisciplinary Field," in T. Rabb and R. Rotberg (eds.), *The Family in Interdisciplinary History* (New York: Octagon), esp. 200–24.
35. See R. Bellah (1986), *Habits of the Heart, Individualism and Commitment in American Life* (New York: Harper & Row). It should be emphasized that this is an ideal-type portrait of postindustrial society; not all of the characteristics described have fully developed yet in America.

11

The Bottom Line: Are Stepfamilies Successful?

If stepfamilies fit into American society, they should prepare children who do not suffer in comparison with children in conventional families, and who as adults are as adjusted as those without such a background. To assess whether or not stepfamilies are successful thus requires asking questions relating to the short- and the long term—whether children in stepfamilies are significantly less well adjusted than children in intact families, and whether adults who have grown up in stepfamilies show long-term damage as a result of the experience. This chapter's two principal parts are addressed to answering these questions. A great deal of research has been done on the first topic, while little has been done on the second. We therefore start with a discussion of what others have found out about stepchildren, and then turn to some new findings about the long-term consequences of stepfamily upbringing.

Stepchildren: Not Much Difference

How do children in stepfamilies compare to children in other types of families? Numerous studies have been conducted to answer this question, and to make sense of them we need to distinguish between different areas of comparison.

Family Relations

Studies of family relations over the last twenty-five years show sometimes inconsistent results, but in general they suggest that there are no striking differences between children in stepfamilies and children in nuclear families.

Stepchildren are not as close to their stepparents as are nuclear family children to their parents, according to a 1962 study of 29,000 secondary school students, of whom over 2,000 were stepchildren. Homes with stepchildren were more likely than intact homes to report stress, ambivalence, and low cohesiveness.[1] Similar results were produced twenty-one years later in a study that found that children in stepfamilies rated their stepfathers less favorably on a standardized adjective checklist than children in intact families rated their fathers.[2] However, the Youth in Transition (YIT) study, a sophisticated survey of 1,650 school children conducted over several years, revealed that in family relationships, children from stepfather families were essentially no different from those in intact families.[3]

Despite the fantasy of stepfamily child abuse that recurs in fairy tales, stepparents do not show higher rates of child abuse than biological parents. The 1981 National Incidence Study of Child Abuse and Neglect reported that in reviewing all cases of child abuse, mothers were involved in 64 percent, and fathers in 40 percent. Stepfathers were involved in 18 percent and stepmothers in 6 percent; these percentages are in line with the prevalence of these types of family. It is thus clearly a myth that stepparents are likely to be abusive to children.[4] The study showed that for sexual abuse, mothers were involved in 43 percent of the cases, fathers in 28 percent, stepfathers in 30 percent and stepmothers in 1 percent. The percentage for mothers includes both active participation in sexual abuse and enabling behaviors that condone sexual abuse by another family member. The higher rate of sexual abuse by a stepfather is consistent with other research.[5]

Attitudes toward family living, marriage, and divorce differ only slightly among adolescents from intact, divorced, and stepfamilies. Youngsters from remarried families are somewhat more tolerant in their opinions about divorce. Adolescent females, in particular, are likely to endorse a positive view of marriage and the family, even those whose personal family experience has been negative. In sum, teenagers' enthusiasm for matrimony and family life is not affected by whether or not their parents' marriage has lasted, ended, or whether their divorced parents have remarried.[6] The same pattern emerges with regard to dating among college students. A study of 365 male and female undergraduates showed little differences in dating activity, whether they were from intact, divorced, or remarried families.[7] And in adulthood, there is no greater likelihood of remaining single if a person was raised in a stepfamily than is the case for a person raised in an intact family.[8]

One aspect of family relations that is strongly affected by remarriage following divorce is people's attitudes toward their biological fathers. A detailed study of postdivorce parent-child relationships examined children's relations with the adult(s) within and outside of their household, in intact, remarried, and divorced single-parent homes. Children were asked if they "often argue with the (step)parent," whether the (step)parent "spends enough time with you," "gives enough affection to you," whether they "frequently do things together" with the (step)parent, if they "feel extremely close to the (step)parent," and if they "would like to be like" the (step)parent when they are grown. Children in stepfamilies felt somewhat more distant from stepparents on all of these questions than did children from their parents in intact families. But children in stepfather stepfamilies felt deeply estranged from their absent biological fathers. Far fewer children in these situations said that their biological fathers gave them enough affection, that they frequently did things together, felt close to them, or wanted to be like them when they grew up.[9]

In another study, children from divorced, unremarried families rate their fathers lowest, while those from intact families most favorable toward their fathers and those from divorced remarried families coming in between these two extremes.[10] Similarly, in a 1981 study of 349 undergraduates, college students rated their biological fathers highest when they came from intact families, and more negatively when their parents had divorced, whether their mothers had remarried or not. But for those whose fathers had died, their mothers' remarriage did not lead these young adults to rate their fathers negatively. The negativity evidently comes from the common pattern of fathers' estrangement following the divorce, rather than from the remarriage of the mothers.[11]

In sum, overall family relations for children in stepfamilies are somewhat more stressful, and the youngsters are relatively more distant from stepparents than from biological parents. This is not surprising, in light of the tales of sometimes harrowing family transformations we looked at in the first part of the book. Children are no more likely to suffer physical or emotional abuse in stepfamilies, although there is a higher than expected incidence of sexual contact between children and stepfathers that reflects the looser and more confused mores associated with stepfamily sexuality. The experience of living in stepfamilies does not affect young people's endorsement of matrimony, dating, and cultural ideals of family life, once again underlining how hope is more powerful than experience in some areas of life. The area where stepchildren are most deeply affected is in their relationships with their biological fathers. The alienation of divorced fathers from their children is a function of assigning virtually automatic custody to mothers, of divorced mothers' manipulating visitation as a way of extracting more or adequate child support, of divorced fathers' concomitant neglect of regular support payments, and of custodial mothers' "bad-mouthing" their ex-husbands to the children. And the possibility cannot be excluded that in some cases a stepfather might well come to "take the place" of the biological father in the eyes of the child over time, in spite of the former's lack of desire to do so.

Psychological Health

Psychologists have looked at stepchildren's mental health by measuring personality development and self-esteem. Although there are some inconsistencies in the studies, stepchildren were found to be as psychologically healthy as children in intact families.

In the 1950s, Jesse Bernard studied over two thousand college students, comparing those who were stepchildren with those who were not in a standard psychological test called the Bernreuter Personality Inventory. Bernard found that there were no differences between the groups of students in stability, self-sufficiency, and dominance.[12] A decade later, in Cedar Rapids, Iowa, 1,500 adolescents from nuclear, single-parent and stepfamilies were compared. No differences were found in personality, school performance, absences, attitudes toward school, extracurricular and community activities, and number of friends.[13] The Youth in Transition survey found that children in stepfather families were no different from children in intact families with regard to five measures of emotional health, including self-esteem and independence.[14]

Although the last two studies found that children with divorced, single mothers were not psychologically different from the other two groups, this result is not consistently reported in other studies. For example, a small (125) sample of college men were tested for psychological development; stepsons were compared to sons from intact and single-parent families. Those from single-parent families showed significant damage, but there was little difference between those from nuclear families and stepfamilies.[15]

Some research also shows greater risk for children in stepfamilies. Anxiety was higher among boys and girls in remarried families, compared both to those in single-parent and intact families, according to a 1983 study of 566 children in Iowa.[16] In a 1965 study of 5,024 high school students, stepchildren were found to have lower self-esteem and more psychosomatic complaints than children in intact families,[17] but more recent research contradicts this finding. A paper published in 1979 found that when the self-concepts of 289 primary school children in intact, step, and single families were compared, there were no significant differences.[18] In a 1980 report, when 738 primary school children were asked to describe themselves in response to a standard list of adjectives, the Personal Attribute Inventory for Children, those from intact, single-parent, and stepfamilies were compared. Those from intact families had the highest self-concept, and those from single-parent families the lowest, while stepfamily children came in the middle.[19]

These differences do not necessarily last into later life. In a 1981 study, 349 college students were asked to respond to the same inventory of adjectives. Their evaluations of themselves did not differ whether they came from nuclear families, stepfamilies, or single-parent families.[20]

Gaining a stepparent does not always improve things for children. In a 1977 study of a poor, black, urban community, the mental health of children from different types of family was compared. Those from single-mother families were the most at risk, but those from stepfamilies were only moderately less so. Mother/grandmother families, however, were an adequate substitute for intact families, implying a more matriarchal orientation of that ethnic subculture.[21]

The psychological evidence seems to be that stepchildren, at least while they are children, are about as well adjusted as children from intact families. Anxiety levels are higher for children in stepfamilies; this is doubtless a reflection of the greater stepfamily stress, albeit short term, mentioned above. The fact that college students reflect no personality-related or self-concept-related differences suggests that these difficulties are temporary and do not last into early adulthood. The strongest evidence that leaps from the page, however, is that there is essentially no difference between stepchildren and children in nuclear families on tests of personality development.

Intellectual Development

Remarriage can have salutary effects for the intellectual development of children from divorced families. Boys, in particular, subsequently benefitted in intelligence tests and academic achievement from the entry of a stepfather into the family when their mothers had been divorced before the youngsters were five years old. Gaining a stepfather did not have the same benefit for girls.[22]

The previously cited 1983 study of 566 children in Iowa found that while children from intact families scored best on a measure of their perception of school performance and children from single-parent families scored lowest, those from remarried families scored in between, again suggesting the mitigating effect of stepfamily life on the damage wrought by divorce.[23]

A similar result was found for older students. Male and female college students from intact, single-mother and stepfather families were compared on a test of perception and SAT scores. Presence or absence of a father or stepfather made no difference to the intellectual performance of females. Males from single-mother families scored less well than those from nuclear families, but the presence of a stepfather caused their performance to improve, approaching that of men from intact families.[24]

On the other hand, there was no difference between children in stepfather families and in nuclear families in several measures of school attitude and performance performed in the YIT study: educational attainment, being held back, mental ability, a child's perception of his own scholastic ability, the value placed by a child on academic achievement, and the average grades received by the child in the ninth and tenth grades.[25] A study of over eleven thousand children in England compared children from the two types of stepfamilies with children from intact and single-parent families on verbal and quantitative achievement, and the number of public exams taken and passed. After background variables were taken into account, no significant differences were found between children from intact and stepfamilies.[26]

To sum up, stepfamily life, at worst, produces somewhat lower measures of intellectual potential and achievement for students, but these are significantly higher than for those in single-parent homes. Acquiring a stepparent in this case clearly improves things for children with divorced or bereaved parents. The salutary effect of stepfamily living is such that some studies show little or no difference between the academic development of stepchildren and children from intact families.

Social Adjustment

Some research on the social adjustment of children in stepfamilies shows them to have some difficulty, some shows that they are not different, and yet other reports indicate superior social skills among stepchildren. Much of the apparent inconsistency results from different types of social adjustment being measured—peer relationships, deviant behavior, crime, delinquency, or feelings of aggression.

Children from intact families scored higher on measures of peer relationships than did children in single-parent families, while those from remarried families scored the lowest, according to a 1983 study of 566 Iowa school children.[27]

Part of the estimation of children's success or failure in social skills also depends on who is asked. A large-scale research project from England found that parents in stepmother and stepfather families perceived the children's behavior to be deviant more often than in conventional families. By contrast, when the children were rated by their teachers, after background factors were accounted for, there were no significant differences in the degree of deviant school behavior of children in the two types of families. When objective measures were used, such as whether a child had been referred for psychological counseling, been arrested, or had contact with the police, children in stepfather families, particularly boys, were found to have more problems.[28]

The YIT study referred to above compared children in characteristics of crime and delinquency—their impulse to commit aggression, delinquent behavior in school, their father's feelings about their troublemaking, and overall delinquency. No differences between children in intact and stepfather families were revealed on any of these measures.[29] These results confirm an earlier study, which also found no greater delinquency among children whose divorced mothers had not remarried.[30]

A small-scale—the total number was only thirty-six—but rigorous observation of the interpersonal skills of children of both sexes in different types of families found that boys in stepfather families actually were more socially adept than boys in nuclear families. They scored higher on measures of warmth, self-esteem, anxiety, anger, demandingness, maturity, sociability, and independence. The differences for girls were less noticeable, but in stepfather families they exhibited more signs of anxiety than in conventional families.[31] A companion study discovered that boys in stepmother families scored less well on these measures than boys in nuclear families, and girls scored higher than boys in stepmother families.[32]

Boys in English stepfather families are more likely to be delinquent, but no greater delinquency or criminality is evinced by children in the United States. And other research shows that boys in stepfather families have better social skills and other positive personality attributes, though boys are less socially adjusted than girls in stepmother families. While the results of the research are not entirely consistent, the overall picture that emerges is that stepchildren are generally not less well socially adjusted than children in nuclear families.[33]

* * * *

Researchers have found little difference between children in stepfamilies and nuclear families on a host of quantitative measures. Depending on the child's sex and age, and the sex of the stepparent, the experience of living in a stepfamily sometimes will result in children's benefiting slightly from stepfamily living, and sometimes in becoming somewhat damaged. In few or no instances are these differences very great. When they are included as a comparison group, children in "single-parent" families tend to score lower in tests of emotional, social, and intellectual development.

In order of preferability for the children, it is evidently best for parents to stay together. However, if divorce is inevitable and does occur, the evidence is that children benefit from, and can overcome divorce's harm as a result of, remarriage of their custodial parent. According to the results of numerous scientific findings, it is safe to conclude that the stepfamily is an adequate and desirable substitute for the nuclear family, at least for children.

We must take these findings with a certain amount of skepticism, however. Quantitative studies are naturally limited, in most cases, to a single point in time. No matter how sophisticated the study, numerical measurements of intricate family relationships are inevitably crude. Over the long run, the effects of stepfamily living could be much more serious than the chronologically limited glimpses of children reviewed above.

Quantitative research is also limited by the fact that the actual processes at work in stepfamilies are much more subtle and continue over much longer periods of time than are assessed in the kind of study we looked at above.[34] Comprehensive reviews of studies on the effects of stepfamily living on children reveal that such quantitative studies fail to show any dramatic differences between children from stepfamilies and children from nuclear families. Yet by contrast, clinical psychologists and social workers strongly emphasize the difficulty of adjustment to stepfamily life. Such studies are naturally based on small samples. They invite the criticism that they are not representative, and few generalizations can be based on them. Yet they cannot be dismissed, if only because clinicians may reveal details of family life that are lost in the larger-scale research.[35]

Studying children while they are still children does not always tell much about how they will turn out as adults. As we pointed out in the discussion of divorce above, even though some earlier quantitative studies indicated that divorce was preferable for children in conflict-ridden families, psychologists are beginning to have second thoughts about the long-term effects of divorce upon children. There may be similar long-term effects of stepfamily upbringing that do not show up in studies comparing children in different types of families while they are still children.

This is why we need also to look at the long run, to see if differences between children raised in different types of families show up years later. It may be that stepfamily upbringing has subsequent effects in adulthood that are not apparent when a person is still young.

How They Turn Out

Are adults brought up in the unsettled family circumstances of a stepfamily somehow different from those who grew up in conventional families?

The General Social Survey (GSS), carried out annually since 1972 by the National Opinion Research Council, provides clues to this question. One question asked by the GSS is "Were you living with both your own mother and father around the time you were sixteen?" The response categories included, among others, intact families, father-stepmother families, and mother-stepfather families. The GSS also asks numerous other questions that make it possible to assess family relations, psychological health, and social adjustment. This makes it possible to compare people who were raised in nuclear families and the two types of stepfamily. Because of the small number of stepfamily respondents in any given year, the GSS respondents from 1972 to 1984 were pooled together for comparison purposes.[36]

In the comparisons that follow, the responses of white Americans only are discussed. As we pointed out at the beginning of the book, the family structures of black Americans are so qualitatively different from those of whites that they cannot conveniently be discussed in this context. The patterns of responses of males and females are differentiated, because some of the studies we looked at in the first part of the chapter suggested that sex is an important factor in people's adaptations to different types of stepfamilies.

Family Relations

Two GSS questions enable us to compare the degree of satisfaction with family relationships experienced by adult stepchildren and adults from intact families. One asks about the happiness of the respondent's marriage and the other about his or her satisfaction with family life in general.

"Taking all things together, how would you describe your marriage? Would you say that your marriage is very happy, pretty happy, or not too happy?"[37]

The answers of males and females to this question are presented in the figures presented below. For comparison's sake, let us look at the "most adjusted" category of respondents, that is, those who report that their marriage is "very happy." For males, there is a difference between respondents from different types of family in the proportion who say they are "very happy." The largest percentage (69.6) is represented by those from intact families; males from stepfather families follow, with 66.2 percent, and those from stepmother families are lowest, with 64.6 percent. The pattern for female respondents is similar. Men from intact families have the highest percentage of "very happy" marriages, 67.1 percent, while those from stepmother families with and those from stepmother families are considerably fewer, some 56.9 percent. The subsequent marital happiness of both males and females is more negatively affected by living in a stepmother family than living in a stepfather family. No matter what their sex, people from conventional families have the largest share of happy marriages.

The second question measuring adjustment in family relations is, "Tell me how much satisfaction you get from . . . your family life: a very great deal/ a great deal/ quite a bit/ a fair amount/ some/ none."[38]

The degrees of satisfaction expressed in response to this question were collapsed into three categories: high (a very great deal, a great deal), moderate (quite a bit, a fair amount), and low (a little, none). The following figures illustrate the male and female satisfaction with family life. Men from intact families account for the largest percentage of those with a high degree of satisfaction with family life (76.1), while those from stepmother families show 73.5 percent and those from stepfather families 70.4. As with men, women from unbroken homes are most likely to be highly satisfied with family life, with 79.5 percent. But females from stepfather families show a higher percentage of highly satisfied respondents (79.5 percent) than those from stepmother families (69.1 percent). Males and females are more positively affected in their satisfaction with family life by having lived with an opposite-sex stepparent. But once again, male and female adults from intact families have the largest share of respondents highly satisfied with their family lives.

Psychological Adjustment

The emotional upheavals accompanying parental discord and divorce, the consolidation of a single parent household, and its interruption by parental dating and parental remarriage all involve unstable and unreliable behavior by significant people in a child's life. When parents and other important adults act in ways that are unpredictable, a child may learn to retreat into wary indifference, coming to see other people as unreliable and selfish, a trait that could persist in later life.

The first three questions used in comparing psychological adjustment of people from different family backgrounds are thus

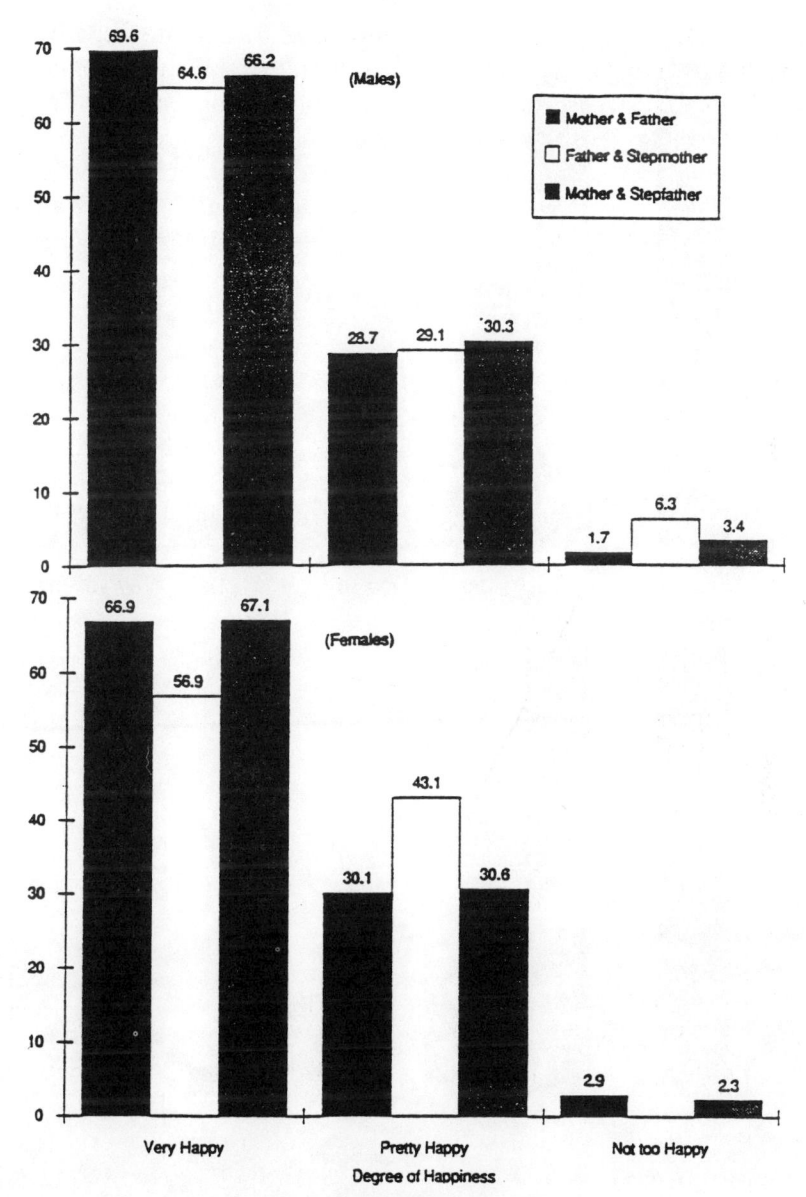

FIGURE 11.1
Happiness of Marriage by Family Type

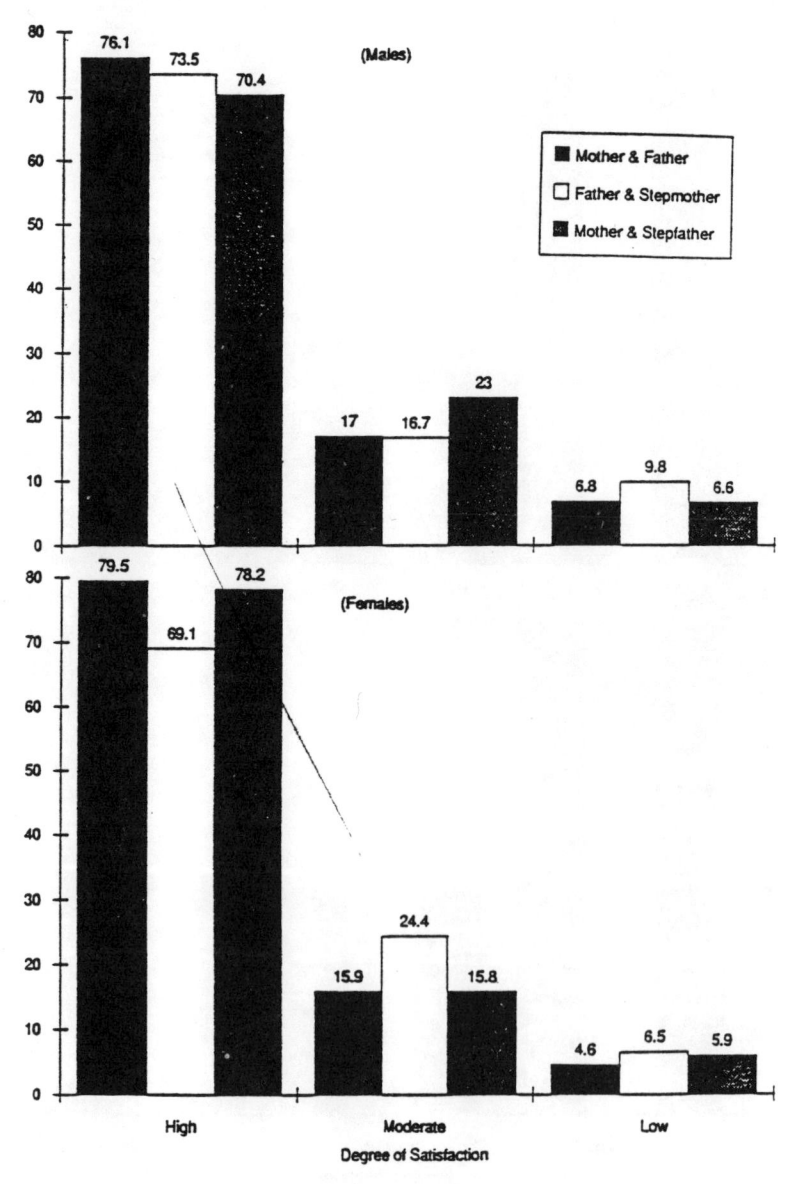

FIGURE 11.2
Satisfaction with Family Life by Family Type

aimed at assessing respondents' trust in others. The responses are presented in the figures that follow.

"Would you say that most of the time people try to be helpful, or that they are mostly just looking out for themselves?"[39]

Male responses to this question show that the largest percentage of people who believe others to be basically helpful come from intact families (50.7 percent), while males from stepfather families (43.4 percent) and stepfather families (41.2 percent) follow. The women who had the greatest belief in others' helpfulness were also most likely to come from nuclear families (59.6 percent), with those from stepfather families (56.6 percent) and stepmother families following (56.1).

Let us now look at responses to the question, "Do you think most people would try to take advantage of you if they got a chance, or would they try to be fair?"[40]

When men answered this question, a larger proportion who thought of other people as fair came from stepmother families (66.3), with men from nuclear families ranking second (62.8 percent), and those from stepfather families a distant third (54.3 percent). Females from nuclear families were most prevalent among those who believe others to be basically fair, with 68.5 percent, and those from stepmother families ranking second (66 percent), while those from stepfather families were proportionally fewest (59.5).

The next question is, "Generally speaking, would you say that most people can be trusted or that you can't be too careful in dealing with people?"[41]

Men from nuclear families, once again, were most likely to say that people can be trusted. Those from both types of stepfamily were considerably less well represented among respondents with basic trust in others (50.8), with those from stepmother families ranking slightly larger than those from stepfather families (41.3 percent, compared to 40.8 percent). Women, too, showed that adults from intact families were most likely to be trusting (46.2 percent), with those from stepmother families (43.8) and stepfather families (41.5) following.

Another way to look at the long-term effects of stepfamily living is to look at people's views of life in general. The purpose of this sort of question is to find out whether people have adopted an

212   **American Stepfamilies**

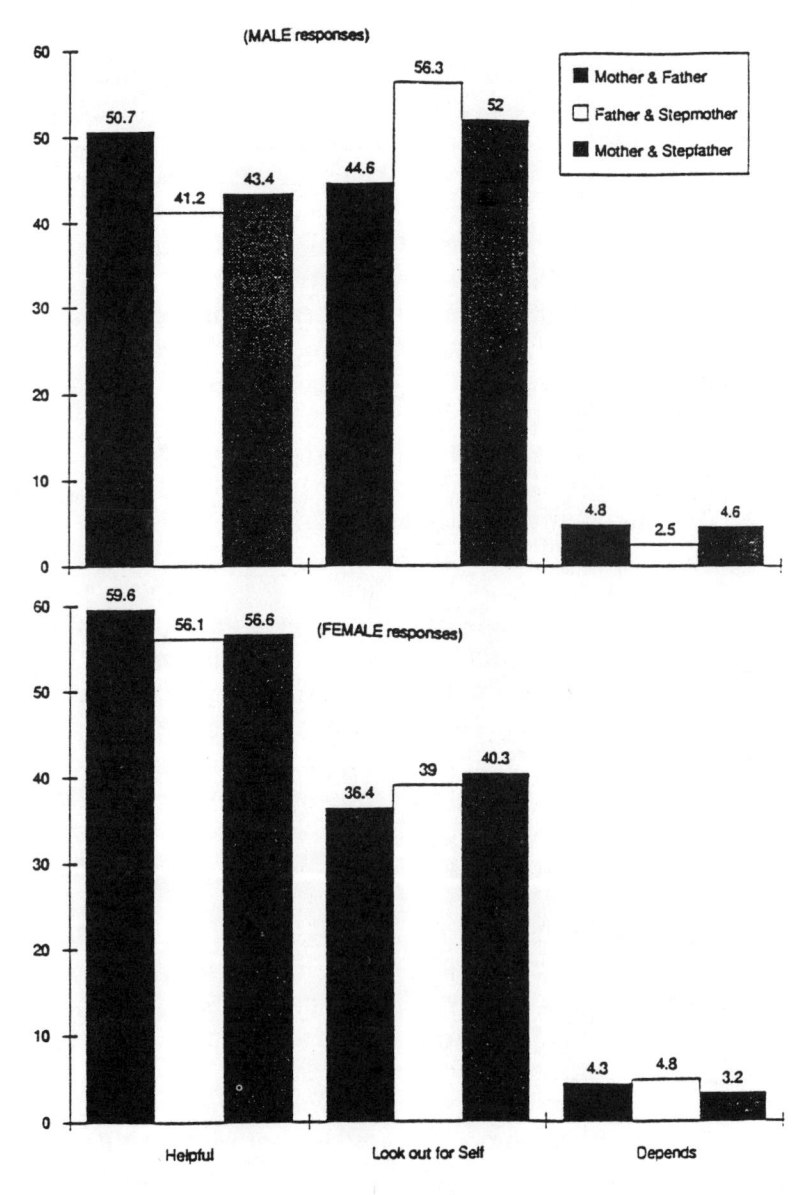

FIGURE 11.3
"Are People Helpful or Looking Out for Themselves?"

The Bottom Line: Are Stepfamilies Successful? 213

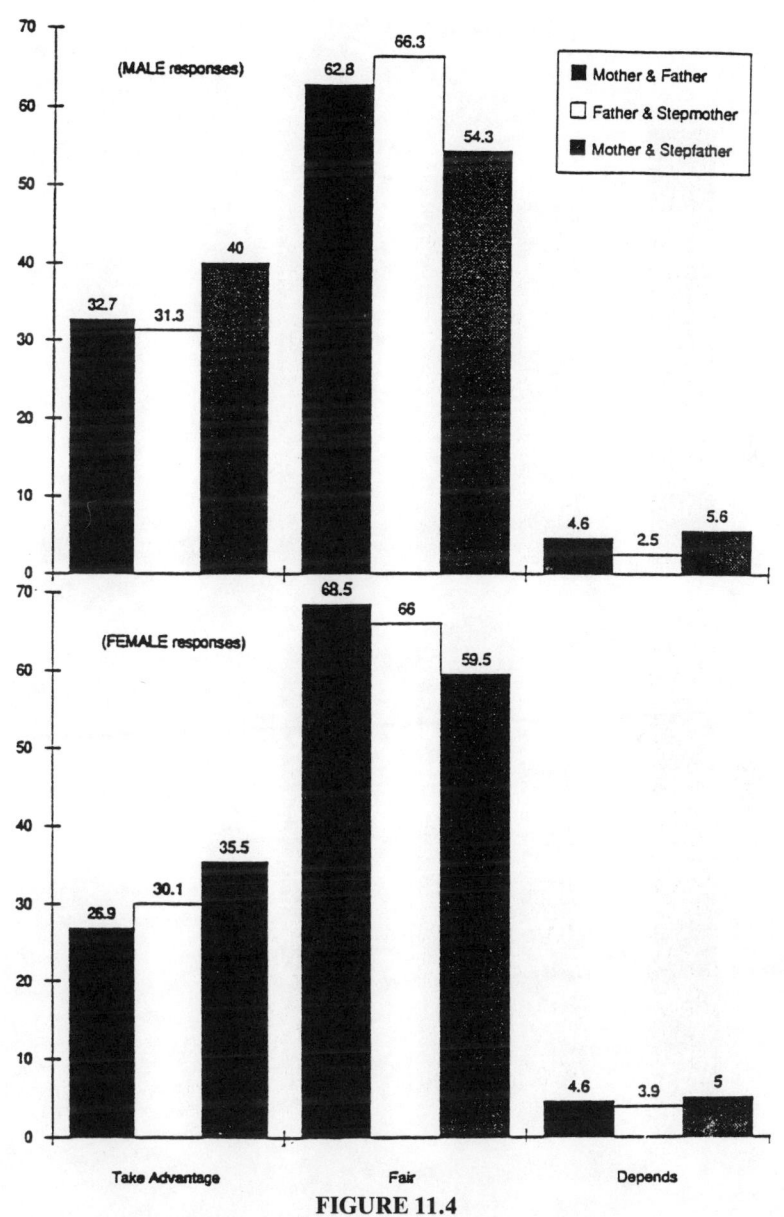

FIGURE 11.4
"Are People Fair or Do They Try to Take Advantage?"

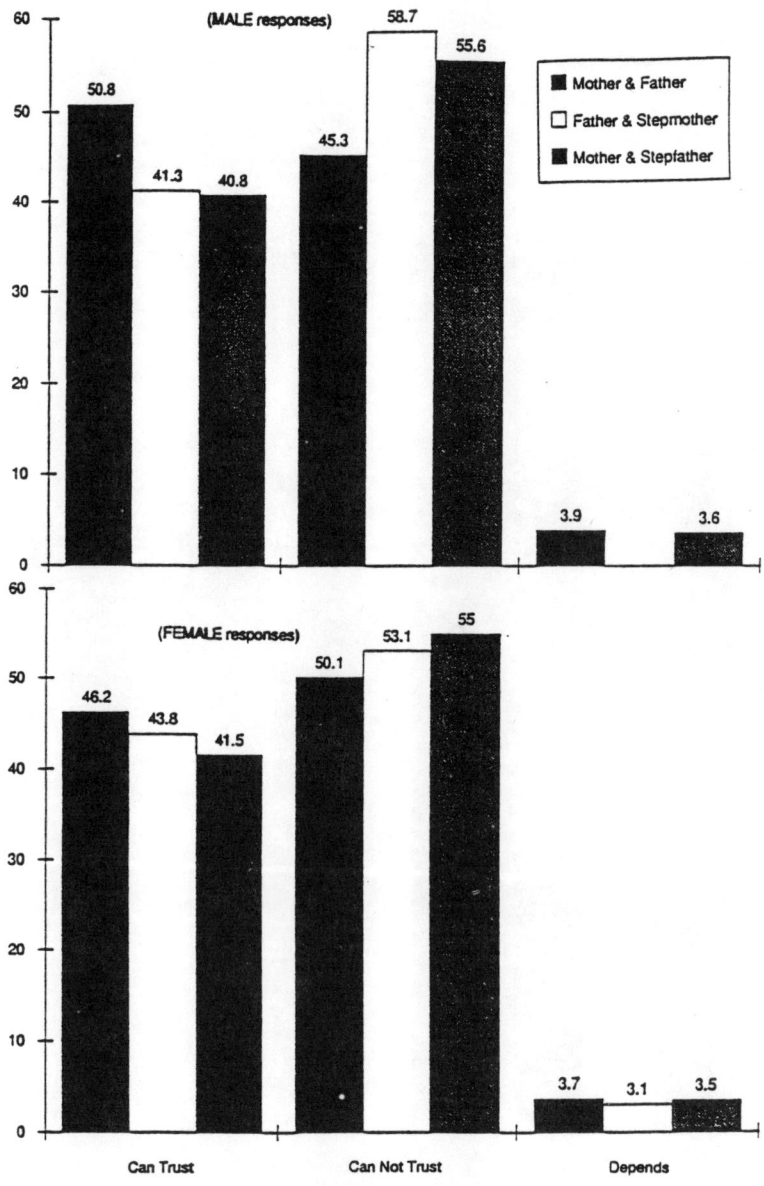

FIGURE 11.5
"Can People Be Trusted?"

outlook of emotional passivity or whether they take relish in everyday events. Here is the wording: "In general, do you find life exciting, pretty routine, or dull?"[42]

The least healthy outcome is for people to regard life as basically dull; if we look at these responses, the lowest proportion come from nuclear families, both for males (3.8 percent) and for females (4.3 percent). For both sexes, having an opposite-sex stepparent produced the highest percentage of people who said life was dull, with 8.5 percent of males with stepfathers and 7 percent of females with stepmothers. The most emotionally healthy responses, however, do not consistently reflect the prevailing pattern of advantage for nuclear families. For males, this is the case, with 50.2 percent of those from conventional families experiencing life as exciting, compared to 43.6 percent of the men from stepfather families and 33.8 percent of those from stepmother families. But for women, those from a stepfather family were most likely to find life exciting (49.2 percent), distantly followed by those from a stepmother family (31.8 percent).

Probably the simplest measure of emotional adjustment is to ask if a person is happy. Granted, many people with problems may be inclined to respond, if asked by a stranger administering a survey, that they are happy when in fact they are not. Yet this GSS question has been used frequently enough to be a valid estimate of emotional well-being: "Taking all things together, would you say things are these days—would you say that you are very happy, pretty happy, or not too happy?"[43]

The responses to this question were inconsistent. Of men who said they were "very happy," those from stepmother families accounted for the largest share (38.4 percent), with those from nuclear families coming second (33.6 percent) and stepfather families a distant third (23.2 percent). But stepmother families also accounted for the largest percentage of the least happy males (14.3), with nuclear families and stepfather families following (11.4 percent and 1.3 percent, respectively). Females are more faithful to the overall pattern, with the larger share of people from nuclear families among the very happy respondents (38.6 percent), those from opposite-sex stepparent families second (34 percent) and from stepmother families third (23.9 percent).

216 American Stepfamilies

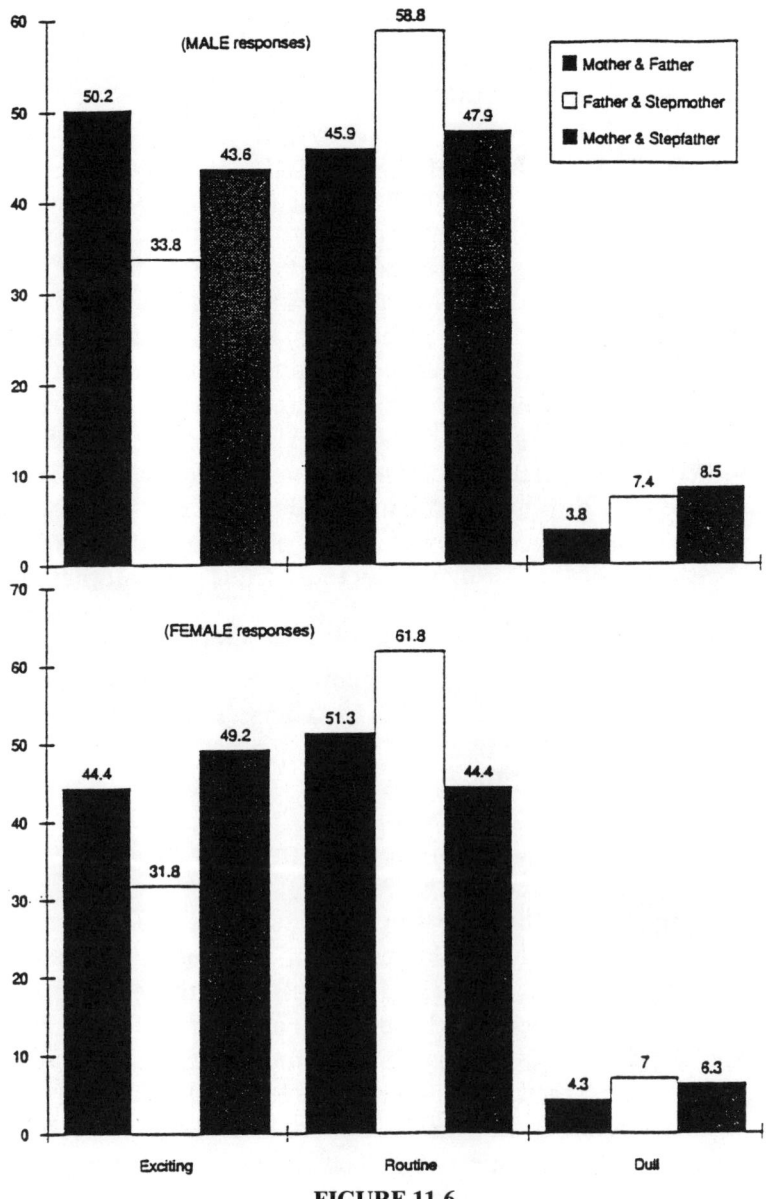

FIGURE 11.6
"Is Life Exciting or Dull?"

The Bottom Line: Are Stepfamilies Successful? 217

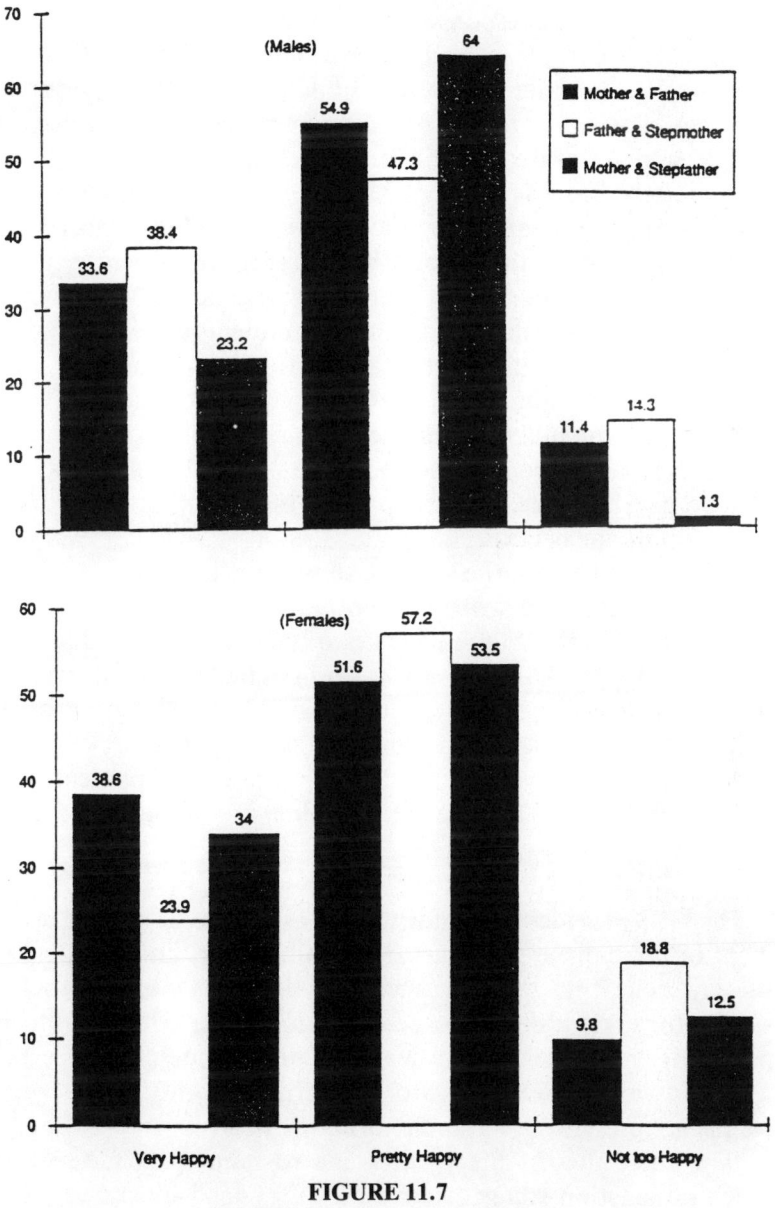

(Males)

	Mother & Father	Father & Stepmother	Mother & Stepfather
Very Happy	33.6	38.4	23.2
Pretty Happy	54.9	47.3	64
Not too Happy	11.4	14.3	1.3

(Females)

	Mother & Father	Father & Stepmother	Mother & Stepfather
Very Happy	38.6	23.9	34
Pretty Happy	51.6	57.2	53.5
Not too Happy	9.8	18.8	12.5

FIGURE 11.7
Happiness by Family Type (Males)

Even though the responses to these questions were not always consistent, a definite overall pattern appears. For males, people from nuclear families were proportionally largest among the "best adjusted" answers for three of the five—those who thought other people were helpful, thought others were trustworthy, and those who thought life was exciting. Men from nuclear families ranked second most prevalent among those who believed that most people were fair and who said they were very happy. For women, a nuclear family background was even more advantageous. Those from nuclear families were relatively the most prevalent in the "best adjusted" answers for four of the five questions; women from intact families who thought life was exciting were second most prevalent. In no cases, for males or females, did respondents from nuclear families rank less than second in the "best adjusted" category. The relative psychological benefits of growing up in an intact family are therefore fairly clear.

On the other hand, the sex of a stepparent in relation to the sex of the adult stepchild does not follow any clear pattern. This corresponds to the lack of definite effect of gender that was discovered among children. Although a few studies cited earlier showed differences between stepsons and stepdaughters depending on the gender of the stepparent, in some cases an opposite-sex stepparent was an apparent advantage, and in some cases an apparent disadvantage. The results for adult stepchildren are similarly mixed.

Social Adjustment

The GSS provides questions that measure people's social adjustment in three different areas: friendship, work, and obedience to the law. The first question measures a person's ability to form satisfactory friendships, the second gauges the extent to which a person is satisfied with the work he or she does, and the third ascertains a respondent's history of trouble with the police. The results are presented in graphic form below.

"For each area of life I am going to name, tell me . . . how much satisfaction you get from . . . your friendships: a very great deal/ a great deal/ quite a bit/ a fair amount/ some/ a little/ none."[44]

The responses to this question, like those for the question about family life discussed above, were compressed into three cat-

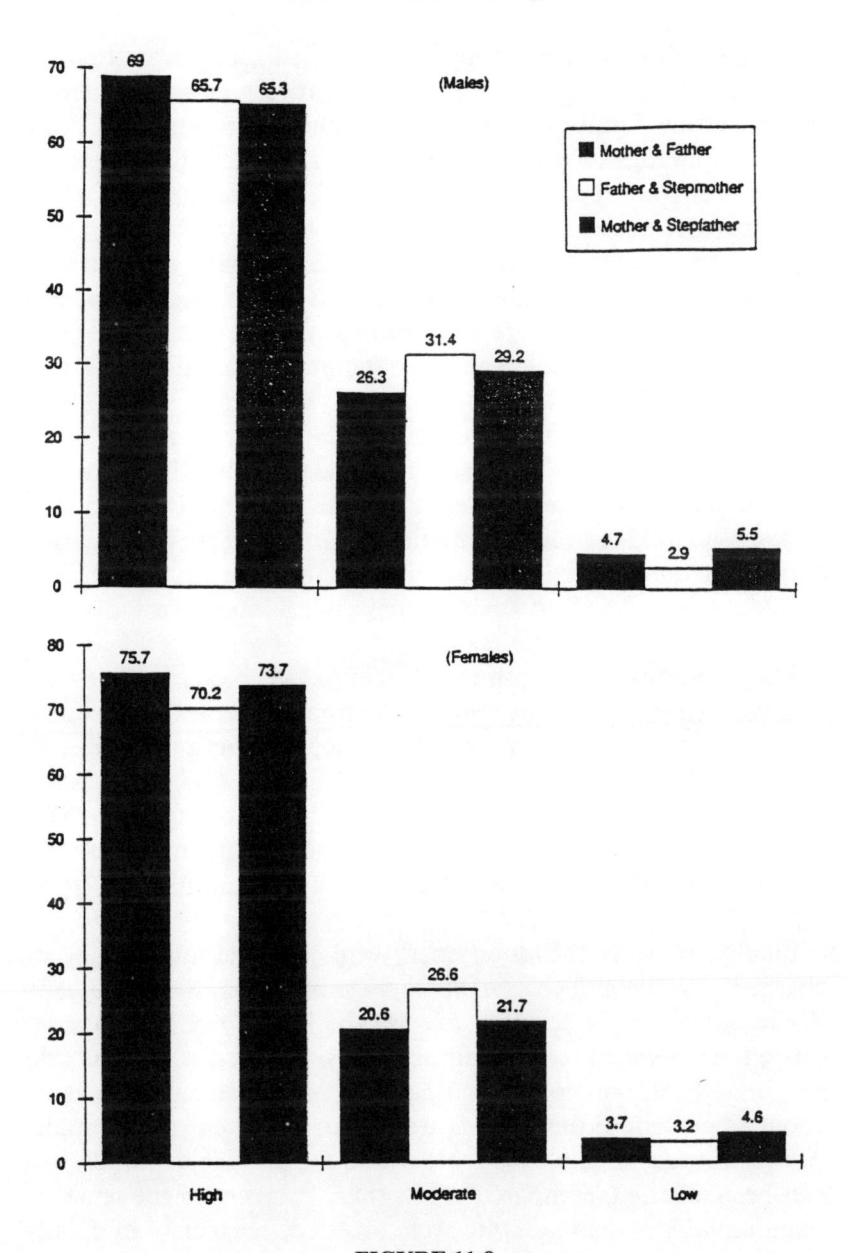

The Bottom Line: Are Stepfamilies Successful? 219

FIGURE 11.8
Satisfaction with Friendships by Family Type

egories—high (a very great deal, a great deal), moderate (quite a bit, a fair amount), and low (some, a little, none). Males from mother-father families represent the highest percentage of those who report a high level of satisfaction with friendships (69 percent) with those from stepmother families (65.7 percent) and stepfather families (65.3 percent) a close second and third. For women, those from intact families have the highest percentage who report a high degree of satisfaction with friendship, but women from opposite-sex stepparent families are proportionally more numerous (73.7 percent) than those from same-sex stepparent families (70.2 percent).

To assess satisfaction with work, the following question was asked. "On the whole, how satisfied are you with the work you do—would you say you are very satisfied, moderately satisfied, a little dissatisfied, or very dissatisfied?"[45] In the figure that follows, "high" corresponds to "very satisfied," "moderate" to "moderately satisfied," and "low" to "a little dissatisfied" and "very dissatisfied."

These responses, for both sexes, followed the pattern of satisfaction with friendships. For males and females, those from nuclear family backgrounds were most likely to report a high level of satisfaction with work, 51.1 and 50.1, respectively. For males, stepmother families (42.9 percent) outranked stepfather families (41.1 percent); for females, stepfather families (50.4 percent) were comparatively better represented than stepmother families (47.7 percent).

Finally, there is the question, "Were you ever picked up, or charged, by the police . . . whether or not you were guilty?"[46] While one might be tempted to view the honesty of responses to this question with a certain amount of skepticism, the results do roughly correspond to the comparative arrest rates of the sexes; about 84 percent of the persons arrested in any given year are male. About 17 percent of all the males in all three types of family had ever been arrested, compared to less than 4 percent of the females. The numbers of females who were arrested, regardless of family type, were so small that they are not discussed. Figure 11.10 does show the results for males, and it is clear that the men from intact families are the least likely to have been arrested, with 16.9 percent

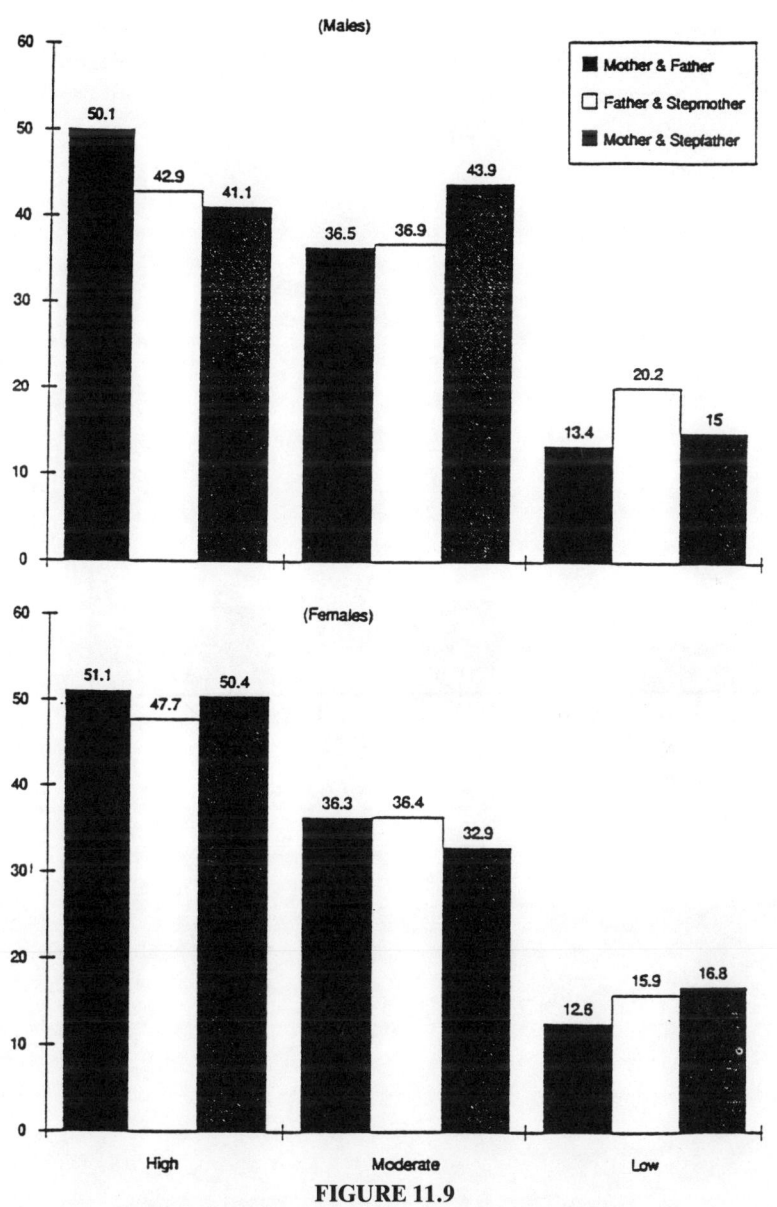

The Bottom Line: Are Stepfamilies Successful? 221

FIGURE 11.9
Satisfaction with Job or Housework by Family Type

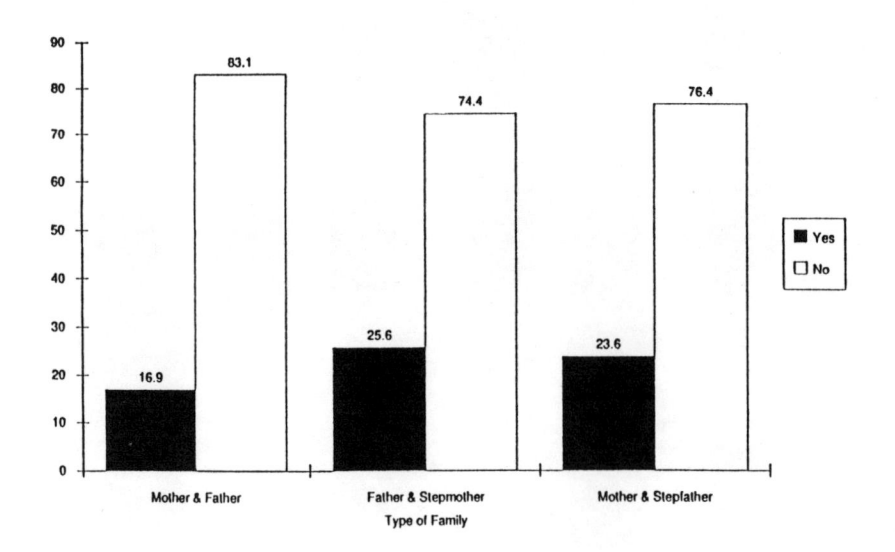

FIGURE 11.10
Male Responses to "Have You Ever Been Picked Up or Arrested by the Police?"

responding "yes" to the question; 25.6 percent from stepmother families, and 23.6 percent from stepfather families.

On the first two of the questions assessing social adjustment, having an opposite-sex stepparent was somewhat less desirable, but the overall advantage of the intact family is unmistakable. On all three of these measures, the pattern of response was the same as that respecting satisfaction with family life: respondents from nuclear families accounted for the largest share of those who gave the most well-adjusted answers.

Half-Empty or Half-Full?

People who grew up in stepfamilies are proportionately fewer than those from intact families among people who are highly satisfied with their family lives and happy in their marriages. People from intact families are more likely than those from stepfamilies to be satisfied with their friendships and jobs and—among men—to have never been arrested. Even in emotional adjustment, adults who grew up in stepfamilies are seldom as prevalent as those from intact homes among those with greatest psychological health. Happiness is relatively more common among men who grew up in stepmother families and a belief in others' fairness among those who grew up in stepfather families. A belief that life is exciting is relatively greater among women from stepfather families. But these are the only exceptions. The evidence is clear: stepfamilies do not produce grown-ups who, on the whole, are as satisfied with their family lives, as emotionally healthy, and as well-adjusted to society as those from nuclear families.

On the other hand, in none of the areas we looked at are people from stepfamilies at a serious disadvantage. Almost everywhere, the difference between the three types of families are within a few percentage points. Even where the differences are greater than 5 percent, these are mainly due to the uneven sizes of the groups; there are so few respondents in the stepfamily groups that a shift of a few individuals can result in apparently substantial differences in percentages. Few of the differences between the family groups are statistically significant. For males the significant differences appear only in happiness of marriage, happiness, trust in others, and a belief that life is exciting. For females, they appear in satisfaction with family life, happiness, and a belief that life is exciting. And statistical analysis shows that even the significant differences do not indicate strong relationships.[47]

Depending on how one looks at it, then, the stepfamily's glass is half-empty or half-full. Children in stepfamilies are not demonstrably different from children from other types of families, at least while they are still children, and at least as far as these differences can be measured by quantitative methods. But clinical psychologists, even though they are biased toward a perception of problems by the very nature of their clientele, suggest that we not be too rash in assuming that there are no long-term consequences to childhood turmoil. And the study of adults from stepfamilies confirms the necessity for such caution, since people from stepfamilies appear less well adjusted than those from intact families.

Yet the bottom line results of stepfamily upbringing are not bleak, because the differences are nowhere very substantial. Although there is no question that it would be better, all other things being equal, to be brought up in a nuclear family, a stepfamily background is at most a minor obstacle to successful adult adjustment to family life, to emotional health, and to society at large. This conclusion permits us to answer the question raised in the previous chapter: To what extent does the stepfamily as an institution carry out the basic task of rearing children who are emotionally and socially competent? The answer is that the stepfamily is a reasonably adequate substitute for the nuclear family when it comes to child rearing.

This is good news, because the social pressures leading to the decline of the nuclear family are well-nigh irresistible, if not necessarily welcome. Whether we like it or not, postindustrial society encourages the kind of adult behavior that leads to divorce, remarriage, and the formation of stepfamilies. A society that emphasizes emotional satisfaction and interpersonal communication as its paramount values is likely to foster a family structure that revolves around adult psychosexual gratification. While children often are forgotten in the parental quest for the perfect partner, it is heartening to see that in the long run, they can overcome the obstacles posed by the consequences of adult vicissitudes.

Notes

1. C. Bowerman and D. Irish (1962), "Some Relationships of Stepchildren to their Parents," *Marriage and Family Living* 24, 113–21.
2. S. Halperin and T. Smith (1983), "Differences in Stepchildren's Perceptions of their Stepfathers and Natural Fathers: Implications for Family Therapy," *Journal of Divorce* 7, 1, 19–30.
3. K. Wilson et al. (1975), "Stepfathers and Stepchildren: An Exploratory Analysis from Two National Surveys," *Journal of Marriage and the Family* 37, 526–36.
4. J. Giles-Sims and D. Finkelhor (1984), "The Stepparent Role: Expectations, Behavior, Sanctions," *Journal of Family Issues* 5, 116–30.
5. D. Russell (1984), "The Prevalence and Seriousness of Incestuous Abuse: Stepfathers vs. Biological Father," *Child Abuse and Neglect* 8, 15–22.
6. L. Ganong, M. Coleman, and G. Brown (1981), "Effect of Family Structure on Marital Attitudes of Adolescents," *Adolescence* 16, 62, 281–88.
7. A. Booth, D. Brinkerhoff, and L. White (1984), "The Impact of Parental Divorce on Courtship," *Journal of Marriage and the Family* 46, 85–94.
8. E. Spreitzer and L. Riley (1974), "Factors Associated with Singlehood," *Journal of Marriage and the Family* 36, 533–42.
9. F. Furstenberg and C. Nord (1985), "Parenting Apart: Patterns of Child-Rearing After Marital Disruption," *Journal of Marriage and the Family* 47, 893–904.
10. T. Parish and J. Dostal, "Evaluations of Self and Parent Figures by Children from Intact, Divorced, and Reconstituted Families," *Journal of Youth and Adolescence* 9, 4, 347–51.
11. T. Parish (1981), "Young Adults' Evaluations of Themselves and Their Parents as a Function of Family Structure and Disposition," *Journal of Youth and Adolescence* 10, 2, 173–78.
12. J. Bernard (1956), *Remarriage: A Study of Marriage* (New York: Holt, Rinehart & Winston).
13. L. Burchinal (1964), "Characteristics of Adolescents from Broken, Unbroken and Reconstituted Families," *Journal of Marriage and the Family* 24, 44–50; see also J. Perry and E. Pfuhl (1963), "Adjustment of Children in 'Solo' and 'Remarriage' Homes," *Marriage and Family Living* 25, 2, 221–23.
14. Wilson et al., "Stepfathers and Stepchildren."
15. H. Oshman and M. Manosevitz (1976), "Father Absence: Effects of Stepfathers upon Psychosocial Development in Males," *Developmental Psychology* 12, 5, 479–80.
16. G. Nunn, T. Parish, and R. Worthing (1983), "Perceptions of Personal and Familial Adjustment by Children from Intact, Single-parent, and Reconstituted Families," *Psychology in the Schools* 20, 166–74.
17. M. Rosenberg (1989), *Society and the Adolescent Self-Image* (New Haven: University Press of New England).
18. H. Raschke and V. Raschke (1979), "Family Conflict and Children's Self-concepts: A Comparison of Intact and Single-Parent Families," *Journal of Marriage and the Family* 41, 367–74.
19. T. Parish and J. Dostal (1980), "Evaluations of Self and Parent Figures by Children from Intact, Divorced, and Reconstituted Families," *Journal of Youth and Adolescence* 9, 4, 347–51.

20. T. Parish (1981), "Young Adults' Evaluations of Themselves and Their Parents as a Function of Family Structure and Disposition," *Journal of Youth and Adolescence* 10, 2, 173-78.
21. S. Kellam, M. Ensminger, and R. Thurner (1977), "Family Structures and the Mental Health of Children," *Archives of General Psychiatry* 34, 9, 1012-22.
22. J. Santrock (1972), "Relation of Type and Onset of Father Absence to Cognitive Development," *Child Development* 43, 455-69.
23. G. Nunn, T. Parish, and R. Worthing (1983), "Perceptions of Personal and Familial Adjustment by Children from Intact, Single-parent and Reconstituted Families," *Psychology in the Schools* 20, 166-74.
24. M. Chapman (1977), "Father Absence, Stepfathers and Cognitive Performance of College Students," *Child Development* 48, 3, 1155-58.
25. Wilson et al., "Stepfathers and Stepchildren."
26. E. Ferri (1984), *Stepchildren: A National Study* (London: NFER-Nelson), 110-15.
27. G. Nunn, T. Parish, and R. Worthing, "Perceptions of Personal and Familial Adjustment."
28. Ferri, *Stepchildren*, 110-14.
29. Wilson et al., "Stepfathers and Stepchildren."
30. Perry and Pfuhl, (1963) "Adjustment of Children in 'Solo' and 'Remarriage' Homes," *Marriage and Family Living* 25, 221-23.
31. J. Santrock et al. (1982), "Children's and Parents' Observed Social Behavior in Stepfather Families," *Child Development* 53, 472-80.
32. J. Santrock, R. Warshak, and G. Elliott (1982), "Social Development and Parent-Child Interaction in Father-Custody and Stepmother Families," in M. E. Lamb (ed.), *Non-traditional Families: Parenting and Child Development* (Hillsdale, N.J.: Erlbaum).
33. The latest summaries of research on stepfamilies show mixed, and not dramatically different, results. For example, Kay Pasley reports that "type of family (divorced, non-divorced, remarried) [is] not correlated with child outcome" and "children in remarriages were identified as having the following poorer behavior: concentration, withdrawal, restlessness, more unhappy." (Kay Pasley, "Survey of 1988-89 Research—Remarriage and Stepparenting," a report from the Wingspread Conference of 1989).
34. E. Hetherington (1979), "Divorce: A Child's Perspective," *American Psychologist* 34, 10, 851-58.
35. L. Ganong and M. Coleman (1984), "The Effects of Remarriage on Children: A Review of the Empirical Literature," *Family Relations* 33, 389-406; L. Ganong and M. Coleman (1986), "A Comparison of the Clinical and Empirical Literature on Children in Stepfamilies," *Journal of Marriage and the Family* 48, 309-18.
36. The drawback of the comparisons discussed below is that they use simple cross-tabulations. This does not permit use of respondent's age as a continuous variable; for this, multiple analysis of variance would have been necessary, a statistical technique not understandable to the lay reader. Also, there are methodological drawbacks to the GSS, paramount among which is the lack of information about the length of time that the respondent lived in a stepfamily. This weakness is inevitable in using data from a survey whose primary purpose is not related to family research.

The Bottom Line: Are Stepfamilies Successful?

37. Of the male respondents, 3,252 were from nuclear families, 79 were from stepmother families, and 145 were from stepfather families; 3,620 of the female respondents were from nuclear families, 65 were from stepmother families, and 173 were from stepfather families.
38. Of the male respondents, 4,641 were from nuclear families, 102 were from stepmother families, and 213 were from stepfather families; 5,677 of the female respondents were from nuclear families, 123 were from stepmother families; and 285 were from stepfather families.
39. Of male respondents, 3,766 were from nuclear families, 80 from stepmother families, and 175 from stepfather families; 4,524 female respondents were from nuclear families, 105 from stepmother families, and 221 from stepfather families.
40. Of male respondents, 3,751 were from nuclear families, 80 from stepmother families, and 175 from stepfather families; 4,517 female respondents were from nuclear families, 103 from stepmother families, and 220 from stepfather families.
41. Of male respondents, 3,629 were from nuclear families, 75 from stepmother families, and 169 from stepfather families; 4,114 female respondents were from nuclear families, 96 from stepmother families, and 200 from stepfather families.
42. Of male respondents, 3,200 were from nuclear families, 68 from stepmother families and 142 from stepfather families; 3,866 female respondents were from nuclear families, 85 from stepmother families, and 189 from stepfather families.
43. Of male respondents, 5,184 were from nuclear families, 112 were from stepmother families, and 228 were from stepfather families; 6,184 female respondents were from nuclear families, 138 were from stepmother families, and 312 from stepfather families.
44. Of male respondents, 4,654 were from nuclear families, 102 were from stepmother families, and 216 were from stepfather families; 5,692 female respondents were from nuclear families, 124 were from stepmother families, and 285 were from stepfather families.
45. Of male respondents, 4,002 were from nuclear families, 84 from stepmother families, and 180 from stepfather families; 5,118 female respondents were from nuclear families, 107 from stepmother families, and 268 from stepfather families.
46. Of male respondents, 3,190 were from nuclear families, 66 from stepmother families, and 144 from stepfather families; 3,826 female respondents were from nuclear families, 86 from stepmother families, and 190 were from stepfather families.
47. When the strength of the significant relationships was measured by means of Cramer's V, none exceeds .048.

Postface:
The Way It Is/The Way It Should Be

In this book I have tried to illustrate, in layman's terms, how stepfamilies actually work, both internally and in American society. It is a sociological work that has deliberately avoided a "how to" approach. This has probably not satisfied readers in search of directions for how to make their own stepfamilies work, and for some advice on how the stepfamily is supposed to function. There are many resources available to stepfamilies who want to improve their chances at success, and I will describe some of the best below. But first, it might be useful to imagine what a stepfamily would be like if everything were working perfectly; this will provide an idea of what sort of ideal stepfamilies can strive for.

The Perfect Stepfamily

The perfect stepfamily would start off with a number of accomplishments behind it. The adults who had been previously married would have recovered from their divorce. This recovery would require having successfully completed the normal stages of grieving, ending with that of acceptance—a renunciation of the past marriage, a realization that it cannot be reconstructed, and that the loss cannot be ascribed to anyone's fault. That both ex-spouses achieve this state of resolution requires that they have gone beyond resentment for pain inflicted during the collapse of their marriage and have abandoned dreams or ploys of revenge stemming from the grudges. In the best circumstance, ex-spouses have remarried or entered otherwise satisfying relationships that minimize their envy. If the remarried spouses should have children together, the ex-spouses regard this with generous good wishes.

The noncustodial father makes all his child support payments in full and on time, and does not withhold checks as a way of retaliating for last-minute or inconvenient changes in visitation. He accepts his ex-wife's remarriage and is sure that his children's stepfather will not try to take his place; the two men are not necessarily friendly but are civil. The noncustodial parent has also come to accept the visitation schedule of the children, and uses the time to promote as normal a parent-child relation as possible. There is no attempt to buy a child's love with gifts, no attempt to make a visit a magical time of nonstop fun. Children have chores and regular bedtimes when they visit the noncustodial parent. Most important, the noncustodial parent in the perfect stepfamily does not use visitation time to express hostility to the ex-spouse to the children, or to use the youngsters as messengers about the custodial parent's shortcomings. The custodial parent does likewise, refraining from withholding contact with the noncustodial parent as a way of extracting more, and more regular, child support payments.

The perfect stepchildren would also have no residual emotions mourning the loss of their first family. In the best circumstance, the children would be so young at the time of the remarriage that they would have no clear memory of the defunct marriage, and while not rejecting the noncustodial parent, would be ready to accept the stepparent without experiencing conflicts of loyalty. The custodial mother has not been a single parent so long that she has elevated the oldest child to a quasi-adult status. If the single parent phase has been of long duration, the single mother has successfully resisted the temptation to rely on one or more of her children as if they were peers, and has maintained a clear generational hierarchy. If they are older, the children have come to accept their biological parents' incompatibility and have stopped having fantasies about reuniting them.

When the adults marry, they find a new dwelling for the stepfamily, one free of old associations and where none of the family members have feelings that it is uniquely their territory. They are free of the illusions that cloud perceptions in beginning stepfamilies—the myths of instant love and of the re-created nuclear family. They anticipate that conflicts may arise, and have tried to devise measures for communicating with each other about it. They have also freed themselves from the emotional baggage from their first marriage(s), particularly the fear that they may be making the same mistake all over again and that they are somehow incapable of forging a healthy family life. First-marrying parents have no illusions that they are heroically intervening to save the other stepfamily members; females do not see themselves as rescuers coming to the aid of helpless children neglected by an inadequate mother, and males do not see themselves as masterfully putting a chaotic house in order. They anticipate and accept the greater legitimacy that the children ascribe to their biological parents.[1]

The perfect stepfamily will have successfully passed through several distinct steps, which can be roughly grouped into early stages, middle stages, and late stages.[2] In the early stages, illusions about stepfamily life have been put aside. The stepfamily has started out aligned on biological lines, and members have realized that this kind of alliance will not make a family that fits together for long, particularly the link between biological parent and child that excludes the stepparent. The stepparent may well at first have reacted to being excluded by insisting even more on being included, which in turn intensifies his exclusion. A stepparent who has survived this experience has managed to distinguish between his spouse's rejection of him as a parent, but not as a mate. At the end of this stage, the stepfamily members will have come to the realization that what does not fit is the way the family is working, rather than any personal shortcoming in themselves.

This realization ushers in the family's middle stages, in which members express their ideas about what is and is not working, and then pass into a phase where they cooperate on setting up new rules and new patterns of behavior that will overcome the misalignments. This is probably the stage in which the perfect biological parent managed to transfer priority from his or her children to the relationship with the remarried spouse. A mixture of new and old rules will make a family sufficiently familiar with new ways of doing things—such as the old bedtimes but with different prebedtime rituals, or going to a restaurant after church on Sunday instead of reading the *New York Times*. The normal period of time for a stepfamily to get to this point is about four years.

The later stages that follow include a time when intimate steprelationships are possible, when stepparents in particular are sufficiently confident that they are comfortable in that role. Couples can honestly share their feelings of ambivalence and pain, and these negative emotions are not perceived as threatening to the remarriage or the other stepfamily relations. In the final stage of the perfect stepfamily's formation, what appears is a realization of the uniqueness and strength of the step-relationship, along with acceptance of its limitations. At this stage, a stepparent would have become a special quasi-parent figure for a stepchild, presenting a unique adult figure that a child can emulate and perhaps share confidences that he or she might prefer not to communicate directly to a biological parent.

A stepfamily that has managed to get to this point will no longer be paralyzed if there arise hostility and sexual tension between stepfather and stepdaughter, jealousy between stepmother and stepdaughter, or refusal of discipline by a stepson. Such reactions may occasionally surface, but the solidity of the relation between the couple, and the confidence of the stepparent in his or her role, make it possible to overcome them. Central to this family flexibility would be a biological parent's acceptance of the unique parenting role of his or her spouse.

Stepsiblings, if they are living in the same household, would have ceased their conflicts over turf and come to accept one another as having the same right to live under the same roof and receive equal treatment from grown-ups, whether biological or stepparents. If they are visiting stepsiblings, the visits have come to be looked upon as a time when peers can be enjoyed, rather than an invasion that has to be weathered. If there is a mix-up in age hierarchies, the children have managed to sort out and preserve their special place as "daddy's little girl" or "the first-born son." Opposite-sex stepsiblings, resident or visiting, have steered a middle course between attraction and loathing, achieving a warm, nonerotic tie that is closer than that usually enjoyed by biological brothers and sisters. The children have succeeded in using their stepsiblings as resources for growing up—as models whom they may want in part to imitate, or as examples they know they do not want to emulate.

If a mutual child is born to the remarried couple, the children will have accepted both the hope and the disappointment it symbolizes. Their disappointment will stem from the realization that any dream they may have had of reuniting their divorced parents is dead. The hope means that the new family is all related by blood now, is bound together biologically and not just legally. The baby is the focus of these hopes, and the hopes are sufficient to overcome the possible resentments by half-siblings, who have only one parent in the family, against an infant who has two.

In the perfect stepfamily, when the children have grown up, they have been equipped to deal more creatively with interpersonal relations than they might have been in an intact family. They have come to accept their upbringing as atypical but not abnormal, and to see its advantages along with its peculiarities. Parent and stepparent, for their part, are happy to see their children mature, and have no guilt or ambivalence about emotional scars that their children or stepchildren may have acquired along the way. Perhaps most importantly, in the perfect stepfamily, grown-up children end up capable of setting out on their own, cutting loose from the family they have worked so hard to join, ready to establish their own families.[3]

Improving Your Chances

The perfect stepfamily described above is obviously a caricature. Divorces are usually messy, leaving raw emotions that last for years. Adversarial court decisions entrench ex-spouses in antagonistic camps solidified around property dispositions and custody agreements. Noncustodial and custodial parents often violate the terms of the divorce decree; fathers disappear and mothers deny them access to their children. Children are used as pawns and bargaining chips. Ex-spouses usually do not go off and get happily married and out of the way; many ex-wives, in particular, remain a financial drain on their remarried ex-husbands' families for many years. Remarrying divorcees are often full of guilt and self-doubt, first-marrying stepparents are seldom prepared for the full impact of instant parenthood. Marital ties are deeply strained by pre-existing biological ties between custodial parent and children; visiting stepchildren are frequently perceived as ill-mannered, invading barbarians. Stepchildren commonly feel deep conflicts over loving a stepparent and keep him or her at arm's length as a way of asserting loyalty to a biological parent. Often a stepfamily cannot move to a new house or apartment, and thus cannot begin anew on neutral ground; a stepparent may well be obliged to sleep in the same room (or even bed) an ex-spouse used to sleep in. Stepsiblings, too, are often galled by having to share "their" room, temporarily or permanently. Half-siblings do not always manage to be heartened by the birth of a mutual child. The list of possible difficulties could go on and on, and the stories in this book described many in painful detail.

There are so many pitfalls along the way that imagining a stepfamily that has come unscathed through all of them is like describing a Utopia. Ordinary, decent human beings who are doing their best often make mistakes, or even cause damage with the best of intentions. Yet for all the impossibility of achieving perfection, people in a stepfamily do have a number of resources at their disposal, which will not make them perfect, but which can serve as helpmates along the way.

Stepfamily members tend to feel that they are alone, that the difficulties they encounter are due to some personal shortcoming on their part, rather than the nature of the stepfamily itself. The major resource thus consists of the realization that they are not alone. What seems like a situation nobody else has ever experienced, with emotions so unanticipated and unaccustomed, is in fact one they share with millions of other Americans.

Others who have already gone through the same experiences can provide sage advice; one of the best ways to end the feeling of isolation and self-blame is through participation in stepfamily self-help groups. These groups, in which newcomers can share their experiences and veterans their suggestions, are proliferating. The largest single organization that sponsors them is the Stepfamily Association of America (SAA), based in Baltimore, Maryland.[4] The SAA has scores of chapters throughout the United States. Many other stepfamily groups, some under the direction of social workers or other mental health professionals, are also available.

Some stepfamilies need more specialized help. Many of the people interviewed for this book mention receiving help from counselors of one sort or another along the way. A psychiatrist, psychologist, social worker, marriage counselor, or clergyman who has been trained to diagnose and treat stepfamily problems is often the key to successfully getting through the difficulties described above. Untangling the issues is a task most stepfamilies cannot do unaided; a group or a counselor is almost a necessity, at least for the rough spots.

The other principal resource for helping stepfamilies survive and thrive lies in self-help books. Numerous books are available, but I will mention those that have been recognized as among the best.[5] A dating couple composed of one or two divorced people who are contemplating marriage should use Jamie Keshet's *Love and Power in the Stepfamily: A Practical Guide* (New York: McGraw-Hill, 1987), since it deals with divorced parenting and dating in divorce. It has useful self-administered questionnaires to help the reader with particularly knotty and common problems. Remarrying couples ought to consult Richard Stuart and Barbara Jacobson's *Second Marriage: Make It Happen! Make It Last!* (New York: Norton, 1985), since it focuses on the relationship between the spouses. It has practical advice, checklists, and is written by a couple who speak from experience. Stepparents should read Emily and John Visher's *How to Win As a Stepfamily* (New York: Dembner, 1982) written by the cofounders of the Stepfamily Association of America. Both are not only trained mental health professionals but veterans in the self-help field for stepfamilies. Stepmothers will find a compendium of practical advice in Cherie Burns's *Stepmotherhood* (New York: Random House, 1985) and stepfathers will find the same in Mark Rosin's *Stepfathering: Stepfathers' Advice on Creating a New Family* (New York: Simon &

Schuster, 1987). Younger stepchildren will enjoy Claire Berman's *What Am I Doing in a Stepfamily?* (Secaucus, N.J.: Lyle Stuart, 1982), and Linda Craven's *Stepfamilies: New Patterns of Harmony* (New York: Messner, 1982) is an excellent book that focuses on common adolescent stepchild issues.

From Generation to Generation

One resource available (though not always solicited) to people in nuclear families is advice from their parents, who by definition have experience in raising children and coping with family life in general. Because stepfamilies are often on their own in constructing their lives, they seldom get experienced advice from their parents on what to do. But the number of stepfamilies has been increasing steadily enough that future stepparents are more and more likely to have come from stepfamilies themselves, and thus can get advice from their own parent or stepparent. The following description of how stepfamily advice was passed on from one visited stepmother to her visited stepmother daughter makes an apt conclusion to the book, since as stepfamilies proliferate, they will be more and more able similarly to tap a well of common knowledge, handing guidance from generation to generation.

> The day that my mother came home from the hospital with her first child, she was only married eleven months, and my father had his daughters over, and my mother said she cried, because she wanted to be alone with him and the new baby. She felt, like, who needed them there? She had just come home from the hospital and she had her first child, and she had two stepchildren in the house. That was when my parents were only married a year. My mother has told me that things weren't great right away, it got better as the years went by. I've asked my mother to help me deal with my stepchildren, and I've often said, "How did you do it? You seem to get along so well with them. Why am I having such a tough time?" And she said, "It didn't happen right away. It kind of evolved over time."
>
> I know that she's talking from experience and so I listen. Other times I get annoyed with her because I feel her experience was a little different and she'll compare it to mine. And not be as sympathetic as I'd like her to be and I get pissed at her.
>
> When I've had a tough time accepting my present husband and the fact that he had a life before me, and he has children that he is financially responsible for and all that stuff, my mother will say, "Well, they are his children, and don't ruin a good thing. What do you want from him? If he didn't provide for them you'd have no respect for him because he'd be a shit. So I understand

money is tight and you resent that he's got to send to them before you get, but that's the way it is; you married him and you knew he had children. What do you want him to do?"

That's the way she is, she kind of sets me straight again. She's also told me, "Hang in, in a few years they'll come less and less, they'll be with you less and less, and before you know it, they'll be off and married and you will be the center of your husband's universe. Hang in there." She's also told me that, because that's what happened with her stepdaughters, "If you really have a good thing with your husband, don't throw it away because of the children. They're not going to be there forever." And she said that out of experience. She also told me that when she married my father, he didn't want any more children, because he already had two daughters. Similarly my husband didn't either, because he already had his family. She said, no sooner did she have us than we became the center of things for him and that's what would happen. She said, "Right now, your stepdaughters are very big focus for your husband because he's just left them. But you will become more and more the center of his universe, just as I did with daddy. Whether you have children or not, your husband will be with you all of the time, and with them some of the time, and what's going to happen over the years, is that you're going to become more of his life than they are.

She explained that, "It seems like a long time but before you know it they'll be twenty-one, and he won't have to support them any more. And then it will be your turn." It was helpful to think of it that way, that it may be difficult for all these years but she's right; it's not forever.

Notes

1. For a summation of some of these pre-remarriage stages, see Ransom, Schlesigner, Derdeyn (1978), *A Stepfamily in Formation*, 36–43.
2. For a full explanation of this process, see Patricia Papernow's brilliant 1984 classic, "The Stepfamily Cycle: An Experiential Model of Stepfamily Development," *Family Relations* 33, 355–63.
3. For an explanation by ten stepparents as to why they believe their stepfamilies have been successful, see K. Starks (1983), "A Descriptive Study of Ten Self-Defined Successful Stepfamilies," *Dissertation Abstracts International* 43, 4058–59.
4. The Stepfamily Association of America, 602 East Joppa Road, Baltimore, Md. 21204. The SAA publishes a quarterly *Stepfamily Bulletin* full of useful and professionally formulated advice.
5. More advice on further reading can be found in two particularly useful sources: (a) a partly annotated bibliography compiled in 1984—with subsequent addenda—for the Stepfamily Association of America by Paul Bohannon and Janice Perlman (this can be ordered from the SAA), and (b) a literature review, M. Coleman and L. Ganong (1989), "Stepfamily Self-Help Books: Brief Annotations and Ratings," *Family Relations* 38, 91–96.

Index

Abortion, 186
Absentee parent, 35
Abuser, 35
Action stage, 80
Adjustment process, 12–13
Adolescents, 135–136, 199
Adult-centered family, 193
Adult stepchildren, 206
    family relations of, 207–208
    psychological adjustment of, 208–218
    social adjustment of, 218–223
Anger, 68
Angier, John, 180
"Angry associates", 34
Anxiety levels, 202
Authority, parental vs. stepparental, 67–68, 87
Awareness stage, 79

Baby boom, 187–188
Bane, Mary Jo, 189
Bell, Daniel, 191
Berman, Claire, 236
Bernard, Jesse, 201
Bernreuter Personality Inventory, 201

Biological fathers, 193, 199–200
Biological parent/child tie, 58, 79, 85–86, 98–99, 125–126, 134–135
Birth control, 186
Bonding, 133–134
Boundaries, unclear, 9
Brothers, 145
Burns, Cherie, 235

Calvinism, 181
Capitalism, 184
Catholic church, 181
Centrifugal children, 125–137
Centripetal children, 135
Chaos-creator, 34
Child abuse, 198
Child-centered family, 184–185, 194
Childless stepfather, 43–46
Children:
    centrifugal, 125–137
    centripetal, 135
    effect on remarriage, 27–28
    emotional damage to from divorce, 191
    ex-spouses and, 36–37
    mutual, 17–18, 83–106

240   Index

Children (*continued*)
  power loss after remarriage, 68
  scapegoating and, 69–71
Child support, 37
Church of England, 182
Coital frequency, 26
Communication, 26
Competition, 34, 121, 122, 158
Complexity, 8–9
Conflict, 26, 29
Connecticut, 182
Contact stage, 80
"Cooperative colleagues," 34
Counseling, 235
Couple relations, 26–30
Craven, Linda, 236
Custodial mother, 107–123
Custodial stepmother, 95
Custody battles, 114

Dating activity, 199
Dating phase, 122
Delinquency, 204
Demos, John, 180–181, 183
Detachment, 133
Difficult ex-spouses, 34–35
Discipline, 12, 118
"Dissolved duos," 34
Division of labor, 86, 184–185, 192–193
Divorce, 33, 126
  no-fault, 190
  rise of as institution, 181–192
Divorce rate, 28
Duberman, Lucile, 27
Duby, Georges, 183

Eastern Europe, 184
Economic expansion, 187
Economics, 27
Education, 27, 187–188
Emotional divorce, 126
England, 180
Equilibrium, 103–105, 130
  shift in, 105–106
Eroticized couple, 191
Ex-spouses:
  birth of mutual child and, 87–88
  children and, 36–37
  difficult types, 34–35
  gender and feelings toward, 35–36
  hostility and, 37–39
  role of, 30–33
  styles adopted by, 33–34

Families of origin, 28
Family, history of, 183–185
Family court, 114
Family members, shifting, 8
Family relations, 198–200, 207–208
Fantasy stage, 79
Female sexuality, 186
Feminine Mystique, The (Friedan), 188
Feminist movement, 188–189
"Fiery foes," 34
First marriages vs. remarriage, 26–30
France, 178, 180
Friedan, Betty, 188

Gender:
  division of labor and, 86, 184–185, 192–193
  feelings toward ex-spouses and, 35–36
  happiness in marriage and, 26–27
  power imbalance between biological vs. stepparent and, 84–85
  stepsibling relations and, 143–144
General Social Survey (GSS), 206–223
Grieving stages, 15–16
Guilt, 16–17, 126, 128

Half-siblings, 83, 161, 164–171
  resident insiders, 162
  resident outsiders, 162
  variety of, 171–172
  visiting outsiders, 162–163
Happiness, 26–27
Higher education, 187–188
Honeymoon phase, 15
Hostility, 37–38
Household technology, 185–186
How to Win As a Stepfamily (Visher), 235

Immersion stage, 79
Impersonal relationships, 194

Index

Incest taboos, 15, 49, 149–152
Industrialism, 184
Inkeles, Alex, 190
Intact family. *See* Nuclear family
Intellectual development, 202–203
Intimacy, 28
Intruder, 34
Italy, 179

Jacobson, Barbara, 235
Jealousy of ex-spouses, 34, 37–38
Johnson, Samuel, 23

Keshet, Jamie, 235
Kinship, 182–183

Ladurie, Emmanuel Leroy, 178
Legal divorce, 126
Love, 134, 144, 184, 186
Love and Power in the Stepfamily: A Practical Guide (Keshet), 235
Loyalty, 79, 132–133, 136

Manipulation, 128–130
Marital loyalty, 133
Masculinity, 37
Massachusetts, 182
Maturity, 26, 28
Mobilization stage, 79–80
Montaillou: The Promised Land of Error (Ladurie), 178
More, Sir Thomas, 180
Mortality rates, 179–180
Mutual child, 17–18, 83–106, 161, 233
  in noncustodial father/custodial mother family, 107–123
Myths, 231

National Incidence Study of Child Abuse and Neglect, 198
National Opinion Research Council, 206
New England, 180–182
No-fault divorce, 190
Noncustodial father, 107–123
Noncustodial mother, 95

Nuclear family, 135, 146, 190–191, 194
  compared with stepfamilies, 197–224
  ideal, 18–19
  rise of, 184–186, 192–193

Oldest child, 14

Parental love, 144
Parent-child dyad, 122, 134
Parenthood, negative feelings about, 192
Parity, parental, 95–99
Patriarchal authority, 192–193
Pecking order, 14
Peer relationships, 204
"Perfect pals," 34
Perfect stepfamily, 229–233
Personal Attribute Inventory for Children, 201
Personality development, 200–202
PINS (Persons in Need of Supervision), 63
Pitfalls in remarriage, 29, 234
Play parent, 122
Postindustrial society, 192–194
Power, 26
  of children in stepfamilies, 126
  children's loss of after remarriage, 68
  imbalance between biological vs. stepparents, 84–85
  mutual child and changes in, 87
Powerlessness, 68–69
Power shifts, 14
Premarital cohabitation, 28
Primary bonding, 133
Pseudo-autonomy, 135
Pseudomutuality, 70–71
Psychological adjustment, 190, 200–202, 208–218
"Pure" stepparents, 40, 43–46
  rescuer role of stepmother, 56–59
  stepfather as sideline player, 47–51
  visited stepmother, 51–59
Puritans, 181–182

Quantitative studies, limitations of, 205–206

Redivorce rate, 28
Remarriage, 23–24, 193–194
    compared with conventional marriage, 25
    couple relations in, 26–30
    second wife and second husband, 30–33
    varieties of stepparenting, 39–41
    war of the ex-spouses, 33–39
Rescuer, 56–59
Resident insiders, 162
Resident outsiders, 162
Resident stepmother, 95–99
Resolution stage, 80, 229–230
Rivalry:
    siblings and, 143
    stepsiblings and, 13–14, 144–149
Romantic love, 186
Rosin, Mark, 235
Rules, 11–12

Scapegoating, 69–71
School performance, 202–203
Secondary bonding, 133–134
Second Marriage: Make It Happen! Make It Last! (Stuart & Jacobson), 235
Second marriages. *See* Remarriage
Self-esteem, 200–202
Self-gratification, 192
Self-help books, 235–236
Self-help groups, 234–235
Serial monogamy, 192
Sex, marital, 15, 26
Sexual abuse, 198
Sexual attraction, 143–144
Shorter, Edward, 177, 191
Sibling rivalry, 143
Sideline player, 47–51
Single-parent phase, 67–68
Sisterhood is Powerful, 189
Sisters, 145
Social adjustment, 203–205, 218–223
Social class, 27
Social institution, 181
Sorrow, 68

South Carolina, 182
South Dakota, 190
State vs. family, 183
Steinem, Gloria, 189
Stepchildren, 85–86, 197, 230–231
    adolescent, 135–136
    family relations studies on, 198–200
    intellectual development studies on, 202–203
    power of, 87
    psychological health studies on, 200–202
    social adjustment studies on, 203–205
    See also Adult stepchildren
Stepdaughter, incest taboo and, 49
Stepfamilies, 175–176
    adjustment process, 12–13
    compared with nuclear families, 1–7, 197–224
    complexity of, 8–9
    grieving stages and, 15–16
    guilt and, 16–17
    in history, 177–181
    mutual child in, 17–18
    nuclear family ideal and, 18–19
    perfect, 229–233
    in postindustrial society, 192–194
    power shifts in, 14
    reality of, 233–234
    rules and, 11–12
    sex and, 15
    shifting members in, 8
    stepsibling rivalry in, 13–14
    successful, 59
    terminological gap in, 9–11
    unclear boundaries in, 9
Stepfamilies: New Patterns of Harmony (Craven), 236
Stepfamily Association of America (SAA), 235
Stepfather:
    childless, 43–46
    factors affecting role of, 47
    limits of role, 19
Stepfathering: Stepfathers' Advice on Creating a New Family (Rosin), 235

Stepmother:
    resident vs. visited, 95–99
    visited, 51–59
Stepmotherhood (Burns), 235
Stepparenting, 39
    compared with biological parenting, 98–99
    pure, 40
    stages of, 79–80
    yours, mine, and ours, 40–41
    yours and mine, 40
    yours and ours, 40
Stepsiblings, 232–233
    birth of mutual child and, 83–85
    rivalry of, 13–14, 144–149
    sexuality and, 149–152
    wider horizons, deeper ambivalence, 155–159
Stone, Lawrence, 180
Stuart, Richard, 235
Successful stepfamily defined, 59
Symmetry, 120–123

Technology, 185–186
Terminology gaps, 9–11
Transitivity, 113–114
Triage, 66–72, 116
Triangular relationships, 108, 115–116, 120–122
    transitivity and, 113–114

Unclear boundaries, 9

Values, traditional, 191–192
Visher, Emily & John, 235

Visitation, 37
Visited stepmother, 51–59, 95–99
Visiting outsiders, 162–163
Voltaire, 181

Weekend children, 57
Weekend stepparent, 57
Weitzman, Lenore, 190
Westoff, Leslie, 26
What Am I Doing in a Stepfamily? (Berman), 236
Wheaton, Robert, 179
White-collar workers, 193
Working women, 189–190
World War II, 187

Youngest child, 14
"Yours, mine, and ours" stepparents, 40–41, 107–113
    triangular relationships and, 113–123
"Yours and mine" stepparents, 40, 61–66, 73–78
    from outsider to intimate, 78–82
    triage and, 66–72
"Yours and ours" stepparents, 40
    affect on ex-spouses, 87–88
    mutual child and, 83–106
    parental parity and, 95–99
    power imbalance and, 84–87
Youth in Transition (YIT) study, 198, 201, 203, 204

Zero-sum competition, 121, 122
Zwingli, Ulrich, 181